"For more than thirty years now, Dr. Cha [...] writing about spiritual warfare. During this [...] his insights and his experiences in at least eight full-length books. In this latest book, Dr. Kraft summarizes his findings and shares from his years of experience his approach to inner healing and deliverance ministries. This book needs to be read by every student studying spiritual formation, by every missiologist engaged in missionary activities and by every pastor and church worker committed to making healthy disciples of the Lord Jesus Christ."

Douglas Hayward, department chair, Graduate Intercultural Studies, Cook School of Intercultural Studies, Biola University

"Personally awakened to the spiritual nature of our Christian faith, Charles Kraft calls us to wake up as well. This book is a must-read for any who seek to understand God's work in the world today from the vantage point of an evangelical who daily engages in spiritual warfare."

Scott Moreau, professor of intercultural studies, Wheaton College Graduate School

"Most Christians are blind to the spiritual realities around us. This book pulls back the veil into the unseen world, where there is a battle. This book will quickly become a classic. Charles is steeped in wisdom in the area of spiritual warfare and has dedicated his life to bringing restoration to the church."

Judith MacNutt, M.A., president and co-founder, Christian Healing Ministries

"Charles Kraft has taken a topic that is still controversial among some in the body of Christ—spiritual warfare—and boiled it down to something we can all agree on: There is an enemy countering expressions of God's love in the lives of believers and lost souls alike that we must combat."

Jennifer LeClaire, senior editor at *Charisma* magazine and director of Awakening House of Prayer in Fort Lauderdale

"Again, Chuck Kraft has reminded us that 'we are at war with a cruel enemy.' This guide to the warfare reflects Dr. Kraft's passion for God's people to experience the full measure of the Father's love. His writing is grace-filled, balanced, thoughtful and practical."

John Shultz, Ph.D., president, Ashland Theogical Seminary

"Chuck Kraft has done it yet again. He has written a book on spiritual warfare that challenges us to rethink theologically and reengage practically. Kraft tethers his insights to Scripture and his own extensive experience with deep healing and deliverance, providing a valuable resource for both academy and congregation. Clearly this is not simply another book on evil supernaturalism, but instead a well-developed manual for spiritual warfare."

Terry Wardle, professor of practical theology,
Ashland Theological Seminary

"Dr. Kraft has removed the veil of mystery that has surrounded deliverance ministry far too long. With truth and honesty, he has opened the door to the evangelical community and gives us the right tools to set the captives free."

Tim Howard, president and founder,
Wellsprings of Freedom International

"There is no evangelical on the planet with a deeper insight into demonic activity or personal experience with deliverance from evil spirits. This book by Charles Kraft is a must-read for anyone in spiritual warfare."

Larry Richards, speaker; author, *The Full Armor of God*,
Spiritual Warfare Jesus' Way and many more

"Charles Kraft has written an informative, practical and timely book on spiritual warfare. I appreciate his humble approach in offering his insights. What he has to say will certainly help many, especially those in ministry who seek greater effectiveness in helping their congregations find spiritual freedom and healing."

Francis Frangipane, Advancing Church Ministries

"Kraft offers an incredibly important resource for all who desire to engage in spiritual warfare. His training in missions, theology and cultural anthropology make him uniquely qualified to write on this topic. His practical experience gives him expert status. Once again he is on the cutting edge. I plan to use this book in my courses."

Bill Payne, Ph.D., professor of evangelism and world missions,
director of chaplaincy studies, Ashland Theological Seminary

THE EVANGELICAL'S GUIDE TO

SPIRITUAL
WARFARE

THE EVANGELICAL'S GUIDE TO

SPIRITUAL WARFARE

SCRIPTURAL INSIGHTS
AND PRACTICAL INSTRUCTION ON
FACING THE ENEMY

CHARLES H. KRAFT

Chosen

a division of Baker Publishing Group
Minneapolis, Minnesota

Published by Chosen Books
11400 Hampshire Avenue South
Bloomington, Minnesota 55438
www.chosenbooks.com

Chosen Books is a division of
Baker Publishing Group, Grand Rapids, Michigan

Printed in the United States of America

Library of Congress Cataloging-in-Publication Data
Kraft, Charles H.
    The evangelical's guide to spiritual warfare : scriptural insights and practical instruction on facing the enemy / Charles H. Kraft.
        pages cm
    Includes bibliographical references and index.
    Summary: "A seminary professor and former missionary offers an accessible, comprehensive resource to help readers lay aside doubts and embrace a biblical, balanced approach to spiritual warfare"— Provided by publisher.
    ISBN 978-0-8007-9615-0 (pbk. : alk. paper)
    1. Spiritual warfare. 2. Evangelicalism. I. Title.
    BV4509.5.K685 2015
    235'.4—dc23   2014041706

Portions of this book were previously published by the author and adapted for this book with permission. The portions revised and adapted for this book include: Charles H. Kraft, *Confronting Powerless Christianity: Evangelicals and the Missing Dimension*, 46–62, 71–72, 115–137, 180–186, 192–233; Charles H. Kraft, "'Christian Animism' or God-Given Authority?" in *Spiritual Power and Missions: Raising the Issues*, ed. Edward Rommen, Evangelical Missiological Society Series, no. 3, 92–94, 103–106, 117–120, 123–132; Charles H. Kraft, *Defeating Dark Angels: Breaking Demonic Oppressions in the Believer's Life*, 33–64, 94–107, 151–172; and Charles H. Kraft, *I Give You Authority: Practicing the Authority Jesus Gave Us*, rev. ed., 43–48, 307–329. Full publication details of all titles in bibliography.

Unless otherwise indicated, Scripture quotations are from the Good News Translation—Second Edition. Copyright © 1992 by American Bible Society. Used by permission.

Scripture quotations identified NASB are from the New American Standard Bible®, copyright © 1960, 1962, 1963, 1968, 1971, 1972, 1973, 1975, 1977, 1995 by The Lockman Foundation. Used by permission.

Scripture quotations identified NIV are from the Holy Bible, New International Version®.

NIV®. Copyright © 1973, 1978, 1984, 2011 by Biblica, Inc.™ Used by permission of Zondervan. All rights reserved worldwide. www.zondervan.com

Scripture quotations identified NKJV are from the New King James Version. Copyright © 1982 by Thomas Nelson, Inc. Used by permission. All rights reserved.

Scripture quotations identified NLT are from the *Holy Bible*, New Living Translation, copyright © 1996, 2004, 2007 by Tyndale House Foundation. Used by permission of Tyndale House Publishers, Inc., Carol Stream, Illinois 60188. All rights reserved.

Scripture quotations identified PHILLIPS are from The New Testament in Modern English, revised edition—J. B. Phillips, translator. © J. B. Phillips 1958, 1960, 1972. Used by permission of Macmillan Publishing Co., Inc.

Scripture quotations identified TLB are from *The Living Bible*, copyright © 1971. Used by permission of Tyndale House Publishers, Inc., Wheaton, Illinois 60189. All rights reserved.

To protect the privacy of those who have shared their experiences with the author, details and names have been changed.

Cover design by LOOK Design Studio

15 16 17 18 19 20 21   7 6 5 4 3 2 1

I dedicate this book to my friend and mentor John Wimber, in gratefulness to God for the miracle that He performed through John in leading this evangelical into a powerful version of Christianity. As a lifelong evangelical, I enjoyed my relationship with Jesus. But I always felt that there was more to Christian faith than I was experiencing. Listening to John and seeing how God used him did the trick. I have not been the same since January 1982, when God used John to change my worldview and then to change my practice. We all miss John, but I will never stop praising God for bringing him across my path.

Contents

Contents

Foreword

I began reading a digital version of the manuscript of this book as I flew back from Malaysia. I had just finished teaching a three-day seminar on spiritual warfare to about three hundred church leaders. As I read, I found myself reflecting on the many ways Charles Kraft had shaped what I had just taught and the profound impact he has had on my own life over the years.

I had read Chuck's book *Christianity with Power* in 1991, but I first met him in person at a conference on spiritual warfare in Southern California in February 1994. I was there because I hoped to learn some things that would help me with the course on spiritual warfare I was teaching at Asbury Theological Seminary. I had never taught a course on the subject and knew very little about it. But because of what God had recently done in my own life and the direction the Spirit was leading, I believed such a course was needed in preparing Christian leaders. So that spring semester I stepped out and offered it.

Much to my surprise, almost a hundred students signed up! Realizing I was in way over my head, I told them the first evening we met that I was not qualified to teach the class, but we would learn together as we went. A few weeks later, I flew out to California for the conference, hoping to learn all I could and meet some people who could help me. That is where I was introduced to Chuck one morning at breakfast.

Then a few months later, he visited our seminary campus in Kentucky to speak at our School of World Mission. He also came to the class I was teaching. But Chuck wanted to do more than just speak. He wanted to minister to students. And it was during those days that I got to work with him as he engaged in healing prayer ministry—especially deliverance ministry—with several of our students. I had never seen anyone minister like he did in such an authentic, credible and pastoral way. What he modeled for me during those days changed my life. Soon afterward, I found myself involved in a similar kind of ministry with seminarians.

Over the years since then, I have connected with Chuck at several conferences and read almost every one of his books. So much of his understanding and practice of spiritual warfare has now become an integral part of my own approach. We do not always agree. His understandings and practices are often different from mine. Sometimes he makes the systematic theologian in me wince! But no one has shaped and influenced me the way he has.

I often tell students they need to make spiritual warfare *one* of the strings on their ministry guitar. It should not be the *only* string, but certainly should be *one* of them. It is firmly rooted in Scripture and the Christian tradition, an important dimension of the Christian life and often needed in the practice of ministry. The guitar definitely plays better and sounds better with this string on it.

Unfortunately, for most of us evangelical Christians in the West, because of our longtime captivity to the naturalistic worldview of the eighteenth century Enlightenment, the spiritual warfare string has been noticeably missing. Since the mid-1980s, Chuck, a lifelong evangelical himself, has been on a mission to help us put that string back on our guitar.

The book that you hold in your hands will definitely help you do that. Here you will find a wonderful compilation of all his writings and his seasoned, best thinking on a wide range of topics related to spiritual warfare. Surely, it is the best of the best of Charles Kraft!

Whether you are a spiritual warfare novice or a seasoned veteran, get ready, then, to be informed and inspired, encouraged and challenged. It is a fitting testament to Chuck's faithful and fruitful life and ministry.

Stephen A. Seamands, professor of Christian doctrine,
Asbury Theological Seminary, Wilmore, Kentucky

Acknowledgments

I want to give special thanks to my editor, Christianne Squires, for carefully going over every word. This is a much better book because of her painstaking attention to the little things. And I am grateful to work again under Jane Campbell's supervision. She and Christianne made the final editing a pleasant experience.

Introduction

The central theme of Christianity is love. "God so loved the world . . ." (John 3:16) is the central verse of the Scriptures. All else in Scripture and life is founded on this one great central theme. We are even told that "God is love" (1 John 4:8).

So, in writing about spiritual warfare, we dare not forget that the reason for a focus on this theme is to enhance our commitment to the central love theme.

However, once we have pointed out that God's love is the central theme, we need to recognize that there is an enemy, a very active and powerful enemy whose main commitment is to counter whatever God is doing. He is anti-love, anti-God, anti-everything God does and stands for. He hates God and uses every means at his disposal to thwart God's activity, especially His loving relationship with His favorite creatures—us.

But many evangelicals act as if that enemy does not exist. In preaching and teaching and our daily lives, we act as if Satan and his forces are not a problem. We go about our business as if the evil in the world is explainable in some way other than that there is an enemy behind it. We emphasize the love part as we should but tend to ignore the context in which that love is expected to flourish—a context of warfare. We live in a battle zone, and we usually do not know what to do about it.

The book you have in your hands seeks to deal with the anti-love context in which we live. I focus on that anti-love context and the enemy's activity not because they are more important than the love message but because they have been neglected, allowing our enemy to work with little hindrance due to our ignorance.

I speak as one who has lived in an evangelical, no-spiritual-warfare type of Christianity. The church I grew up in was a sound evangelical church where I was challenged to read the Scriptures and to follow them. I was so sincere that during my high school days I got up faithfully at 5:00 a.m. to study the Scriptures and to read biographies of Christian heroes, especially of missionaries. During those days I pledged my life to become a missionary. This commitment was strengthened in Christian camp and my home church, soon leading to a focus on Africa. But there was never a solid focus on dealing with the spirit world. In fact, we learned to steer clear of hyperemotionalism and Pentecostals.

To prepare for missionary service, then, I applied to Wheaton College, the college one of my mother's cousins had attended to prepare for missionary service in Africa. I applied nowhere else. I simply assumed I would be admitted. And I was.

At Wheaton I followed the recommendation of a prospective missionary to major in anthropology, which I did. I also fell in love with a woman who agreed to marry me and go to Africa with me. But I cannot recall ever meeting a Pentecostal or charismatic there, either, or in the evangelical seminary that I attended after Wheaton. To this point, still no attention was paid to the Holy Spirit or to spiritual warfare.

In Nigeria, however, it became obvious that within my strong evangelicalism I had learned nothing to assist me in dealing with the spirit world. I asked the Nigerian leaders I was expected to help what was their most important problem. Without hesitation, they answered, "Evil spirits." It became clear, then, that I could not help them with their biggest problem.

The Lord was good, however. I was never pressed into embarrassing situations in this area. And the Nigerian leaders were able to handle things on their own. But I was left with a guilty conscience and a feeling of deep inability to help my Nigerian brothers.

We came home and were not able to return. But the Lord led me into a missionary training position at Fuller Seminary in Pasadena, California, where I was to teach and write about issues of Christianity's relationship with culture. Among our student body, there was a trickle of charismatic students who kept asking, "Where is the Holy Spirit?" I did not know.

In 1982, my thirteenth year of teaching at Fuller, we invited John Wimber to teach us on healing. Though it was a course for students, I decided to attend, in hopes that the course would help me to understand what was missing in my Christianity. I was not disappointed. John was not hyper-emotional. That would have put me off. He was scripturally sound and personally balanced. What he offered, I could accept and fit into that hole in my theology.

I still consider myself an evangelical, though one who believes in and practices a more biblical Christianity than I had been trained in. That part of Christianity that my mentors ignored has been filled in, both theoretically and, most importantly, in practice. I have become a practitioner of what Jesus practiced in setting captives free. Christianity is brand-new for me.

My prayer is that this book can be of help in transforming you into a more completely biblical Christian. Not all of the book is new. I have written chapters in other books on this subject, and since those chapters embody my latest thinking on the subject, I have included several of them in this book. Much of this material was taken from *Confronting Powerless Christianity, Defeating Dark Angels, I Give You Authority* and my chapter in *Spiritual Power and Missions*.

To counter this ignorance, we need to deal solidly with our basic assumptions. These make up our worldview. I have written comprehensively about worldview in my book *Worldview for Christian Witness*[1] but summarize some of that material here to alert us to a basic problem that affects us as we attempt to move from ignorance to understanding in this area.

I also deal with the very important subject of experience. The enemy has no problem with those who believe in his existence but do not practice against him. He has the most trouble with those who have correct assumptions and oppose him actively—those who believe he is alive and well and who practice setting people free from satanic captivity.

Jesus was a practitioner, and He expects us to be practitioners as well. He expects us to fill His shoes in today's world by freeing captives from

---

1. Charles H. Kraft, *Worldview for Christian Witness* (Pasadena, Calif.: William Carey Library, 2008).

17

the enemy's clutches. Let this book, then, be a call to action, a call to participate in the warfare that made up so much of Jesus' life and ministry. It is not enough to know the truth academically. We need to know it in practice. That kind of knowledge and experience is the kind of love Jesus has called us to incarnate.

There are two major events in a Christian's life—salvation and freedom. Millions of God's people are saved but not free. But as the apostle Paul points out, it is freedom that God calls us to—freedom beyond salvation (see Galatians 1:4; 5:1). A major aim of this book is to enable God's people to bring freedom to those who are saved but still in captivity. May God bless you richly as you read and apply what you learn.

Charles H. Kraft
Pasadena, California
February 2015

Part 1

Introduction to

SPIRITUAL
WARFARE

1

A Concern for Spiritual Warfare

Recently, I attended a two-day gathering of evangelical leaders where a series of presentations was made with the aim of instructing and challenging the leaders to greater effectiveness in their ministries. The leaders would all claim to be biblical, but not a word was said to help us challenge Satan. To that group of evangelical leaders, it is as if the enemy does not exist, as if the softer themes of love and faithfulness are all there is to focus on in ministry, as if the considerable amount of attention Jesus, our model, gave to challenging and defeating this enemy was not to be imitated.

But there is another group of evangelicals just as committed to the softer themes but also concerned about what the enemy is doing and what we need to do to confront and defeat him. These leaders have been awakened by the many books and seminars that have come into existence recently. They recognize that our enemy is alive and well and very active in our world and even in our churches. This group has discovered that we do not have to become weird to be concerned about spiritual warfare.

The fairly recent cooling of the historical antipathy of evangelicals toward Pentecostals has opened many of us up to learning from Pentecostals and charismatics. We have even been named. We are called the Third Wave. We have been learning to take more seriously than evangelicals usually do the spiritual power aspects of biblical Christianity. Jesus predicted, "Those who believe in me will do what I do" (John 14:12). We note that what Jesus did and predicted we would do includes challenging Satan in spiritual warfare.

My experience as a "card-carrying evangelical" is a case in point. I was led through a paradigm shift and a practice shift into power ministry,[1] which has transformed my life and allowed me to work with God to bring spiritual freedom to hundreds of God's children.

One of the authors who has awakened many is Frank Peretti, through his books *This Present Darkness* and *Piercing the Darkness*. With regard to him, the question in many people's minds is, Since Peretti's books are fiction, how well does his portrayal of spiritual warfare correspond to what happens in real life? The answers given to this question, then, divide us into two camps: those with experience dealing with the spirit world and those without experience.

> I grant a high degree of credibility to Peretti's picture of the spirit world.

My thirty-plus years of working in spiritual warfare, during which I have ministered to several hundred demonized people, leads me to grant a high degree of credibility to Peretti's picture of the spirit world. He portrays a very active, well-organized realm of evil spirits—a realm assumed by the authors of Scripture. He then imagines what goes on between the spirits that inhabit that realm—evil spirits and angels of God—and human beings. He clearly describes the great evil power that operates as satanic conspiracy and the attempts of the evil spirits to defeat God by thwarting and attacking the people of God and their institutions. He observes the need for partnership between humans and God to counter that power. He correctly views prayer

---

1. For more information on power ministry, see Charles H. Kraft, *Christianity with Power: Your Worldview and Your Experience of the Supernatural* (Eugene, Ore.: Wipf & Stock, 2005). (Originally published Ann Arbor, Mich.: Vine, 1989.)

as an act of warfare and the primary means of obtaining the spiritual power that enables us to attack the enemy and win.

Many, especially those coming from a theological perspective, have tried to discredit Peretti.[2] These critics usually have had no experience in dealing with the spirit world. Those with experience join me in recognizing that Peretti knows better than his critics what he is talking about.

So, when evangelicals ask me how to gain insight into what is going on in the spirit world, I frequently recommend reading *This Present Darkness* and *Piercing the Darkness*. Though Peretti uses imagination to construct his stories, he offers great insight into what probably goes on in the invisible spirit world. He knows what he is dealing with and deserves to be taken seriously.

Other helpful books have also sprung up recently. Just to mention my own, I have written *Christianity with Power; Confronting Powerless Christianity; I Give You Authority; Deep Wounds, Deep Healing; Defeating Dark Angels; Behind Enemy Lines; The Rules of Engagement* and *Two Hours to Freedom*. You can also find an extensive list of resources in the bibliography at the end of this book.

Is It Right for Us to Ignore This Topic?

For generations, spiritual power issues have "belonged" to Pentecostals and charismatics. We evangelicals have tended to reject such concerns and connect them to emotionalism and going overboard on tongues, prophecy and other gifts of the Spirit. We take a more rational, less emotional approach that we claim is more biblical than Pentecostal emotionalism. Though our major doctrines are pretty much the same as those of the Pentecostals, we consider ourselves more composed, more reason-oriented and less emotional. "We know. We don't need to feel," we say, "for feelings will mislead us."

Typical of our attitude is the response of an evangelical pastor I once asked about demons. I said, "If demons exist, would you rather know or

2. See, for example, Robert Guelich, "Spiritual Warfare: Jesus, Paul and Peretti," in *Pneuma* 13 (1991): 33–64.

not know?" He answered, as probably most evangelicals would if they were being honest, "I'd rather not know!" He was living rather comfortably in a kind of Christianity quite unlike that of Jesus.

Jesus' Christianity had a lot of room for demons. Yes, His was a message of love. But it was also a message of freedom, recognizing that many people are in captivity both to sin and to Satan. His mandate was to free them from that captivity (see Luke 4:18). And just before Jesus left the earth, He promised that anyone who has faith in Him would do the works He was doing here on earth (see John 14:12).

When Jesus left the world, He gave us the Holy Spirit. Since the Holy Spirit lives within us, then, in the spirit world we are like elephants and demons are like mice. The myth is that elephants are terrified by mice. They run when they see them, even though elephants have much more power than mice. Mice win in their encounters by bluff, not by power. They bluff elephants into fear.

So it is with us. The enemy easily bluffs us into fearing evil spirits, even though we carry infinitely more power than satanic "mice." We choose to be ignorant rather than to challenge our enemy, though he terrorizes our people. We fear, giving the enemy a victory he should not have. We have enough to do, we say, dealing with other aspects of our message and mission without opening this can of worms. The result, though, is a sub-biblical Christianity—a Christianity without power, a secular Christianity so affected by Western secular assumptions that we deny in practice, if not in theory, the existence of the invisible supernatural world. But our people are looking for a faith with power as well as insight. Our worldview is a basic problem here, and we will deal with this worldview in the following chapters.

Evangelical theologians, to the extent that they deal with the spirit world at all, tend to spend their time discussing whether or not demons exist today. Often they follow liberal thinking by suggesting that what the New Testament portrayed as demons was merely a pre-scientific understanding of what we know now were psychological problems. Many pastors join them, eliminating spiritual warfare from their agendas. In addition, evangelical scholars and pastors have bought into the secular assumption that emotional problems are all psychological, not spiritual. The result of such assumptions is that Jesus is trusted when He talks about love or sin but not when He assumes demonic influence, as He often did.

But should we not assume that Jesus is as right about demons as He is about love and sin? Could it be that people in our churches are inhabited by demons, as they were in the synagogues of Jesus' day? Is it right to assume that Jesus' war against satanic emissaries is over? Did Jesus rid the world of demons once and for all? Or are demons smart enough to keep themselves hidden from people who question their existence, lest Christians wake up to the power they have and start using it?

We notice that some go to excess. Some blame everything on demons and avoid their own responsibility for their actions. "The devil made me do it" is their way of explaining aberrant behavior. We do not want to be associated with people like that. We do not want a reputation of believing what they believe and behaving like them. Some of us would rather turn away from this area that was important to Jesus than to be labeled Pentecostal or charismatic.

> **Should we not assume that Jesus is as right about demons as He is about love and sin?**

But Jesus knew something we may not. He could see that the world is full of spirits, many of them on Satan's side, whose job is to make life as difficult as possible for the followers of Jesus. And He showed us what to do about it. He did not treat demonization as a psychological problem. Psychological problems do not talk to us. Demons do.

Jesus was not simply accommodating to a pre-scientific worldview that believed psychological problems were demonic beings. He saw what I have called "capital *R*" Reality (God's reality) and acted accordingly. He knew that there are alien beings who serve Satan, hate humans and actively disrupt whatever they can. He knew that these beings were very much a part of His world. They are also an active part of our world.

With Jesus on our side, do we do well to fear or ignore this area? No. We should not approach this area fearfully. But we do need to learn a few things. We have all the power of God on our side—much more power than our enemy has. But there are rules of engagement. Jesus did not go into battle unprepared. Nor dare we. There is help. And we do not have to become like the hyperemotional, weird ones who—so unlike Jesus—make spiritual warfare look so distasteful to us evangelicals.

The Bible Does Not Ignore It

The Bible has a lot to say about Satan and demons. These issues are taken very seriously throughout Scripture. Throughout the Old Testament, the evil kingdom is always lurking in the background and affecting what goes on in the human realm. Each of the kings of Israel and Judah were evaluated as good or bad on the basis of what each did with the satanic strongholds called "high places." They were not simply graded on a human scale. They left as their legacy what they did spiritually. That is what the biblical authors considered most important.

Satan is not omnipresent. He has to depend on his principalities, powers, rulers and ground-level demons to carry out his plans (see Ephesians 6:12). Whether in the Garden of Eden or afflicting Job, whether through activities during Israel's wars or by influencing Israel's kings and the pagan nations, these messengers of evil have been the agents of Satan.

In the New Testament, ground-level demonic spirits influenced those who killed the babies when Jesus was a child (see Matthew 2:16–18). Though Satan himself confronted Jesus in the wilderness (see Luke 4:1–13), he was undoubtedly accompanied by a host of demonic spirits. Satan and his minions were very active when Jesus was on earth. We frequently see Jesus exposing and casting them out. Satanic beings must have been behind the Pharisees and the other Jewish leaders as they developed their opposition to Jesus.

We see demonic beings visible in many of the events recorded in the book of Acts (e.g., Ananias and Sapphira, Acts 5:1–11; the demonized slave-girl, Acts 16:16–18) and in activities recorded throughout the epistles and Revelation (e.g., the table of demons, 1 Corinthians 10:21; the blinding of those who do not believe, 2 Corinthians 4:4; the teachings of demons, 1 Timothy 4:1; and many of the activities recorded in the book of Revelation). The apostle Paul summarizes the situation as follows: "For our struggle is not against flesh and blood, but against the rulers, against the authorities, against the powers of this dark world and against the spiritual forces of evil in the heavenly realms" (Ephesians 6:12 NIV).

Jesus and the other New Testament personages took Satan and his hosts seriously, but they were not alarmed by the satanic kingdom or its activities. They did not fear evil spirits. They were not impressed by them at all. When confronted, they dealt with them matter-of-factly, knowing that God's Kingdom and His power are infinitely greater. They acknowledged the existence of these evil spirits and used the power of the Holy Spirit to fight them.

The satanic kingdom wants us to fear it. But when we realize how little power that kingdom has when compared to the power of God, very little fear is left. We should respect Satan and demons and never take them lightly, but most of what looks like power on their part is either deceit or bluff or both. They really have little more power than that given them by the person they inhabit. If that person's will is engaged against the demons in partnership with Jesus—usually with the help of someone else—it is only a matter of time before the demons must go. A struggle may take place at first if the person's will is not yet on God's side or if he or she has a lot of inner healing work to do. But as soon as the person is willing to deal with their inner work and someone knowledgeable helps them, the tough part is over.

Speaking about the Kingdom of God and demonstrating the power that is its hallmark were among the most important things Jesus did. He pointed to this power when He stated that His driving out demons "proves that the Kingdom of God has already come to you" (Luke 11:20). Jesus clearly operated in God-anointed spiritual authority and power. He came to defeat Satan both during His life and through the cross and resurrection. He ministered in power, defeating the enemy every time He took him on. A major part of the gospels is devoted to accounts of the authority and power demonstrations that characterize Jesus' battles with the enemy.

Jesus made it plain that He wanted His followers to minister in His power and authority. During His earthly ministry, He conferred on His apostles (see Luke 9) and the 72 (see Luke 10) the "power and authority to drive out all demons and to cure diseases" (Luke 9:1). With this authority and power, Jesus' followers were to heal the sick and let people know that "the Kingdom of God has come near" (Luke 10:9). Then Jesus said to the disciples and to us, "As the Father sent me, so I send you" (John

20:21). His intent was that His followers imitate His approach to witness, accompanying words with power (see Acts 1:8).

From Matthew 28:20, we learn that Jesus meant for His followers to pass along to their followers the things He had taught them. He stated that they were to teach their followers "to obey everything [He had] commanded [them]." He then promised, "Whoever believes in me will do the works I have been doing, and they will do even greater things than these, because I am going to the Father" (John 14:12 NIV). We can assume that doing what Jesus has been doing includes exercising His power to deal with demons. So let's turn our attention to a deeper reflection on what this means.

> **Jesus made it plain that He wanted His followers to minister in His power and authority.**

2

Issues in Spiritual Warfare

There are a number of issues to be dealt with under the general heading of *spiritual warfare*. Though most preaching and teaching tend to emphasize what might be called the peaceful side of our faith, there is also a very important warfare side to it. Love, faith, peace and the like are what I am calling the peaceful side. This is the side James Kallas calls the "Godward view."[1] As Kallas points out, though, the majority of the Scriptures deal with what he calls the "Satanward view," the warfare part of the gospels and human life. (We will discuss Kallas's insights in greater depth in chapter 8.)

I choose to refer to the Satanward side as *warfare*, though there are those who rightly object to the term since it is often assumed either side can win in a war. These people prefer a term like *spiritual plundering*, since there is no chance the satanic side can win. However, those of us who prefer the

1. See James G. Kallas, *The Satanward View: A Study in Pauline Theology* (Philadelphia: Westminster Press, 1966).

term *warfare* can point out that it is not necessary to assume either side can win for the term to be used. For example, during the Second World War, Germany was still fighting what was considered a war for nearly a year after its defeat was assured. And some of the bloodiest encounters of the war took place between June 1944 and May 1945, when the unconditional surrender was signed. So, even though the defeat of Satan is assured, the fighting continues until God wraps things up. Plus, it feels like war.

Whatever we call it, there are a number of important issues to deal with, eight of which I will highlight below and others of which will emerge as we deal with our subject.

Issue 1: The Bible Speaks of Demons

The first issue is the fact that, according to the Bible, there is a spirit world that includes noncorporeal, spiritual entities that serve Satan (see Ephesians 6:12). We call them demons.

Though the influence of Enlightenment rationalism has been quite effective in causing many evangelical traditions to deny the existence of Satan and demons, or at least to minimize their activity, we claim to take the Bible seriously. And the Bible takes Satan, demons and their activities very seriously.

> Psychological problems are not separate beings that can talk to people and be cast out.

It is not, as some claim, simply an outmoded primitive worldview that holds that demons exist. Nor is Jesus simply a good psychologist. Both the New Testament and ministry experience show that demons, unlike psychological problems, are separate beings that live in people, can talk and can be eliminated through the authoritative use of the power of Jesus Christ. Psychological problems, though very real, are not separate beings that can talk to people and be cast out.

As we might expect from representatives of the kingdom of darkness and deceit, demons are very good at hiding and keeping people unaware of their presence. I myself was completely unaware of demonic activity—though I would have said I believed in demons—for the first 38 years of my Christian experience. When, however, demons are challenged in the name of Jesus Christ, they can be forced to reveal their presence. And they can reply, convey information and, unlike psychological problems, be cast out.

I have now worked with several hundred demonized people and become keenly aware of the presence and activity of these scripturally authenticated beings. I may have been fooled a few times over the course of the past thirty-plus years since I met my first demon, but I have not been fooled hundreds of times. Demons do exist, just as Scripture indicates they do, and they are alive and active today.

Those who come to the Bible and life with no experience identifying and dealing with demons may claim that demons do not exist or that they are not an important factor in human experience. Even seminary professors and pastors, who are assumed to be conversant with spiritual things, are often more influenced by their naturalistic, humanistic, secular worldview than by Jesus' words and teachings in this area. They often try to explain Jesus' activities by portraying Him as a good psychologist.

Some, especially those who have had a bit of psychology, see what we call demonization as the psychological disorder now referred to as dissociative identity disorder (DID, formerly called multiple personality disorder, or MPD). But their lack of experience plus their Western worldview mislead them. I have worked with several hundred demonized people and at least a hundred persons with DID/MPD and can testify that demons are quite distinct from the dissociated parts that characterize DID. Experience with demonized people and those with DID enables one to clearly differentiate between "person parts" and the alien beings we call demons, though demonization usually accompanies DID. Thus, in every DID client with whom I have worked, I have also found demonization.

When a person dissociates in order to survive, his or her angry and fearful reactions provide fertile ground for the entrance of demons into each of the person parts that respond in that way. So when we find that a client is dissociative, we look for and find demons in almost every dissociated part. Though we may be puzzled at first, it usually becomes clear fairly soon that the demons and the person parts are quite distinct from each other. (We will discuss MPD and DID in greater detail in chapters 9 and 11.)

Issue 2: The Bible Portrays a Context of Conflict

Not only does the Bible speak of demons, but it also portrays a context of conflict between God's Kingdom and Satan's.

The Old Testament portrays God as waging a constant battle against animism and idolatry among His chosen people. God commands His people to put Him first among the gods (see Exodus 20:5). Then He constantly condemns the kings of Israel and Judah for whoring after these other gods (see 2 Chronicles 21:13; Jeremiah 3:2; Ezekiel 16:15–26). We see a constant battle going on for the will of His people. God shows us what took place in the human realm when God's people either followed Him or ignored Him. But behind the scenes, we see clearly implied that as people "do their thing," a cosmic battle rages between God and Satan.

When we look at Job 1, Daniel 10, Isaiah 14 and Ezekiel 28, we get a better view of what is going on in the heavenlies. But even then, that area is none too clear for us. However, when we look at people today with the Old Testament perspective in our awareness, we see a propensity in humans today to imitate the unfaithfulness of the Israelites. It seems, then, that we should be taking seriously this spiritual dimension of the Old Testament.

In the New Testament, too, we see Jesus and the apostles constantly at war with evil invisible beings. Jesus stated He came to set captives free (see Luke 4:18–19), implying that someone out there has put people into captivity. John, then, underlined what Jesus said when he stated that "the Son of God appeared . . . to destroy what the Devil had done" (1 John 3:8). And Paul was so concerned about spiritual conflict that he commanded us to put on full spiritual armor (see Ephesians 6:10–18). Many more references could be cited, pointing to the fact that we are in a battle first for people's souls but also to rescue them from demonization and sickness. It is clear that the Bible presents us living in a battle zone.

Though traditional evangelical seminaries and Bible schools claim to be biblical, they usually provide little or no instruction in this important area. Evangelical teachers and pastors, even those who are most critical of the "demythologizing" of liberals, tend to treat anything to do with demons as if they do not exist today. And if the teachers do recognize the existence of demons, they have no idea how to deal with them and so ignore them.

Ignoring the activity of satanic forces allows them to run rampant within our churches and training institutions.

This area was neglected in my own evangelical background, though I contended for the Scriptures. My seminary training provided hardly a glimpse into dealing with Satan and demons, even though one of our textbooks had a section in it dealing with the enemy kingdom. However, we never got to that part of the book before the term ended! Most of us in seminary learned to give lip service to the fact that we are in conflict with Satan, but we gave no attention to that conflict beyond the need to win souls away from the enemy.

Things changed for me when I experienced an awakening in my own life in 1982. I found myself for the first time getting insight into a question my Nigerian brothers had asked: What can we do about evil spirits? I did not know the answer in the '50s in Nigeria, but I was learning in the '80s under the tutelage of John Wimber in a class we started at Fuller Seminary.

I started attending that class with many questions, such as: What involvement should evangelicals have in the spiritual warfare part of Jesus' total cause? We have done well to emphasize the winning of souls, but what about the freedom Jesus promised? Can we be content to simply deal with things at the human level and ignore the spirit level? Does our obedience to Christ commit us to do more?

Issue 3: Deliverance and Healing Were Modeled by Jesus

Jesus neither ignored the presence of demons, as evangelical pastors and seminary teachers traditionally do, nor treated demons as the cause of every problem, as certain Pentecostals do. He dealt with both demons and healing matter-of-factly, without making a show of it. He then gave His followers authority over both demons and diseases (see Luke 9:1; 10:19) and promised that we would do the works that He did (see John 14:12). These works undoubtedly included the casting out of demons and healing in the power of the Holy Spirit.

Having led His disciples into power ministry, Jesus then commanded them to teach their followers everything He had commanded them (see Matthew 28:20). He wanted those He taught to teach their followers—coming down to us today—both the love message and the warfare message. As such, we are to both practice and teach healing and deliverance as Jesus and His followers did.

When we look at Scripture and Jesus' expectations for His followers, it is clear that it is those who do not get involved in ministering deliverance and healing who have to justify their behavior, not those who are active in these areas. For Jesus, this kind of ministry was normal. It should be for us also, if we claim to be following His example. Those for whom such ministry is not normal are the ones who have some explaining to do.

For most of us, following Jesus' example in these power areas requires two shifts: a paradigm shift and a practice shift. It requires a change of perspective and a change in behavior.[2] We need to understand that Jesus has empowered us to do His deliverance and healing ministry. Then we need to get busy doing the ministry—healing and delivering people from demons.

Issue 4: Jesus Would Do the Same Today

If Jesus were a part of our churches and training institutions today, would He not be actively engaged in fighting the enemy and setting captives free, just like He did during His time on earth before? He said He came to set captives free (see Luke 4:18–19), and He would not be content to simply talk about setting them free. He would do ministry. He would be setting captives free from the enemy. He taught through works as well as words. He assumed that we live in a world of conflict between God and Satan, and He did what He could to free people from the enemy. His early followers did the same.

Freeing people from emotional and spiritual problems—including the demonic—is an important ministry endorsed by Jesus and meant to be part of the experience of every Christian. Such ministry is thoroughly appropriate to churches and educational institutions that purport to be ministering to people and freeing them spiritually.

Those of us involved in teaching ministries need to add person-to-person ministry to our lecturing and writing, modeling what Jesus modeled for us,

2. For more on this topic, see Kraft, *Christianity with Power*.

which includes freeing our students from emotional and spiritual problems. In addition, we need to be instructing our students by word and deed how to deal with spiritual problems to which demons may be attached.

Some ministerial training institutions give a lot of attention to counseling. This is well and good, except that these institutions are usually teaching secular psychology with precious little spiritual input and no attention given to dealing with spiritual beings and power.

I am afraid the church has bought into the view of secularists, who try to make a picture of a three-hundred-piece puzzle but ignore one hundred of the pieces. Reality presents us with a life made up of material, human and spiritual aspects. The world tries to explain everything in terms of the two hundred pieces of material and human life, as if that is all there is, but ignores the hundred pieces that represent spiritual reality. It tries to make the complete picture with just two hundred pieces, and it does not work for them, yet we imitate them, trying to make sense of reality, too, by explaining it in terms of our knowledge of material and human insight alone.

Jesus would not do it that way. If Jesus were invited to work within such a secularized curriculum, He would infuse it with spiritual concern and ministry and spend His time demonstrating that the neglected spiritual dimension is the crucial part of any help such teaching is expected to bring.

Issue 5: Our Church Leaders Must Learn Warfare

Today's world, like that of Jesus, is full of evidence that Satan and his demons are very active in all areas of human life, including church life. Such problems as homosexuality, pornography, divorce, abortion, suicide, violence, abuse and even nominalism and religiosity are not merely human problems (though they are that). They also have spiritual, often demonic dimensions.

Church leaders today need to learn how to deal with the spiritual dimensions of these problems. It is not enough to teach secular approaches to these major life issues. Nor is it enough to teach our students to deal only with the human end of such problems. Evangelical training institutions claim to deal with spiritual reality but virtually ignore the spiritual power dimension that for Jesus and the rest of the New Testament was a very important area. And since faculty and administration ignore it, our students go out ill-prepared to deal with this dimension, as did nearly all of us who presently teach in such institutions.

Jesus taught by doing as well as by talking. We cannot effectively teach spiritual warfare by simply talking about it. We need apprentices who will put insight into practice. Our training needs to be more like medical internships than like the average classroom in which information is bought and sold. When we teach preaching, we believe a student needs to get up in front and do it. The student cannot pass preaching class simply by talking about it. Nor can a soldier or an athlete win by simply talking about the battles or the game.

> **We cannot effectively teach spiritual warfare by simply talking about it.**

The same applies to spiritual warfare—we do not learn to do it simply by talking about it, as we have learned to do with most subjects in our school classes. Students learn what they do. If they talk about it, they learn to talk about it. If the subject is ignored, they learn to ignore the subject. If they watch people do something and then practice it themselves, they learn to do it.

Issue 6: It Does Not Have to Be Crazy

The models of faith healing, deliverance from demons and other types of spiritual warfare we may see on TV and in healing campaigns often turn people away from this ministry, seeing it as crazy. This is most unfortunate. If we look at Jesus, we see none of the hyperemotionalism and showmanship that many contemporary ministries seem to major on.

Many evangelicals react against such showiness and assume that anyone who gets into power ministry is unbalanced at best and a charlatan at worst. They cannot imagine the possibility of a more balanced approach so they dismiss the ministry as well as the purveyors of the ministry. They evaluate in terms of their stereotypes of those attempting to minister in a sane way without asking if there is a more sane approach to power ministry.

Jesus seemed to go about His ministry calm, cool and collected, more like noncharismatics than like extreme Pentecostals. He demonstrated that such ministry can be done in a reasonable manner.

I understand where people are coming from who insist that spiritual power ministries and ministers are wacky. Many of them are. I myself was once put off by any mention of dealing with demons because the wacky approach was all I knew. But I have found that we can learn to do spiritual warfare in more balanced ways, and I am trying to prove it in my own practice.

We of the Third Wave regret unscriptural doctrinal aberrations, such as the "name it, claim it" teaching, the "demon under every bush" teaching and the teaching that we do not have to take responsibility for our sinful behavior because demons are to blame. I label these teachings heretical and unbiblical. Unfortunately, they are taught by some very visible "faith healers," some of them very gifted in ministry and as communicators.

I believe as evangelicals who are into spiritual power, we can demonstrate a better way. For one thing, we tend to have a more solid biblical base than those who fit the stereotype of Pentecostals and charismatics, even though we have erred in not paying more attention to spiritual power. We also tend to be less emotional. Further, we are potentially less given to exaggerating the importance of lesser gifts in favor of more important and practical emphases, such as healing and deliverance.

It is a shame that many evangelicals, in reaction against the excesses of certain Pentecostal and charismatic ministries, have turned completely away from this ministry that Jesus felt to be so important.

Issue 7: Our Institutions Need to Outgrow Fear

As Third Wave evangelicals, we have tried to exemplify a balanced form of evangelicalism in our ministries and in our training. We have aimed to be biblical and to follow Jesus' example. But we have been infected by the rationalism, secularism and humanism of the society around us and moved into what might be called a secular Christianity. In dealing with spiritual power, then, we have tended to embrace the extreme views of certain Reformed and dispensational theologians (e.g., Warfield, Darby) while navigating away from the insights of Pentecostal and charismatic Christianity.

In recent days, however, there has been a cooling of the antipathy toward Pentecostals and charismatics by certain evangelical leaders who have begun to accept them as long as they are not too wild. These Pentecostals and charismatics have been admitted into traditional evangelical organizations, even into leadership in traditionally noncharismatic evangelical groups (e.g., National Association of Evangelicals, Gordon-Conwell Theological Seminary, Fuller Theological Seminary, Biola University, Dallas Theological Seminary, Asbury Theological Seminary). Sadly, some of these Pentecostals and charismatics have gained acceptance by downplaying their distinctives and, I am told by some, have lost their concern for healing and deliverance. "We might as well be Presbyterian!" one Pentecostal leader once said to me.

> **Spiritual power issues can be dealt with in a balanced, scriptural way.**

With this new openness to charismatic concerns, we can hope that traditional evangelicals and our institutions can outgrow their fear and suspicion of those who deal with these distinctive emphases of Pentecostal and charismatic Christianity. We need to learn that these issues can be dealt with in a balanced, scriptural way. This book aims at presenting the issues of spiritual warfare in just such a way.

Unfortunately, traditional evangelicalism has offered largely secular answers to pastoral, emotional and missionary problems. Theologically, we are primarily rationalists, working in a secular form of activity much like secular philosophy. In counseling, we advocate secular psychology, even though the practitioners are Christian. In missiology, we have become known—at least before 1982—for offering secular approaches to church growth, culture and communication. Educationally, our educational institutions are more like secular universities than the kind of relationally based learning community that Jesus developed.

During my first decade at Fuller, one of the questions I heard most insistently from Pentecostal and charismatic students was, "Where is the Holy Spirit?" I was teaching missionaries some very helpful things about

Christianity in relation to culture but did not know how to answer that question. Out of that sense of need, then, I sought to learn from John Wimber where and how the Holy Spirit was working. I opened myself to seeking how to combine the best of Pentecostal and charismatic insight and practice with the great scriptural and intellectual foundation that evangelicalism has provided.

With what seems to be a new openness on the part of some evangelical pastors and institutions, there may be more hope today than previously that we can see some changes. Requests coming to me for seminars on spiritual power are frequent. And my courses on spiritual power at Fuller were very well attended. My books dealing with spiritual power for evangelicals sell well. Some evangelical churches and many students are interested. And mission faculty both at Fuller and elsewhere are coming to see the importance of expertise in the area of spiritual power to Christian missions both in the non-Western world and in North America.

Though church leaders who are in established positions and are not looking for controversy may be resistant, it is encouraging that there are some who are looking for answers to real-world spiritual problems.

Issue 8: Demons Are a Secondary Problem

Our experience dealing with demons has led us to recognize they are a secondary problem. The primary problem is the amount and kind of spiritual and emotional garbage that is at work in a person's life. Dealing with the garbage, therefore, is the most important thing to do. In ministry, we spend most of our time (approximately three-quarters of it) dealing with this garbage. This is an inner healing type of counseling with the overt presence and activity of the Holy Spirit playing an integral part. It is a counseling approach to setting captives free.

Ignoring demons when they are present, as in approaches in which the client is only counseled, leaves a person understanding more of his or her condition but still unhealed and unfree. So we also deal with the demons and get rid of them. Complete healing does not come unless both the emotional and the spiritual components of a person's problems are dealt with. This means dealing primarily with the emotional garbage but also with the spiritual "rats" that make their home in that garbage, and in that order.

Most deliverance ministries err by assuming that the demons (rats) are the biggest problem and that getting rid of them should lead to healing. So they go after the demons with little or no dealing with the emotional and spiritual problems. On the other hand, ministries that involve only counseling, dealing with the garbage, tend to assume the only problems are human problems.

Our ministry approach is to assume that both human problems and demons are there. We deal with the human problems first. Then, when the garbage on which the demons have fed is taken care of, they are left with little or no ability to fight. In this way, we very seldom have any violence in getting them out.

What I refer to as garbage includes both *spiritual problems*, such as sin, curses, commitments to occult organizations, dedication to evil spirits or the gods of other religions, and *emotional problems*, such as unforgiveness, hatred, anger, fear, shame, guilt, lust and the like. Demons are attached to these problems. For the person to receive complete healing, then, both the garbage and the rats need to be dealt with.

As we have seen, there are significant issues to contend with if we, as evangelicals, are to continue closing our eyes to the presence and activity of the spirit realm. We have reviewed a range of these issues, including the witnesses of Scripture, culture and experience. All point to the clear acknowledgment of the spirit realm and warfare reality and what to do about it. Reader, how will you respond?

Part 2

The
PERSPECTIVE

3

Principles
of Interpretation

It is clear to most of us that our traditional Western worldview patterns affect our understanding of reality in such a way that the existence of invisible things is denied unless proven by secular science (e.g., germs, radio and TV waves). Though this is changing a bit as Westerners become more interested in and often involved with the occult, the unfamiliarity of Christians with the spiritual realm makes us very insecure in our quest to accept and understand more of spiritual reality.

Though some of us have now gotten over the habit of denying spiritual reality, we may retain a measure of insecurity concerning how to interpret Scripture and life. In what follows, we will explore spiritual reality in light of Scripture and experience with a focus on how we interpret each. The theological area we are working in here is called *hermeneutics*.

The Problem of Scripture

An important hermeneutical problem in our attempts to make sense out of these matters stems from the nature of Scripture. Throughout Scripture, we are given bare-bones, surface-level descriptions of events, usually without any attempt to explain what the motivations were of the persons involved or what were the underlying spiritual dynamics. We are left to infer both. Whether it is Peter's denials of Jesus (see Matthew 26:69–75) or David's sin with Bathsheba (see 2 Samuel 11) or the reason for the delay in answering Daniel's fervent prayer (see Daniel 10) or why, contrary to Jewish custom, Jesus needed to go through Samaria in John 4:4, we are usually not told what biblical characters were thinking or even what God was thinking at the time.

Likewise with regard to the spiritual dynamics behind given human events. Except for the conversation between God and Satan concerning Job (see Job 1) and between Jesus and Satan at Jesus' temptations (see Luke 4:1–13), plus a few other events, we are left to speculate what Satan was doing in the background. We have very little direct information concerning how he operates or the rules by which his activities are governed. We are largely left to infer both from the surface-level descriptions we read.

Jesus tells us that people are in captivity to Satan (see Luke 4:18–19), that Satan is the ruler of the world (see John 14:30) and that Satan has a kingdom that, Jesus infers, is active and well organized (see Matthew 12:25–26). Jesus demonstrates that His Kingdom and the power He gives His followers (see Luke 9:1) are greater than the kingdom and power of Satan. He calls even a physical healing a release from the enemy's grip (see Luke 13:10–17). But neither Jesus nor the biblical authors who recorded the events explain the principles behind God's Kingdom and power.

Due to the surface, human-level nature of the descriptions of these events, we often can at least infer the influence of human sin in them. We are shown, for example, that Adam, David and many others disobeyed God and sinned, thus bringing about judgment by God. But when the disciples attempted to infer sin as the cause of the plight of the man born blind (see John 9) or of those killed when a tower fell (see Luke 13:4), Jesus denied sin was the reason but gave no insight into the behind-the-scenes spiritual dynamics that influenced these events.

Nor are we informed as to why curses and blessings work, when they work and what might be the conditions under which they might not work.

My own translation of Proverbs 26:2—"A curse unwarranted is like a bird that flutters around but cannot land"—helps a little but does not explain most of what we, as well as the translators of Proverbs unacquainted with these spiritual dynamics, would like to know. Nor do the descriptions help us much in our attempts to understand the principles at work in Jacob's blessings (see Genesis 48–49) or in the curse God led Elijah to put on Ahab's family because of what Ahab did to Naboth (see 1 Kings 21:20–24) or of the strange dynamics involved in Balaam's activities in Numbers 22–24 or in scores of similar scriptural events.

> **Our Western worldview greatly interferes with our attempts to gain insight into spiritual reality.**

One thing that is clear, however, is that our Western worldview greatly interferes with our attempts to gain insight into the spiritual realities behind such events. From the perspective of our Western evangelicalism, we can read the descriptions and easily pick up the human factors. However, our worldview blindness in the spiritual area results in our having untrustworthy instincts when trying to understand what is going on in the spirit world.

The Problem of Causality

Another important—and rarely noticed—Western worldview influence is our habit of reducing every effect to a single cause. In dealing with demonization, for example, I am frequently asked, "Is this a demon or a psychological problem?" The underlying assumption, stemming from our worldview, is that it is one or the other. People frequently are pushed into cognitive dissonance when I reply that it is both—for demons must have something to attach to. Again, they are like rats, which cannot exist unless there is garbage for them to feed on. The garbage, then, is usually emotional or spiritual damage. So, with respect to demonization and most other spiritual issues, there is *dual causation*.

Likewise with regard to the issue of territorial spirits. The argument over whether we have the right to pray against (or, rather, take authority over) higher-level demons is often couched in either-or terms. For example, many will say we ought to deal with the sin and repentance of a people group rather than with higher-level demons because sin and repentance are the root issue. I contend, however, that there is dual causation with these higher-level problems, just as there is for the individual demonized person. That is, dealing with territorial spirits automatically means we also need to deal with the garbage of sin that requires repentance on the part of the group. We are not turning people away from the scriptural mandate to deal with the internal stuff. We are simply saying that spirit problems, whether connected to individuals or groups, need to be addressed at both the human and suprahuman levels.

The Problem of Anthropology

There are, in addition, certain issues of interpretation in the anthropological area. Chief among them is the question raised by some of our critics whether certain of our practices are to be considered the use of animism and magic or as the use of God-given authority.[1] If they are magic, how does one keep from accusing Jesus and biblical peoples of the same? How we see the cultural issues, then, interacts with our understanding of how God has set things up in the universe and how Satan, whom we know is a counterfeiter, is able to work.

If, as I contend in my book *Behind Enemy Lines*,[2] the rules of operation in the spirit realm are largely the same for both sides—as are the rules in the material and human realms—it should not surprise us if the forms by means of which spiritual power is conveyed are the same for both God and Satan. For example, the law of gravity and all other physical laws apply to both the righteous and the unrighteous. The major differences in the operation of spiritual principles lie in the *source* of the power and the *way* the principles are used, not in the principles themselves. In application

1. See Robert J. Priest, Thomas Campbell, and Bradford A. Mullen, "Missiological Syncretism: The New Animistic Paradigm," in *Spiritual Power and Missions*, ed. Edward Rommen (Pasadena, Calif.: William Carey Library, 1995), 9–87.

2. Charles H. Kraft, ed., with Mark White, *Behind Enemy Lines: An Advanced Guide to Spiritual Warfare* (Eugene, Ore.: Wipf & Stock, 2000). (Originally published Ann Arbor, Mich.: Vine, 1994.)

of these principles, then, the methods and techniques used by Satan and those used by God for blessing, healing, dedication, worship and the like will be largely the same, in spite of the fact that the power comes from opposite sources.

Though we use such terms as *animism* and *magic* to designate the satanic use of certain spiritual principles, then, we should not assume that those principles, put into creation by God Himself, cannot be used—with some differences, to be sure—under the power of God for the purposes for which He originally intended them.

The Problem of Experience

Among the important problems we have to deal with in interpretation is the differential in experience. There is usually a very large experience gap between those who criticize a warfare perspective and those of us being criticized. In a discussion with one of our severest critics, Richard Priest,[3] I asked him if he had ever cast out a demon. He said no. My response is that his lack of experience contrasts with the experience I have had in working with several hundred demonized people.

This fact explains a lot concerning why his and my perspectives differ. He criticizes us but offers no experience to qualify him to comment on our ministries. Further, he does not seem to notice there are a multitude of marvelous results flowing from our ministries. Knowing the importance of experience in our interpretation of both Scripture and life, I find it hard to take his criticisms seriously.

Critiques of a spiritual warfare approach usually take a standard evangelical position with regard to the untrustworthiness of experience. (This may be because experience, from an evangelical perspective, tends to be falsely equated with feeling.) But that stance against experience is based on the myth that it is possible to interpret Scripture in some objective way without reference to one's own life situation and experience. This, of course, is impossible unless one simply accepts someone else's interpretations based on that person's experience.

3. See Priest, Campbell, and Mullen, "Missiological Syncretism."

All interpretation, whether of Scripture or of life, is closely tied to experience or lack of experience. We believe the experiences recorded in Scripture are endorsed by God as conveying His truth and are, therefore, to be regarded as authoritative though not exhaustive. But as soon as we interact with the Scriptures, the understanding that we derive is pervasively affected by the perspective we bring to the process of interpretation—a perspective strongly influenced by experience.

This means interpreting our own experiences in light of Scripture brings us into a cross-cultural situation, where we apply what seems to be similar in Scripture to the events of our own situations. This cross-cultural perspective gives us a further handle on understanding scriptural events while opening us up to experiencing spiritual events in our day.

Because of this, we need not be afraid of launching out beyond Scripture. I see Scripture like a diving board from which we launch out into the waters of experience. We need to launch out into spiritual waters, experimenting with the Holy Spirit's guidance, based on our best understandings of Scripture and of life.

Lastly, I will say that there are at least three kinds of knowledge: intellectual, observational and experiential. Though, as Westerners, we tend to understand knowledge as an intellectual thing, the consistent emphasis of both the Old Testament and the New Testament is knowledge based on and validated through experience.[4] How are we to know, then? It is experience that is the measure, whether we are focused on knowing God in a redemptive relationship, knowing the truth (see John 8:32) or knowing what is involved in areas like the empowerment of objects, curses, inheritance of demons and territorial spirits.

Those who criticize us in these and other areas tend to know what they are talking about only intellectually. They have not observed much, if any, spiritual warfare. Their observational knowledge is, therefore, lacking. Nor have they experienced the use of God's power that Jesus modeled for us in healing and deliverance from demons. This leaves their experiential knowledge lacking as well.

4. Gerhard Kittel and Gerhard Friedrich, eds., *Theological Dictionary of the New Testament*, trans G. W. Bromiley (Grand Rapids, Mich.: Eerdmans, 1985), 119.

The Problem of Dual Allegiance

I believe the biggest problem in worldwide Christianity is what I call *dual allegiance*.[5] With this term I label the kind of situation found with many new believers in which Christians, though they have committed themselves to Christ, turn to animism by continuing to go to shamans and diviners and to engage in other animistic practices to meet their felt need for spiritual power. The Gospel message has encountered them at the point of allegiance to Christ, and they study the Scriptures to discover God's truths, but they have not come to experience anything within Christianity that confronts and replaces their previous sources of spiritual power.[6]

> **Even Christians turn to shamans and diviners to meet their felt need for spiritual power.**

It is an unfortunate fact that Christians all over the world are practicing a Christianity devoid of the ability to deal with the spirit world. They are practicing the powerless Christianity the missionaries brought them, and they either ignore spirit-world experiences (to the extent that they can) or go about trying to deal with the spirit world in really strange ways. Thus, largely because of deficiencies in the worldviews of the missionaries who helped them come to faith but rendered their faith powerless, the Christianity practiced in much of the world is animistic.

Fortunately, many Western missiologists are beginning to recognize these deficiencies and to try to do something about them. Some of us are learning not to ignore or condemn the concern for power among non-Western (or even Western) peoples. In an attitude of repentance over the ignorance that led many of us to ignore or mislead those we worked with, we are seeking to learn and teach Christianity with power. For if the Christianity of missionized areas (and of Euroamerica as well) is to be properly biblical, issues of spiritual power need to be on the front burner of our training and

5. For more on this concept, see Charles H. Kraft and Marguerite G. Kraft, "The Power of God for Christians Who Ride Two Horses," in *The Kingdom and the Power*, ed. Gary S. Grieg and Kevin N. Springer (Ventura, Calif.: Regal, 1993), 345–356.

6. Charles H. Kraft, "What Kind of Encounters Do We Need in Our Christian Witness?" *Evangelical Missions Quarterly* 27 (1991): 258–265.

practice, as they were for Jesus. We evangelicals have ignored the power side of our faith for too long.

As we explore matters pertaining to the spirit world, we are attempting to pioneer in an area heretofore virtually unexplored by evangelicals. We do so with a desire to learn as well as to share what God has been teaching us. In addition, we want to work carefully and wisely in this area so that what we come up with will be biblical, balanced and helpful both at home and abroad.

The issue of what to do about spiritual power was once at the heart of the way we Westerners understood our mission to the non-Western world. Missionaries of a century ago understood that the essence of mission was the confrontation between God and Satan. Unfortunately, mission practice was usually built on the assumption that God had so influenced Western cultures and Satan had so influenced pagan cultures that the encounter between God and Satan involved the stamping out of their Satan-infected way of life and replacing it with our "God-ordained Christian culture." To bring this about, we introduced Western schools, churches and medicine as if these were the God-ordained instruments for Christianizing the non-Christian world. And through these techniques, we secularized the missionized peoples in hopes that they would become Christian.

In reaction, along came a generation of Christian practitioners who, influenced in part by anthropological thinking, focused on appreciating, accepting and using even the cultures of pagans for the sake of the Gospel. We began to understand and teach that non-Western cultures are not totally bad while Western cultures are not totally good and that every culture is usable by God for His purposes.[7] In our optimism about culture, however, we tended to pay too little attention to the fact that Satan also uses culture, precipitating the kind of spiritual warfare we see throughout the non-Christian world as well as throughout the Bible.

Though we encountered people at the point of their need to commit themselves to Christ and pointed them to the truths of Scripture and Christian experience, we evangelicals had nothing to offer them either to confront

7. See Charles H. Kraft, *Christianity in Culture: A Study in Biblical Theologizing in Cross-Cultural Perspective*, rev. ed. (Maryknoll, N.Y.: Orbis, 1979, 2005); and Charles H. Kraft, *Anthropology for Christian Witness* (Maryknoll, N.Y.: Orbis, 1996).

or to replace their sources of spiritual power.[8] We thus grew a powerless or dual-allegiance Christianity much like ours at home, and large numbers of non-Western Christians to this day follow a powerless Christ and go to native priests, diviners, shamans and medical practitioners when they need healing or supernatural guidance.[9]

We had learned that culture is not the enemy but did not know what to do about the one who *is* the enemy and who operates in every cultural context. Into this void for me came a credible witness named John Wimber—an evangelical whom God had led into a calm but powerful healing ministry. He taught us by word and demonstration what God had been teaching him concerning the authority Jesus gave believers to minister in the power of the Holy Spirit (see Luke 9:1; John 14:12; Matthew 28:19–20; Acts 1:8). He also taught us that the Great Commission, like Jesus' life and ministry, has two parts to it: a proclaim part and a heal part (see Luke 9:2). We began to learn that Jesus is keeping His promise—that we who have faith in Him have the authority to do what He did while He was on earth (see John 14:12).

> **The Great Commission has two parts to it: a proclaim part and a heal part.**

We began to see and participate in healings and deliverances. These happened as we operated in the authority Jesus gave us to claim the power of God for healing and deliverance. We also began to listen to God more and to experience what are often called *words of knowledge* (see 1 Corinthians 12:8)—insight given by God to assist in ministry. This is a way God has used throughout history to reveal things to humans. In this way, both Old Testament and New Testament servants of God regularly received guidance directly from Him.

For example, it was through a word of knowledge that the disciples heard from the Holy Spirit that they should choose Barnabas and Saul "to do the work to which [God had] called them" (Acts 13:2). This was also the way Jesus got insight, since in obedience to the Father He did not use His divine attributes (including His omniscience) while on earth. Had He

8. See Kraft, "What Kind of Encounters Do We Need in Our Christian Witness?"
9. See Kraft and Kraft, "The Power of God for Christians Who Ride Two Horses."

retained His omniscience, He could not have claimed not to know concerning the end times in Mark 13:32.

Being exposed to Wimber's ministry has brought about in us Third Wave evangelicals profound paradigm and practice shifts, shifts that enable us to approach mission and life in a different way. Those changes will be a major factor at several points in our discussion here where there are differences of interpretation of Scripture and of life experience—not that these shifts make our understanding more correct than that of our critics. They do mean, though, that we often see different things when looking at the same data. For myself, after 38 years of solid evangelical Christian experience, the Bible has become in the last 30 years a new book, a book testifying to a much deeper spiritual level than I had ever seen before.

4

Our Power
and Authority

A major satanic tactic is to keep us from knowing the power and authority we have been given by our Lord. Satan and his kingdom are jealous of us. Satan used to be in second place in the universe, just below God. But when God created humans and gave us authority over the world (see Genesis 1:26), Satan got dropped to third place—a distant third, below God and humans.

I believe the fact that we are now just a little lower than God Himself (see Psalm 8:5, when correctly translated) angers Satan. So he commits himself to doing whatever he can do either to regain second or first place or to destroy whatever God is doing with humans. He hates God and therefore hates God's favorite creatures. He challenged God and lost, but he feels he can hurt God by picking on us.

I have become convinced, through working in inner healing and deliverance, that the enemy's primary area of attack is on our self-image. *Satan does not want us to discover who we are.* I work with victimized, abused and defeated people whose lives are often characterized by severe hopelessness or depression. Yet they are often brimming with hidden talents and untapped spiritual gifts given to them by God at conception. The enemy, knowing what these gifts and talents are, has done his best to keep these people from knowing their abilities. And he has destroyed—or nearly destroyed—their perception of who they are intended to be.

A woman recently converted out of the occult reported that while serving Satan, she had the ability to "see" the amount of spiritual power different people carry with them. She could spot a Christian immediately, even at a great distance, by noting the amount of spiritual power he or she carried. But she and the other occultists felt no threat from the vast majority of Christians, since most Christians had no idea what to do with the Holy Spirit power they carried. When these occultists ran into Christians who did know how to use this power, they steered clear of them.

Fortune-tellers and occultic healers discover they cannot function smoothly when there are Christians around. A former student of mine told me of a time when he and a group of other Christians were waiting at a bus stop in front of a building that had a fortune-teller sign on it. While they were waiting, a woman came out of the building and asked them to leave. She said those working inside could not hear the spirits as long as the Christians were there!

We were created in second place in the universe, created to rule over it.

How different things would be for a lot of Christians if only we realized how much power we carry and used it!

The satanic kingdom wants us to fear it. Satan and his demons rejoice when the stereotype of powerful spirits and weak humans is portrayed in the media. They love *The Exorcist*. They love stories of knock-down, drag-out deliverance events that showcase satanic power. They want us to ignore the fact that we have more power than they do.

But when we realize the power differential between that kingdom and ours, we should have very little fear left. We should respect Satan and his demons and never take them lightly, of course, but most of what looks

54

like power on their part is either deceit or bluff. They have only the power given them by the person in whom they are living. The more garbage in the person they inhabit, the more powerful the demons can be. When the garbage is taken away, their power lessens and dissipates. Demonic power is calibrated to the amount and kind of garbage in a person.

If we are to live and minister effectively for Christ, we need to know who we are and what that means. As Dean Sherman says in *Spiritual Warfare for Every Christian*, "If we are unsure of ourselves, it is because we do not yet know who we are, or in whose authority we operate."[1]

Twelve Truths about Who We Are

Understanding all this, then, we need to recognize just who we are and the authority and power God has granted us. Let me summarize twelve important points relative to who we are. These are things we can tell ourselves and the enemy, who does not want us to lift our heads in appropriate pride and feel the wonder of who God made us to be.

1. Only We Are Created in God's Image

Though it may be hard to imagine, there is something about us that is like God Himself (see Genesis 1:26). We, not the angels nor any other part of God's creation, are His masterpieces, created in His image and likeness.

2. We Are Created "Only a Little Lower Than God"

Psalm 8:5, when translated properly, as in the New Living Translation, says that we are created just a little lower than God Himself. Our position at creation was far above all created beings, including the angels. We were created in second place in the universe, meant to rule over it. We must never forget this, for the enemy will not be content until he can blot it out of our minds.

1. Dean Sherman, *Spiritual Warfare for Every Christian: How to Live in Victory and Retake the Land* (Seattle: YWAM Publishing, 1990).

3. God Has Stepped In and Redeemed Us

Through the Fall, we dropped to a position below the wicked angel Satan, who had challenged God for first place and lost. But God did not leave things that way. He made it possible through Jesus, the second Adam (see 1 Corinthians 15:45–47), for us to be reestablished in our rightful position just under God.

4. God Made a Way Back for Us but Not for the Angels

This is a significant point. Though both we and Satan rebelled, only we have been redeemed. We must be more valuable than angels. This makes our enemy anxious to keep us from discovering who we are. He envies us the attention God showers on us and the position He gives us. Satan knows that with the Holy Spirit within us, we have more power than he does.

5. We Are the Adopted Children of God

As John says of those who have committed themselves to Christ, "See how much the Father has loved us! His love is so great that we are called God's children—and so, in fact, we are" (1 John 3:1). As God's beloved children, we even inherit with Christ (see Romans 8:17; Galatians 4:7). God has adopted us and chosen us (see Ephesians 1:4), much as a child-less couple chooses and adopts a child into their family. By His choice, not ours, we are part of God's family, restored through redemption to our original position above Satan. And the universe, including Satan's hosts, has to recognize this fact.

6. God Gives Us the Holy Spirit to Live Within Us

As family members, we get to carry infinitely more power than all the satanic kingdom put together! Within us lives God Himself, the Creator and Sustainer of the universe and of all the angels, including Satan. When we realize this, we are different persons in relation to the enemy and the universe, for we know this world really belongs to our Father, even though Satan has control of it for the present (see 1 John 5:19).

56

It was difficult for the disciples to understand why Jesus needed to go away to release the Holy Spirit to come to them (see John 16:7). The disciples may have wondered how anything could be better than Jesus' presence. But I believe Jesus was pointing to the time when the Holy Spirit would not simply be *with* them but *in* them (see John 14:17).

For up to the coming of the Holy Spirit in Acts 2, the relationship between the followers of Jesus and the Holy Spirit seemed to be an external one. Jesus was with them, guiding them, giving them authority and empowering them (see, for example, Luke 9:1–6). But since the Holy Spirit came on all of them in Acts 2, God Himself has come to live *in* us, bringing with Him power (see Acts 1:8), gifting (see 1 Corinthians 12:1), fruit (see Galatians 5:22–23) and the very presence of God permanently from within.

7. God in Jesus Has United with Us for Eternity

God could not have united with an angel or animal—only with one who bears His image. So God in Jesus joined Himself to humanity, forever uniting Creator and creature. In His ascension, Jesus never went back to simply being God. He is still a human being, one of us, and will be for eternity! And because of this, we get to share with Him the inheritance reserved for the siblings of the King (see Romans 8:17; Galatians 4:7).

8. We Are Children of the King

This is our true identity, giving us special rights and privileges with our famous Father. We have, among other things, special permission as His princes and princesses to come into the King's presence at any time (see Hebrews 4:16). It reminds me of a book that was written about life with a famous grandfather, called *I Called Him Grand Dad*.[2] Though many would have given their right arms to spend time with this person's famous grandfather, only the grandson, the author of the book, got to come into that man's presence at any time, without an appointment.

That is the way it is with us and God. The awesome Creator of the universe, the One whose name strikes fear into the hearts of those who

2. Thomas T. Fields Jr., *I Called Him Grand Dad* (Bloomington, Ind.: Xlibris, 2009).

have offended Him—this God, this fearsome One, is our Father or Grand-father. We need have no fear in His presence, as Isaiah did (see Isaiah 6:5), or uncertainty over whether the King will extend His favor to us, as Esther did (see Esther 4:11). We have been invited to come boldly and confidently into His presence (see Hebrews 4:16), running even into His throne room, knowing we are welcome because we are His (grand)children. And we call Him *Abba,* our dad (see Romans 8:15; Galatians 4:6).

Allowing this truth to penetrate the deepest parts of me has transformed me. It has destroyed and replaced my negative self-image. I lived most of my life with a Charlie Brown or Murphy's Law attitude that said, "It's normal for things to go wrong, so if anything goes right, it must be a mistake." With this attitude, I felt God must have made a mistake by linking up with me. What freedom I have found in allowing myself to accept and bask in the truth of what God thinks of me! And what confidence in operating in the authority and power He has entrusted to us!

We are saved by God's grace (see Ephesians 2:8). We are also adopted, given position and empowered by that grace. All of this is incredible—totally beyond anything we deserve. Yet God Himself has chosen to arrange things this way. So we stand in the universe as the fully privileged children of God Himself. We have been given all the rights and privileges of family members, including the right to operate in the power and authority of the Maker and Sustainer of the universe.

9. We Get to Partner with God to Make New Humans

The children we make are eternal beings, completely new creations, all made in the image of God Himself. Angels cannot do this. Animals cannot do this. Only we, with God, can create brand-new beings who will live forever.

10. God Trusts Us

Something within me says He should have known better than to entrust His work to us. But just as Jesus forgave and trusted the adulteress (see John 8:1–11); forgave, reinstated and trusted Peter (see John 21:15–19); and trusted His disciples enough to turn the Kingdom over to them; so He trusts us.

When Jesus left the earth, He entrusted us with the Holy Spirit and predicted that with Him we "will do what [He did]—yes, [we] will do even greater things" than He did (John 14:12). Jesus trusted the disciples and us so much that He calls us His friends—those entrusted with "everything [He] heard from [His] Father" (John 15:15). The Kingdom, then, is our Kingdom as well as His (see Luke 12:32; 22:29–30). Knowing who we are enables us to work in partnership with the Lord, tapping into the riches of our position in Christ.

Back when there were genuine kings and queens on the earth, their rule was absolute. The princes and princesses had authority as well, and all the subjects of the kingdom had to yield to their authority. As God's princes and princesses, we carry the same authority in the spiritual realm. When we understand that identity and use the power of Jesus' name appropriately, the spiritual realm has to obey. We have "every spiritual blessing in the heavenly world" available to us (Ephesians 1:3). If only we could grasp how much God wants us to appropriate the authority and power that rightly belongs to us based on our position in Christ! The satanic kingdom trembles to think what that would mean.

The position God has given us is awesome. We are in such an elevated place that the angels watch us curiously (see 1 Corinthians 4:9; 11:10; 1 Timothy 5:21; 1 Peter 1:12) and serve us (see Hebrews 1:14). Furthermore, we will get to judge them (see 1 Corinthians 6:3). Again, God did not think highly enough of the angels to rescue those who followed Satan; He redeemed only us. What grace and love! What privilege is ours to belong to God's family! We must never forget who we are, even when we do not feel like it is true.

11. Spiritual Authority Is Part of Who We Are

Our spiritual authority is recognized by God and by the enemy world as flowing from our very beings. As Christians, we have no choice as to whether or not we possess this authority. It comes in the package when the Holy Spirit is given to us. Our only choice is whether we will learn how to use the authority—and then actually make use of it. It is kind of like a credit card. We can use it or not. When, however, the card is given to us to use in service to our Lord, it is irresponsible not to use it.

12. *We Have Jesus' Authority*

Jesus did things that made it clear that He operated in spiritual authority. He defeated Satan both during His life and through the cross and resurrection. He said the fact that He drove out demons "proves that the Kingdom of God has already come to you" (Luke 11:20). Over and over we see Him exercise His spiritual authority over the enemy.

Over half of the book of Mark is devoted to Jesus' demonstrations of His authority through healing and deliverance. But Jesus did not limit this authority to Himself. He conferred it on His apostles, the twelve (see Luke 9) and the 72 (see Luke 10), giving them the "power and authority to drive out all demons and to cure diseases" (Luke 9:1). With this authority and power, they were to go about healing the sick and letting people know "the Kingdom of God has come near you" (Luke 10:9).

Then Jesus said to His followers, "As the Father sent me, so I send you" (John 20:21). It was His intent that His followers imitate His approach to witness, accompanying words with power (see Acts 1:8). In Matthew 28:20, then, we learn that He meant for His followers to teach their followers the things He had taught them. They were to teach their followers "to obey everything [He had] commanded [them]."

That this teaching was to include how to operate in the authority of Jesus to perform signs and wonders seems clear from His promise in John 14:12, where He said, "Whoever believes in me will do the works I have been doing, and they will do even greater things than these, because I am going to the Father" (NIV).

Three Hindrances to Asserting Power

Paul's prayer for us was that we understand our power and authority:

> I pray that you will begin to understand how incredibly great his power is to help those who believe him. It is that same mighty power that raised Christ from the dead and seated him in the place of honor at God's right hand in heaven.
>
> Ephesians 1:19–20 TLB

To reiterate, we are God's precious children, even to the extent of being adopted as brothers and sisters of Jesus and inheriting with Him (see Romans 8:15–17; Galatians 4:5–7). We are children of the King, princes and princesses in His Kingdom. And part of our inheritance as His children is incredibly great power—the same power that raised Christ from the dead. This power within each of God's children is greater than that of the entire satanic kingdom. And Satan knows this, whether or not we do.

Why, then, do so many Christians have trouble believing in the spiritual authority God has given us? And why do many go even further and question their status as God's precious children? Many of you are probably struggling this very minute with what I am saying about your inheritance and authority as God's child. You would like to believe that you are a prince or princess, but deep within, you wonder if that is really true. *It is.* The enemy, however, is committed to keeping you from knowing who you are and the authority and power that is yours because of who you are.

Let me assure you of the truth that as a Christian, you are God's precious child and have inherited His power and authority. However, some stumbling blocks may be in your path, as they were in mine. Following are some common ones and what to do about them.

1. You May Not Have the Freedom of Christ

It is difficult to appropriate the riches of our inheritance in Christ, including the authority and power He has given us, unless we are experiencing His freedom in our own lives. As Paul says, "Freedom is what we have—Christ has set us free!" (Galatians 5:1). The fact is, however, that many Christians are not free. We may have given our lives to Christ and even been used by Him in ministry, but inside we find that living and working for Jesus involves a constant fight with problems that never seem to go away completely.

There may be emotional wounds—what I call garbage—resulting from reactions to hurts we have experienced, often during childhood and the teenage years. When we are hurt, we react—usually with anger, resentment, fear or similar negative emotions. These are not inappropriate reactions, given the fact that someone has done or said something that hurts us. The problem arises, however, when we hang on to these emotions and wallow in them.

Jesus does not deny our right to our feelings. He showed intense anger on at least one notable occasion. But He did not let these emotions lead Him into sin. Rather, He gave them to the Father before the end of the day, lest He give the devil a chance to come in (see Ephesians 4:26–27). Jesus did not want the devil to find something by means of which to gain a hold on Him (see John 14:30 NIV).

Unfortunately, many of us have not learned what can be referred to—please pardon the analogy—as the law of "spiritual excretion." In our physical bodies, we have an excretory system. It sees to it that material that cannot be used or could hurt us is regularly eliminated. If, for some reason, that system gets blocked or does not function properly, we get poisoned from inside. The same is true in the spiritual and emotional realms—except that we have to control our spiritual and emotional excretion by acts of our will. This process does not take place as automatically as the physical one does.

Just as we feel a sense of relief after physical elimination, we feel at peace or rested after spiritual excretion. The process involves simply giving up our right to anger, bitterness, revenge and like emotions and giving our feelings to Jesus. By so doing, we allow Him to take on Himself our impossibly heavy burdens (see Matthew 11:28) and to repay anyone who has hurt us (see Romans 12:17–21). This is, I believe, what Jesus was referring to when He said:

> "Come to me, all of you who are tired from carrying heavy loads, and I will give you rest. Take my yoke and put it on you, and learn from me, because I am gentle and humble in spirit; and you will find rest. For the yoke I will give you is easy, and the load I will put on you is light."
>
> Matthew 11:28–30

The stakes are high, both for you and for the plans God has for you, if you let the enemy continue to have a hold on you. If he has a grip on you, you are a spiritual prisoner of war in the cosmic battle between God's Kingdom and that of Satan. You have been disarmed so that your weapons will do you no good. Neither will the authority and power that Jesus has given you. You are locked up in a prison and may not know that Jesus has made it possible for you to be released and set free from those things Satan has used to bind you.

The fact that many do not know what freedom feels like has been brought home to me by the reactions of several people just after they were delivered from demons. They remarked that they now felt very strange. Though it is usual for a person to feel free and light, a young man I will call Art exclaimed, "I feel weird!" Art just lounged there on the couch where he had been sitting with a strange look on his face. My thoughts, which he seemed to read, were something like, *Oh no, we've got more work to do.* But he interrupted to explain that in all of his eighteen years, he had not experienced this "feel of freedom" that now washed over him. He had heard of it but never known what it felt like. Now, as freedom flowed over him, he just wanted to sit for a while and enjoy it. I met Art a couple of years later and learned that the "feel of freedom" had never left him.

> **You may be a spiritual prisoner of war in the cosmic battle between God's Kingdom and that of Satan.**

In a second situation, a missionary I will call Julie also did not recognize the feel of freedom. Julie had grown up as the oldest daughter in a family with an alcoholic father. She had, therefore, been forced to take major responsibility in her home from about age nine. In the process, seeking help for a task much too big for her, she had opened herself up to a strong demon of control.

When I met Julie in the country where she and her husband served as missionaries, she had been nearly incapacitated for almost a year with deep depression. When we freed her from the stronger demon of control and the weaker one of depression, plus several others, it was obvious to her that something had changed. But since she could not remember ever having felt freedom, she did not know how to interpret the change. She thought she was back in depression until some of her co-workers helped her understand what had truly happened. Now, several years later, she is still enjoying that freedom.

2. *You May Have a Self-Image Problem*

As mentioned earlier, the enemy is especially hard on us in the self-image area. Several aspects of Western society are very helpful to our enemy in enabling him to put us down. Individualism and a competitive spirit cut us off from relationships with others. We are taught to define ourselves in comparison with others according to what we do, how we look, how we feel we are accepted and how much we have achieved, rather than in terms of who we are. Our normal standards of comparison with others are usually based on such ephemeral things as possessions, physical attractiveness (especially for women), the number of friendships we have and how well we have assimilated and can regurgitate what is often irrelevant information.

In all of this, there is great opportunity to discover and focus on those areas where we fall short in comparison to others. Many of us live our days constantly falling short of our own standards and feeling we are unacceptable to ourselves, others and God. We seem neither to know that our standards are unattainable nor that God's standards are quite different.

We really want to believe God loves us. We want to take our place as a prince or princess in His Kingdom. We want to believe in the tremendous power available for us as His children. But our self-condemnation keeps us from accepting what is rightfully our inheritance.

For years, I had a negative tape inside my head continually playing the enemy's lies. He said things like:

"Reject yourself. You're no good."

"You are a failure-prone sinner and will never be anything else."

"Carry your guilt. Your sins are too great for even God to forgive."

"See how unworthy and inadequate you are? You're always messing things up."

"Worry about what others think of you."

"Fear that you're going to fail again."

In short, those messages were telling me I was unacceptable and unworthy to be the prince God has adopted me to be. They kept me continually defeated.

One day, however, a friend of mine asked, "Why don't you use a mirror and tell yourself the truth?" He said I could break habits of self-rejection and self-hatred in this way and teach myself a new habit, a habit that conformed to God's attitude toward me. So I began to talk to myself in a mirror daily. I said things like "I love you" and "You are a prince of the Most High God" and "Jesus has really forgiven that thing you have done." After several weeks, I found that my attitude toward myself was changing. I was developing a new habit—from self-hatred to self-love, from self-condemnation to self-acceptance.

By telling myself God's truth, I was being reprogrammed by Jesus and was learning from Him to receive His acceptance and love. The tape Jesus plays in my mind now conveys quite different messages than the old ones— messages of truth to confront the lies I had been believing. He says to me:

"Because I have accepted you as you are, you can accept yourself."

"I love and accept you for who you are, not simply for what you do or don't do."

"You are forgiven. You don't need to feel guilty anymore."

"I chose you. Don't argue with My choice."

"I have made you worthy and adequate."

"I will never leave you or forsake you."

"Don't fear. Cast all your cares on Me, for I care for you."

I am blown away by the fact that I now can accept that the King of the universe thinks enough of me to grant me far more love and acceptance than I deserve and that I have granted myself for most of my life.

He wants us all to hear Him saying the same things to us. His desire is that we truly understand, deep within us, His love for us and our place in His Kingdom.

In his book *The Seven Gifts*, Bernard Kelly uses a powerful analogy to help us understand the difficulty Christians have in accepting their inheritance. Kelly likens the struggle to a slum child who was adopted by a royal family. At first the slum child rejoiced that he was out of the slum and living in a palace. The child's new father, the king, told the slum child that he no longer needed to live in the dark, hateful streets where he once lived. Furthermore, the king told his new son that all of the royal family treasures now belonged to him as their adopted child.

In spite of this joyful inheritance, the child remembered the way people in the slum had treated him and the abuse he had suffered. Something within him cried out, "It can't be true!"

Unfortunately, this poor slum child had brought much "slum baggage" with him to his new palace. The royal family could take him out of the slum, but getting the slum out of him was another matter. Fortunately, his new, loving parents understood this and took him by the hand to teach him to trust their unconditional love. Caringly, patiently, they helped him along until he could truly acknowledge and accept his new life and inheritance.[3]

Many Christians react exactly like that slum child! They have been given a new life and inheritance as children of the Most High King, but like the slum child, they too bring their baggage of hurts and wounds into their new life. They have internal tapes that cry out, "It can't be true!" It is here that we need to give the Holy Spirit our hand and seek healing of the wounds that block our acceptance of our rightful inheritance. Jesus desires that our stumbling blocks—our self-hatred, our low self-esteem, our fears, our unworthiness—be removed. He wants to help us step forward to claim our rightful place as His children through inner healing.

We will discuss inner healing in greater depth in chapter 12, but for now, know that inner healing and the freedom that follows are possible through God's powerful ministry to you. To begin to experience this, sit quietly before the Holy Spirit and ask Him to bring to mind events in which your self-image was damaged. Ask Him to let you see Jesus in each event, and allow the Lord to minister to you. As He does, accept your true relationship with Him and thank Him for who you are. Between such intimate times with Jesus, continually affirm for yourself the truths of Scripture concerning who you are to ward off and overcome the attacks of the enemy on your mind and emotions.

3. You May Not Have a Proper View of God

Satan does not want us to understand who God is and the implications of this truth. The enemy is especially anxious to keep us from discovering

3. Bernard Kelly, *The Seven Gifts* (London: Sheed & Ward, 1941), 12–14.

who God wants to be to us. God wants to be our Father in the fullest sense of the word, but the meaning we attach to the word *father* is often the biggest roadblock to our letting Him become to us all He seeks to be.

When we give ourselves to Christ, we are adopted by a heavenly Father in whose presence we are welcome at any time. We are invited to "approach the throne of grace with fullest confidence, that we may receive mercy for our failures and grace to help in the hour of need" (Hebrews 4:16 PHILLIPS). Many of us, however, struggle with the reality of a heavenly Father who unconditionally loves and accepts us. The reason may be that we have not experienced such love and acceptance from our earthly father. Many of us have endured neglect and even abuse from our fathers, and we cannot imagine any other kind of treatment from someone else called by that name.

I have ministered to a large number of people whose concept of father had been damaged in major ways. One woman's definition of *father* had become "someone who always stands in my way whenever I really want to do something." Another's came out in the statement "Whenever I picture Jesus, I see Him with a stick in His hand." For still others, a father may be someone who has abandoned the family or is distant and unconcerned or has abused them psychologically, physically or sexually. Such people usually find that at the deepest level, they cannot accept the truth that God is not like their earthly father—even though they have accepted that truth on a rational level.

Another problem for many people is their anger at God for allowing bad things to happen to them or to someone else. They have been taught that God can do anything He wants. When they have experienced difficulty, they reason, it must be because God did not care enough about them to protect them. So they are angry at God and convinced He endorses their low opinion of themselves. We can be certain that Satan is involved in supporting this lie.

The fact that these people miss is that God has put limits on Himself. He cannot be limited by anything outside Himself, but He has made rules for the operation of the universe that He Himself obeys. One of these rules is that He does not normally interfere as humans exercise their free will. Another rule is that He seldom acts in the human arena without a human partner.

Though He promises to be with us always (see Matthew 28:20) and never to allow us to experience events that are too big for us (see 1 Corinthians 10:13), God seldom interferes with human free will, even when the person is working under Satan. But when we cooperate with Jesus in partnership, He does marvelous things.

False perceptions of our heavenly Father provide some of the greatest blocks to understanding and functioning in our spiritual authority. Faulty pictures of the Father or of Jesus need to be corrected before we can take our rightful place as God's princes and princesses. We must renounce and refuse to listen any longer to the lies we have been hearing about our Father.

The key to becoming free to understand and relate properly to God the Father is forgiveness. If we are angry at God, we need to forgive Him. By forgiving God, I mean to stop holding anger and bitterness toward Him for allowing things to happen that we feel He should have prevented. We do not understand why He allows people to get hurt, and He usually does not explain (He did not explain to Job). But since His ways and thoughts are as far above ours as the heavens are above the earth (see Isaiah 55:9), we have to give up our attempts to understand God and simply accept that the God we relate to will do right (see Genesis 18:25). We then give up our right to be angry at Him, committing ourselves to trusting Him and refusing to dictate how He should run things.

> **False perceptions of our heavenly Father provide some of the greatest blocks to understanding and functioning in our spiritual authority.**

Having forgiven God, it is critical that we also forgive our earthly father, no matter what he may have done to us and no matter how often he did it. Again, it is no sin to become angry or even to desire revenge. We have the right to that revenge! But Jesus asks us to give Him our right to revenge.

However, there are other rules. If we assert our right to anger or revenge, the harvest is predictable. In the emotional area, as in every other area, the law of the harvest governs the outcome. That law is that we reap what we sow (see Galatians 6:7). Sow the seeds of anger, revenge, bitterness and hate, and the fruit will be such things as emotional instability, negativism that ruins relationships, and physical illnesses such as cancer, arthritis, diabetes and the like—plus demons to reinforce such problems.

The solution, though, is simple. Just as with sin, we are to acknowledge our emotional attitudes, confess them to God, give them to Him and never take them back. We are then to forgive the guilty person unconditionally, just as completely as God has forgiven us. The rule is, "If you forgive others the wrongs they have done to you, your Father in heaven will also forgive you. But if you do not forgive others, then your Father will not forgive the wrongs you have done" (Matthew 6:14–15). And you get imprisoned by your own unforgiveness.

The result of forgiveness—the fruit of sowing forgiveness—is that both the one forgiven and the one who forgives go free! Having forgiven our earthly father, we are free to love him and thereby come to a new understanding of our heavenly Father.

Additionally, we need to be careful how we evaluate the behavior of our earthly father and other relatives toward us. Most of those who have abused their own children have suffered similar or worse abuse themselves. This does not excuse them. They still are guilty and responsible for their actions. This fact does, however, enable us to understand that their behavior usually was not willful but *driven*.

Behind their behavior was not a cool evaluation of what they were doing and a choice that they believed was right. Rather, they were not in control of their behavior but were driven by emotions, such as anger, bitterness and the desire for revenge, all of which were rooted in their own life experiences and usually reinforced by demons. In reality, their outbursts were not aimed at us but at those in their own backgrounds who had hurt them. They are more to be pitied than condemned.

Even fathers who are not abusive often make mistakes, and big ones. Often we fathers have simply capitulated to our own insecurities and feelings of low self-worth at the expense of our children. We may have simply followed the dictates of a society that gives us points for what we do in our careers but no points for being good fathers. Accordingly, we have worked hard to be successful in the eyes of our co-workers and others at the expense of our children. If your father was like that, please forgive him for neglecting you. He needs your forgiveness. And recognize that your heavenly Father is not like your earthly father at his worst, though your earthly father may have been like God at his best. Our heavenly Father is never too busy to spend time with you. Indeed, He says, "I will never leave you; I will never abandon you" (Hebrews 13:5).

Our Greatest Weapon

"Not by might nor by power, but by my Spirit," says the Lord Almighty.

Zechariah 4:6 NIV

Our greatest weapon in fighting satanic influence—whether in ourselves or in others—is our intimacy with Jesus. Jesus set the example by living His life in constant closeness to the Father. He was listening to the Father at all times; thus, He could say, "I say only what the Father has instructed me to say" (John 8:28). He was continually watching what the Father was doing; thus, He could say, "The Son . . . does only what he sees his Father doing. What the Father does, the Son also does" (John 5:19). Jesus lived in absolute dependence on the Father; thus, He could say, "By myself I can do nothing. As I hear, I judge, and my judgment is true because I do not live to please myself but to do the will of the Father who sent me" (John 5:30 Phillips).

Those were Jesus' day-by-day directives. To be certain, His sights were lined up with those of the Father, with whom He regularly spent time alone. Over and over again, we read that Jesus withdrew "to a solitary place" (Matthew 14:13 NIV) to be alone with the Father.

As we reach out to bring healing and deliverance to those in need, it quickly becomes apparent that we are not the healers. Healing and deliverance do not happen because we are gifted. People are touched, healed and delivered because God Himself is with us. It is important to remember that it is not by our might or power but by His Spirit that God gets things done. Cultivating an intimacy with Jesus that enables constant working with and dependence on His Spirit is, therefore, the first order of business.

Such intimacy is not the mysterious thing many people make it out to be. It does not have to involve religious ritual. People often ask me, "How do you prepare for a deliverance session?" The truth is, I seldom do anything special. Rather, I try to stay prepared constantly, because I never know when I will be called upon. The other day I received a telephone call out of the blue from someone I had never met. Within half an hour, I was interacting with and casting out demons. Whether over the phone or in person, that is often about as much warning as I get. So I try always to be prepared by staying close to Jesus.

Spiritual authority is, I believe, in direct proportion to spiritual intimacy. Our power comes from the indwelling Holy Spirit. Our authority comes from keeping on good terms with our Lord.

Part 3

Worldview
BLOCKAGE

5

Our Problem
as Westerners

There was a time when Western society was very aware of the spirit world and its power. The Church, too, believed in healing, deliverance and spiritual manifestations. We are told that Martin Luther was so aware of Satan's presence on one occasion that he threw an inkwell at him. Though some of the things reported were questionable, such as statues crying, they could still have been the legitimate result of either godly or satanic power.

Then changes in philosophy turned our forebears from a God-centered approach concerning the interpretation of life to a human being–centered approach. And under the influence of the philosophical movements that culminated in what has been labeled the Enlightenment, we have become "Enlightenment Christians." We evangelicals followed our society in the worldview changes that led our people into secularism. The Reformation and the rise of universities played a major part in this movement, turning people toward interpreting advancements as purely human accomplishments and away from seeing God behind those accomplishments.

This has led the majority of Western Christians, in keeping with the rest of society, to see spiritual beings and forces as either belonging to the realm of superstition or make-believe, not as real. And this in face of the fact that the Bible speaks a lot about satanic beings and shows how to handle them! The majority of Christians interpret life and even the Bible as if these beings and powers do not exist. For most Western Christians, spiritual power is a mystery and much of the Bible seems like fairy stories.

A major hindrance faced by evangelicals who are trying to understand spiritual warfare, then, is our Western worldview. In what is called the West, we learn from infancy to focus on what we can see and to ignore the unseen world that Scripture addresses.

We are like people putting together a picture puzzle that has three hundred pieces, but we learn to work with only two hundred pieces. There are another hundred pieces out there, but we do not even see them or, if we do get glimpses of them, we do not know what to do about them.

We are taught about the first one hundred pieces that deal with the physical world, and we see that reality pretty clearly. The second hundred pieces picture the human world, with all of the ins and outs of human activity, and though there is much to learn in this area, we spend a lot of time dealing with it because we know that these pieces, too, are an important part of reality.

But there are another hundred pieces to the puzzle. They picture spiritual reality. We learn as we grow up to ignore these pieces. We may know that the puzzle is incomplete without these pieces, but few know what to do about the situation. As a result, we attempt to interpret spiritual things as if they fit into the two hundred pieces. We do not recognize that there is another important area of reality not covered by the things we have learned. Like the pastor I referenced in chapter 1 who said he would rather not know that demons exist even if they do, we ignore it. Our Western worldview assumptions leave no room for spiritual reality.

The apostle Paul made a statement that relates well to what we call *worldview* in 1 Corinthians 13:12. He said:

> What we see now is like a dim image in a mirror; then we shall see face-to-face. What I know now is only partial; then it will be complete—as complete as God's knowledge of me.

J. B. Phillips translates this passage to say we are like those "looking at puzzling reflections in a mirror." Another possible translation is, "Now we see as through a dirty window." We may refer to this thing that limits our vision as worldview. We do not see things or know things as God sees and knows. He works with all three hundred pieces of the puzzle! Our sight is dim and our knowledge partial, so we attempt to interpret spiritual reality using only the two hundred pieces we know.

God, however, sees clearly and completely. I like to call His view *Reality*— a perfect, unobstructed, capital *R* view. Our view, on the other hand, can be labeled *reality* (small *r*)—perception that is limited and faces interference by various factors. We are promised that someday we will be able to see and know as God does—but not yet.

When we look at what we see around us, we look at Reality (capital *R*) as it exists. However, when we interpret that Reality, we come up with *our* reality (small *r*), which is our perception of what we see. This interpretation is based on some combination of what we have accepted of what we have been taught and our own creativity. This is our worldview.

We have been learning the elements that make up our worldview reality from the time we grew up, even before birth. Our parents and teachers convey information and perspectives to us in a myriad of ways as we adopt our society's structuring and perception of reality. The result is our worldview—the assumptions, values and commitments that constitute the core of our culture.

We Can Change Our Worldview

It is common to speak of the power of one's culture or worldview to make one do certain things. "His culture made him do it," we say, or we speak similar words that are easily offered to explain differences in behavior between people of different societies. But that is not true. Culture does not cause anything.

Culture and worldview are structural things, providing patterns in terms of which people interpret and behave. They are like the script an actor uses or the roads we drive on. The script or road is just there. It does not cause anything, though it is intended to guide behavior and becomes the unconscious basis for that behavior. It may also be ignored or changed according to the desire of the one using it.

Worldview assumptions, like all of culture, are there to be used. They have no power in and of themselves. When worldview assumptions are acted on, however, they are empowered. People choose, though usually unconsciously, to follow and thus empower the cultural patterns they have been taught. *But the power is in the habits of the people*, not in the worldview assumptions or even in the broader cultural patterns.

> **We are creatures who think, interpret and behave largely according to the habits we learned as we grew up.**

We are taught our worldview assumptions and patterns and practice them so predictably that we make habits of them. And those habits provide the power by means of which we operate our lives. We habitually follow the patterns of our worldview. We are creatures who think, interpret and behave largely according to the habits we learned as we grew up.

But even though we are creatures of habit, that is not the whole story. We are also creative. We refuse to do things the same way forever. So we change things. We may replace old attitudes with new ones that are then turned into habits.

Most Americans, being two-hundred-piece people, have the worldview-governed habit of paying attention to physical and emotional reality but not to spiritual reality. If we experience a demonic manifestation, then, we are pushed to consider something not accounted for by our two-hundred-piece worldview. We may, then, either attempt to explain the event as psychological, in accord with the two hundred pieces we have been taught, thereby keeping our existing worldview, or we may take the event seriously and change our interpretation of things. If we decide to change, we establish a new habit.

The pastor I asked about believing in demons said he would rather not know if there are demons. He would rather hold to his present worldview habit than to open himself up to a new understanding. He would cling to the naturalistic interpretation provided by his existing worldview rather than deal with an interpretation that would require him to take seriously the missing hundred pieces of the puzzle. He feared such a change. His approach to life and even to ministry, then, is basically secular.

As an example from Scripture, we may point to the Pharisees, who saw how Jesus worked in spiritual power but refused to change their worldview assumptions. They assumed that Moses had come from God (see John 9:28–29) but chose to reject Jesus, who showed even more closeness to God than Moses did. They kept their worldview and rejected Jesus because He posed a threat to their worldview and to their social and political power.

The question that faces many who consider making worldview changes is, What would people think if I made this change? For instance, one of my problems as I considered making changes in a charismatic direction was the stereotype in my mind of Pentecostals and charismatics. I did not want to become or be regarded as one of them.

For many evangelicals, it is the teaching we have received against the exercise of spiritual gifts in our day and age that hinders change. Those infected with the teaching of dispensationalism or Reformed theology often flatly deny that spiritual gifts are for today.

There are also issues of temperament or fear of criticism that lead people to fear stepping out. A wrong view of God can also weaken our will to change. We may believe that only God can do something, missing the fact that He works in partnership with humans. We will deal with these issues as we go along.

So, if we are to change any part of our worldview, we need to experience a shift in perspective and practice.[1] What really cements any change, however, is a change of practice.[2]

We Need an Evangelical Shift

As I have said, evangelical theology has been strongly affected by Enlightenment philosophy, leading it to be highly rational and academic. It has thus become weak on invisible reality, even to the point of ignoring or denying it. As Western Christians, we may be concerned with power, but

1. For more on this, see Kraft, *Christianity with Power*.
2. You can learn more about worldview in Kraft, *Worldview for Christian Witness*.

the power we are concerned with tends to be about the material world or perhaps economic or political power.

Furthermore, evangelicals tend to focus on the peaceful activities of faith, characterized by such things as love, repentance, peace, faith, righteousness, grace, obedience and human responsibility—again, what James Kallas calls the "Godward view" of our faith, which we will discuss in greater depth in chapter 8. These things are very important. In addition, evangelicals are strong on the fact that God is in charge and will win out in the end. He is omnipotent and therefore cannot be defeated. He loves us and will do what is best for us. He relates to us with grace and forgiveness. He is righteous and requires righteousness and obedience of us.

But there is another side. Without denying the truth of these Godward characteristics, evangelicals have, by and large, ignored the war motif that is also prominent in Scripture. This part, according to Kallas, makes up 80 percent of the Synoptic gospels and Pauline epistles![3] We tend to ignore what Satan is doing and the authority we have been given to tackle and defeat him. The partnership in war that Jesus invites us into may be discussed from time to time but is usually done without insight into our part in defeating the enemy.

When we have turned our attention to spiritual warfare, we have tended to focus on God's part in the war, ignoring what we are expected to do. Pastors usually ignore the need and responsibility to "clean up" their parishioners from demonization. And the training we receive in our Christian colleges and seminaries tends to be information-oriented (i.e., secular) rather than ministry-oriented. Would Jesus be as lax as we are in dealing with this "Satanward view" in our churches and training programs?

The humanity of Jesus and His total dependence on the direction of the Holy Spirit and its implications for our lives tend to be weakly and often poorly dealt with. We may debate the relationship between Jesus' deity and His humanity without recognizing that He fought the enemy totally as a human being filled with the Spirit and that we are to do the same. We may focus on the way suffering fits into God's plan for our lives without recognizing that suffering is a wartime casualty, not God's plan.

We are at war and need to understand that we are expected by God to play a role in the battles. We do not do well if we are simply content to

3. Kallas, 32.

practice the more peaceful aspects of our faith, leaving the warfare aspects to God. Every pastor and every layperson is expected by God to minister deliverance and healing as Jesus did.

We Have to Know the Nature of Jesus

A major worldview problem in dealing with spiritual warfare, then, is our view of Jesus. As evangelicals, we believe Jesus was and is both God and man. It is easy to assume He did miracles as God under His divine nature. As evangelicals, we have strongly defended Jesus' deity and seen His miracles as proving His deity. We also believe He was man, but we have not often emphasized His humanity.[4]

It is important to ask, then, Just how did Jesus work? Was His life merely a drama with all the lines memorized? Or did He shift back and forth between being God and being man (the most common evangelical position)? Did He really operate in all His divine power and knowledge but hide it frequently? In Matthew 24:36, where He says He did not know the day or the hour of the Son of man's return, did He really know but not admit it? Did He lie? If He did not know, how do we understand that He was God? Doesn't God know everything?

Furthermore, since we are not God, can we really be expected to do His works, as He promised in John 14:12? I wrestled over this matter my whole life and excused myself from being expected to deal with healing and deliverance because of this very assumption—that Jesus could do miracles because He was and is God but that I cannot because I am not.

As evangelicals, we assert that Jesus was 100 percent God and 100 percent human. But there are several theories that help us understand His activities, especially those attributed to His divine nature.

Theory 1: Jesus as Mystery

The first of these theories is that Jesus was a total mystery. In this view, we should simply give up any attempt to understand Him. He is God and

4. C. Peter Wagner does an excellent job discussing this in C. Peter Wagner, *Confronting the Powers* (Ventura, Calif.: Regal, 1996).

cannot be explained. He was the God-man, and His nature is beyond our ability as mere mortals to understand. We just have to take Him by faith. This view appeals to many who feel that trying to understand Jesus takes too much energy, so they go about their business and give up trying to understand. They might even strongly declare that God, by definition, is beyond our comprehension.

Theory 2: Jesus as Human

A second view is that Jesus was only human. This is the view of most theological liberals. They deny His divinity and see Him as simply a human, very gifted and worthy of great honor but not God. As evangelicals, we certainly want to reject this view.

Theory 3: Jesus as God

A third view holds that Jesus was totally God, though in human flesh. This view holds on tightly to Jesus' deity and denies His humanity. It does not try to reconcile His two natures.

Theory 4: Jesus on Two Channels

The fourth view is what Wagner calls the "two-channel theory."[5] This is probably the most prevalent evangelical view, holding that since Jesus was both divine and human, this means He constantly switched back and forth between the two natures. He would walk and talk as a man but turn on His "God power" to do miracles, alternating between the two as He went through His life.

According to this theory, Jesus regularly hid His divine knowledge from His human consciousness. If He chose to act as God, He could. If He chose to act as man, He would simply turn on His humanity. During that time, His knowledge was limited, as we see in Matthew 24:36, where He said that only God the Father knows when the end of the age will come. Jesus would be making that claim as a man, saying, "*Humanly speaking*, I do not know . . ."

5. Ibid., 121–139.

To me, this is an unsatisfactory interpretation, even though I once held it myself—it was the best I could do. But I have changed my understanding (my worldview assumption). In order to change, though, I needed to understand what Jesus was saying in John 5:19, where He stated that He did only what the Father led Him to do. This statement indicates that Jesus worked in total dependence on the Father rather than dependence on His own divinity.

Theory 5: Jesus as Incarnation

A much more satisfying understanding, then, is what may be called the incarnation theory. This position is articulated in Philippians 2:6–8, which indicates that Jesus always had the nature of God but did not cling to it to assert His equality with God. Instead of this, of His own free will, He turned His back on using His deity and took on the nature of a servant. He became a man, living as a human being in humility, walking the path of obedience all the way to death—His death on the cross.

This position affirms that Jesus was 100 percent God but that He chose to put aside His divinity for a time, not by giving it up but by agreeing with the Father that He would never use it, *functioning totally as a human being*.

He had both a divine nature and a human one, but in agreement with the Father and the Holy Spirit, He took on human beingness and lived in obedience to God the Father as His servant/slave while on earth. He agreed to suspend His use of divine attributes while on earth. He still possessed these attributes but agreed with the Father and Holy Spirit not to use them.

He lived, then, as a human being without ever appealing to His deity, even to the extent of refusing to help Himself when He was taken to trial. He acknowledged His divine nature but never used it (such as when He accepted worship during His triumphal entry into Jerusalem in Matthew 21:1–17; see also Luke 19:28–40 and John 20:24–29). As He was taken to His death, He said, "Don't you know that I could call on my Father for help, and at once He would send me more than twelve armies of angels?" (Matthew 26:53). But had He done this, He would have broken His agreement with the Father.

Jesus only used His human nature, never His divine nature, while on earth. He faced and conquered everything as a human—the true second Adam (see 1 Corinthians 15:47). In Luke 4:1–13, the temptations are recorded in which He was tempted by Satan to use His divine attributes and break His agreement with the Father. But He refused.

We hold, then, that Jesus was totally human with one difference. He had no earthly father. This means He did not inherit original sin, since that is inherited through the male line. He had no inherited sin nature, since the sin nature is carried as spiritual inheritance along the male line.

Jesus' deity was there, but He did not use it. He was tempted in every way that we are (see Hebrews 4:15). He lived without the power and authority of His divinity. So He did what He did in dependence on God the Father. As He said in John 5:30, "I can do nothing of myself."

Support for this position comes from the fact that He did no miracles before the Holy Spirit came on Him at His baptism (see Luke 3:21–22). From then on, He healed, cast out demons and spoke like no one else had ever spoken. And the people of His hometown, Nazareth (a village of four hundred people), were amazed. He had lived among them, and they saw none of this activity during the thirty years that passed until He started His ministry (see Matthew 13:54–56). Then, after the Holy Spirit came upon Him at His baptism, He began doing miracles under the Holy Spirit's power, not the power of His own divinity.

How, then, did He know things others did not? Often He knew what people were thinking, but not always. God showed Him through words of knowledge (see John 5:30)—a kind of direct revelation available to us also (see 1 Corinthians 12:8). He also got instructions during nights in prayer He spent with the Father (see Luke 5:16; 6:12). He heard from God (see John 8:26, 28, 38). Otherwise His knowledge was just as limited as ours. *When He said He did not know, then, He really did not know.*

The worldview change demanded by these considerations is crucial to the way we understand spiritual warfare. If Jesus did miraculous things out of His divine nature, we have no right to expect any of us mere humans to do them. We have no right to expect us humans to participate in freeing people from infirmity, from demons, from curses or from any other of Satan's activities.

But since Jesus lived and worked totally as a human, working in obedience to the Father, working in the power of the Holy Spirit to defeat Satan and then giving this power and authority to us (see John 14:12), *we can do what He did.* We can receive the same Holy Spirit that empowered Jesus and do the same works that He did.

An additional fact to note here is that Jesus never returned to simply being God. He was incarnated, thus becoming a human being forever. He will return as He left us—as a human being (see Acts 1:10–11).

We Cannot Forget Dual Causality

As I mentioned in chapter 3, one major worldview problem for us Westerners is our either-or thinking. With regard to any event, we look for *the* cause, believing it to be singular. It is common for people to ask me if a certain behavior is human or demonic. The answer I give them is yes. It is both. Because of our worldview assumption that everything has but a single cause, we have great difficulty understanding multi-cause analyses of events. By ignoring the hundred pieces of the puzzle that represent spiritual reality, we Westerners limit ourselves to single-cause assumptions.

When we shift to a dual-cause basic assumption, then, some of our critics suggest we are off the track. They contend that we are off base in seeking spirit-level explanations in addition to human-level ones when, they say, Scripture puts the blame for human problems only on human sinfulness. In criticizing us for advocating dual causality, however, they are demonstrating their captivity to a mono-cause, either-or perspective. They assume that by suggesting there is a spiritual dimension to a given event, we are advocating that there is only a spirit cause. We are not. We are saying that there are two causes.

For example, with regard to human sinfulness, Scripture holds that there is both human responsibility and evil spiritual pressure. We cannot simply say, "The devil made me do it," and avoid responsibility for our behavior. But we are also wrong to ignore the fact that spirit beings are working 24/7, tempting us to use our free will to disobey God. Judas is a good example of this dual causality. His actions at the time of Jesus' crucifixion are both his fault and the result of satanic activity in his life.

As mentioned, I believe every event has both a human dimension and a spirit dimension. What we do at the human level affects what goes on in the spirit world. Our worldview, however, hinders us from awareness of the fact that what we do has spiritual implications. It hinders—and for many, completely blots out—our attempts to see spiritual reality. When we do things, even if we are aware of the spiritual dimension, we are usually focused completely on human-level behavior and have to infer the spiritual dimension.

If, for example, we are asked to list the things in the room we are sitting in, we describe the physical things and the human things and omit the invisible objects. There are spirits, good and evil, in this room. There is also air in the room, plus radio and TV waves, and probably other invisible things. But only the physical and human things draw our attention, and we seldom even recognize the existence of the spiritual things.

> **What is going on in the spirit world while you are reading this book?**

And what is going on in the spirit world while you are reading this book? I think we can assume that the enemy is interested in what you are doing. Does he want you reading books like this? Might he be afraid that you will learn to do something that would curtail his activities? Has it been difficult to get into this book or into others like it? Could it be that our enemy is trying to hinder your learning and especially your activity in this area?

While we are doing our human things, an evil spirit world exists that has its own agenda. And the beings in that world do not want you getting active in spiritual warfare. We pray and engage in warfare activity because there is a very active enemy kingdom that seeks to thwart God's activity. This is the third hundred pieces of the puzzle that our society ignores or even denies.

In a church service, while the preacher is speaking on a biblical passage, what is going on in the spirit world? What about during worship? Both preaching and worship seek to draw us closer to God. Drawing closer to God may or may not be happening at the human level. At the spirit level, God is reaching out to us and hopefully is connecting.

I am afraid that much of what goes on during church services on Sunday mornings stays in the human realm, not really connecting with God as He reaches out for us. The services may, then, be more pleasing to Satan than to God. Sermons may be primarily informational (i.e., secular), and so may hymns. What is going on in the evil kingdom when these activities are happening?

Ideally, what goes on in church pleases God and disturbs the enemy. It has been my own experience and that of many others that contemporary worship, with all of its limitations, moves us into the spirit realm, closer to Jesus. I believe contemporary worship is the most important thing that has come into our church life in this generation.

When contemporary worship is done well, the heavens open and genuine contact is made between at least some of us and God. At the human level, we sing. At the spirit level, we are in contact with God and have moved into the missing third of Reality.

Prayer is probably the most obvious example of activity in the human world paralleled by activity in the spirit world. At the human level, we can describe things like posture and words spoken. At the spirit level, we know God listens and determines what to do about our prayers. It is clear that activity is expected at both levels.

Prayer is partnership with God. It is also an act of warfare. There is nothing Satan hates more than prayer. In prayer, we are joining the spirit world on God's side, partnering with God and enabling Him to defeat the enemy spirits, who are constantly active in promoting their cause.

On the negative side, what is going on in the spirit world when abortion is happening in the human world? Power is released when blood is shed. When Jesus died, the power released in the spirit world was so great that people came out of their graves (see Matthew 27:51–53)! When power is released unjustly, our enemy wins big-time. How much power is released in the U.S. when the number of babies murdered climbs to more than fifty million?

Or how much power is released when God's plan for marriage is disobeyed? Advocates of same-sex marriage have foisted on the world the lie that same-sex marriage is a matter of fairness. In advocating same-sex marriage, however, these individuals have broken spiritual laws and thereby given a big advantage to the enemy in his attempts to destroy our society.

In fact, unrighteousness of any kind at the ground level breaks God's rules and gives the enemy big victories in the air, greatly enhancing his attempts to destroy what God has created. There is a human cause, manifested in human misbehavior, which is the misuse of God's gift of free will. This misbehavior, then, automatically gives Satan and his forces a victory in the spirit realm.

There are a large number of activities performed at the human level that have powerful ramifications in the spirit realm. These include dedications, blessings, curses, thievery, dishonesty and loyalty pledged to spirits, whether conscious or unconscious. In short, any acts of disobedience to God's laws give Satan victories.

On the positive side, righteousness of any kind is a type of obedience, a partnership between us and God. And obedience at the human level enhances God's power at the spirit level. When Christians live righteously, gather to worship, fast, pray and help others, angels are mobilized and God's side is strengthened.

Examples from Scripture

Scriptural examples of human-spirit interaction abound, and in some few cases we are given insight into what is going on at both levels. In Genesis 3, we are shown both the human and the spiritual sides of disobedience, though there are many unanswered questions concerning how acts that seem to be fairly small could have such large-scale ramifications as some of them do. In Genesis 4, we are told that as the murder of Abel happened on the human level, his blood cried out spiritually to God (see Genesis 4:10). Perhaps the clearest account of what takes place at both spirit and human ends is the report in the book of Job, chapter 1, of the conversation between Satan and God (though after that chapter we are mostly left on our own to figure out what is going on in the spirit world).

When we get to the book of Ruth, we find details about human events but nothing explaining what was going on in the spirit world. With the story of Ahab and Jezebel in 1 Kings 16:29–33, we find a lot of detail about the human side of things with a clear implication that something is going on in the spiritual arena, but we are not told what.

In the historical books of the Old Testament, we are told that the difference between the good kings and the bad ones is symbolized by what they did with the shrines that reverenced other gods. There was so much power in this behavior that when a king set out to destroy the shrines, the people turned to God. When, however, a king honored the shrines, the whole nation turned away from God.

Another biblical example is the conflict between Israel and the Philistines. The Israelite army takes on the Philistines at the human level. The God of the Israelites takes on the gods of the Philistines at the spirit level, and the win is interpreted spiritually as the win of the god of the winning army.

A startling example of the need to recognize and analyze causality at both human and spirit levels is recorded in 2 Kings 3:24ff. Israel is defeating the Moabites to such an extent that the latter are driven back into their walled capital city. The Moabite king, in desperation, takes seven hundred of his swordsmen and tries to force his way through Israel's lines to get help from the king of Syria (verse 26). But in vain. So, we read, "he took his oldest son, who was to succeed him as king, and offered him on the city wall as a sacrifice to the god of Moab" (verse 27)—and the Israelite army turned and went home! Why?

At the human level, Israel was winning in a big way. The king of Moab, however, through the sacrifice of the heir to the throne, was able to throw so much spiritual power at Israel that they turned and ran—without, sadly, remembering that they could have appealed to a greater spiritual power and won at the spirit level just as they had been winning at the human level.

In the New Testament, we are shown both the human and spiritual sides of the events surrounding the virgin birth of Jesus. When the baby is in danger from a jealous King Herod, it is a message from the spirit world that alerts Joseph to take the baby away, thus thwarting the plan of Satan to destroy Jesus (see Matthew 2:13–15).

We could point to many more examples of this principle, but these few are enough to point to the fact that spirit activity and human activity operate parallel to each other, producing parallel causes to the events of human life. I contend, therefore, that no human problem is completely analyzed until both the human-level and the spirit-level causes are taken into account. Throughout the Bible, whenever a conflict takes place, it takes place on both levels. An individual is tempted, producing both internal factors, stemming from his or her sin nature, and external factors, stemming from the fact that the members of the satanic kingdom, "the spiritual powers in space" (Ephesians 2:2), are always there to empower temptations. These events are examples of dual causality.

Reminder of Our Enemy

Scripture tells us there is an enemy who is very active and whose commitment is to "steal, kill, and destroy" (John 10:10) as much as he can in the human context. And we are expected, like the New Testament Christians were, to "know what [Satan's] plans are" (2 Corinthians 2:11). When Jesus announced His reason for coming to earth, He spoke of humans as "captives" and "oppressed" (Luke 4:18). He later referred to Satan as "the ruler of this world" (John 14:30).

Both Jesus and the New Testament writers were very conscious of Satan's activities in the world—much more conscious than we are. Paul calls the enemy "the ruler of the spiritual powers in space" (Ephesians 2:2) and points out that "we are not [simply] fighting against human beings but against the wicked spiritual forces in the heavenly world, the rulers, authorities, and cosmic powers of this dark age" (Ephesians 6:12). Peter, then, describes the enemy as one who "roams around like a roaring lion, looking for someone to devour" (1 Peter 5:8).

When dealing with the demonic, we soon learn that we have to work at both the human and the spirit levels. Those who tend to ignore the activity of Satan miss this, probably because they do not know how to understand spiritual reality. Though it is difficult, we who are participating in spiritual warfare are attempting to understand the dual causality of Scripture. I believe everything that happens needs to be seen at both levels—though there are human causes for most things, there are also influences coming from the spirit level.

Example of Our Part

One of the things we who are involved in spiritual warfare have learned is that demons can live in a person only if there is something within that person for them to attach to. This can be sin, though most of the Christians I work with have already taken care of things ordinarily thought of as sin. The things that attract demons are more often reactions to life experiences, like unforgiveness, wallowing in anger, deep feelings of rejection, lust or any number of other reactions that may rightly be called sin but usually are not thought of when that term is used. Or there may be an inherited satanic grip on them stemming from ancestral vows, curses, dedications or the sins of their ancestors. Whatever the garbage that gives the demons their rights, we need to speak of two causes (garbage and demons), not just one.

Likewise with respect to cosmic-level relationships between human and spirit beings. In order for higher-level spirits to have influence, there needs to be some vulnerability at the human level. (We will discuss this further in chapters 14 and 15.) When, therefore, groups of people are organized according to territorial groupings, such as nations or cities, or band themselves together in institutions, businesses, clubs and the like by promoting racism, occult involvement, pornography, prostitution, abortion, homosexuality, gambling or any number of other sinful activities, they give higher-level spirits legal rights in their society. For example, it is critical that a people group repent of, say, racism, if the power of the higher-level spirits whose job it is to keep the sin active is to be broken. Just as there are two causes to deal with in individual demonization, then, we need to deal with both the human and the spirit world when contending with higher-level spirits as well.

Partnership Between the Two

All of these examples witness, I believe, to a rule of the universe: Humans can cooperate with spirit beings, enabling humans to do more than they would otherwise be able to do. On the Christian side of the fence, we can, through prayer and obedience, enable God to do what He wants to do. God works with us in partnership, choosing to work in the human arena when we partner with Him (again, two causes) and choosing to not do His work when we refuse to cooperate.

Those who obey Satan, then, have to obey the same rule. When people choose to partner with Satan, he is enabled to do his work. When people follow Satan, that enables him to succeed, within the limits set by God, in his schemes. The rule seems to be that either God or Satan is enabled to carry out schemes when their followers commit themselves to the scheme.

There is, then, continuous interaction and quite a bit of interdependence between humans and spirit beings on both God's side and Satan's side. When we obey God, He is enabled to do more of what He wants to do. And when we fail Him, His will may not get done (unless He overrules the situation in some way). Thus, Jesus prayed that God's will would be done "on earth as it is in heaven" (Matthew 6:10) because God's will is not automatic. God does not want any to perish (see 2 Peter 3:9), but His will can be thwarted and people can perish if they choose to partner with Satan and reject God's offer. Refusal to partner with God automatically results in partnership with Satan. God and Satan make their choice; humans make their choice, too.

> **Refusal to partner with God automatically results in partnership with Satan.**

In spite of what we have said concerning the need for something at the human level to enable spirit-level activity, there is also some degree of activity possible within the spirit world, independent of human permission. We would contend, for example, that God can, still within the rules He has put into the universe, exert influence on people who seem, at least, to have no use for Him. (Consider, for example, the conversion of the apostle Paul in Acts 9 or the seven years Nebuchadnezzar was driven into the wilderness in Daniel 4:31–37.) God can restrain, protect and attack within those rules.

It should not seem strange to us, then, that Satan, working under the same rules, though not with the same degree of autonomy, can exert similar kinds of influence in the human arena. We have the example of Job, where God was protecting him and Satan requested and received permission from God to attack him, even to the extent of killing his family (see Job 1:1–2:10). Interestingly, though, the enemy allowed Job's wife to live, to partner with Satan, in order that she could convey Satan's message to Job: "Curse God and die" (Job 2:9). This part of the story shows, again, dual causality. Satan gave the words (see Satan's prediction that Job would curse God in Job 1:11), and Job's wife partnered with Satan and spoke the very words Satan had predicted.

Satan also tried to kill Jesus as a child (see Matthew 2:16). In order to do this, he partnered with a human, King Herod, who would do Satan's will by ordering the killing. God, however, was able to partner with Joseph and Mary, who responded to a dream in which God's angel instructed them to flee to Egypt. In both cases, we see this partnership rule in action—there are spirit and human components to the events. Dual causality.

I contend, then, that the rules of the universe allow Satan a certain amount of autonomy to exert influence both on those who serve him and, to some extent, on those he does not have rights over. With Job, he requested and gained more rights than were his previously. With us as sinners, he has certain rights because of our sinful condition. As a part of his right to tempt us, he seems to be able to put thoughts into our minds. Apparently, he also has the right to test us and perhaps even, on occasion, to capture us, judging from the words Jesus used in the Lord's Prayer: "Do not bring us to hard testing, but keep us safe [deliver us, NIV] from the Evil One" (Matthew 6:13). Satan's ability to influence both pagans and the people of God, then, is abundantly clear from the events recorded in the Scriptures, as well as from contemporary experience.

In any event, our attempts to understand and analyze need to take into account the human and the spirit influences in any given situation. This is what I am calling dual causality. And we may need to confront and change our worldview assumptions if we are to properly understand spiritual power and its exercise.

6

Forms, Meanings
and Empowerment

I apologize for the technicality of what follows, but it provides an important foundation for the points I want to make in this chapter. The issues I deal with here are directly related to worldview interpretation and its relationship to spiritual power.

A very important issue in any discussion of worldview and spiritual issues is the matter of cultural forms, meanings and empowerment. The form-meaning distinction is basic to any discussion of culture and life. We use the term *form* to label every cultural item or event—all of the customs, structures, material objects, rituals, music and beliefs visible and invisible—that make up a culture. These items may be material objects (e.g., jewelry, houses, chairs, idols) or nonmaterial entities (e.g., words, rituals, baptisms, songs). The forms are the building blocks of culture. All of the visible and invisible items and events of a people's life are cultural forms. The cultural forms, then, are the items that people interpret and to which they assign *meaning*. And the meanings people assign can affect them powerfully.

We learn from communication theory that meanings exist not in the cultural or linguistic forms themselves but in the people who use the forms. Meanings are attached by people to cultural forms according to the customary agreements of the people who use the forms. In other words, we can talk to each other intelligibly only if both of us agree to attach the same meanings to the words and sentences we make. These words and sentences are the language forms a person uses with the expectation that the other person will interpret them to mean what the first person means by them. The forms are the parts of a culture and language. The meanings are created according to the agreements of the persons who use the cultural forms. People participating in the same sociocultural group agree with each other as to what significance each cultural form has, and thus they can communicate with each other. If they do not agree, as when one speaks in a language that the other person does not know, they cannot communicate.

In addition to being the vehicles of meaning, cultural forms can be spiritually *empowered*—either by God's power or by Satan's. We do not wrestle simply over meanings that people attach to forms but with real, live, invisible beings who have the ability to inhabit cultural forms (see Ephesians 6:12). Cultural forms that have been dedicated to spirit beings, whether God or Satan, carry spiritual power. This fact is important in dealing with spiritual warfare.

How This Relates to Spiritual Warfare

When an object is dedicated to God or to Satan (usually in the name of a god or spirit), a meaning is given to it. For example, I have had the experience of being blocked in attempting to cast out a demon because the person in whom that demon lived was wearing a dedicated ring. When I noticed the ring and had the person lay it aside, I was able to kick out the demon. There was enough spiritual power in the ring to block God's power from releasing the person from the demon until we laid aside the ring.

A further example: I wear a gold cross necklace that I have empowered by blessing it in the name of Jesus. On occasion, when working to free a person from demons, I show the demon the cross. This act usually breaks the demon's power, enabling me to cast it out. Note that the symbol of the cross carries an important meaning. But in addition, the cross has been empowered by my blessing it in Jesus' name to assist in banishing demons.

Western Christians show some awareness of this principle when they dedicate church buildings, the elements of Communion, anointing oil and babies to our God. In addition, we bless individuals and, in benedictions, whole congregations in the name of Jesus Christ. Though some people believe such dedications and blessings are merely rituals, significant only because of their meanings, I do not. I believe these acts have meaning. But multiple experiences of blessing or anointing a person and witnessing an immediate and surprising reaction have convinced me that we also are dealing with God's empowerment.

James recommends that we use anointing oil to bring healing to the sick (see James 5:14). If the oil is to be effective, however, it must be dedicated in the name of Jesus and thus empowered. The elements used in the Lord's Supper also can and should be dedicated. This is likely what Paul meant in 1 Corinthians 10:16 when he referred to the Communion cup as blessed (NASB).[1] He intended for the elements to be thus empowered. This empowerment makes it dangerous to participate in the Lord's Supper unworthily (see 1 Corinthians 11:28–32). Paul's handkerchiefs and aprons also were empowered so that people received healing through them (see Acts 19:12). So, I believe, was Jesus' robe (see Luke 8:43–48).

God regularly flows His power through words such as *in Jesus' name* and the commands we give to demons. When such words convey God's power, we can call them *empowered language forms*. When we dedicate buildings or objects to Jesus, we are using His authority to empower them for His purposes.

But cultural objects (material forms) can carry evil spiritual power as well. Many missionaries and travelers have experienced strange occurrences in their homes that stopped when they took authority to cancel the power of or destroy certain objects that were carrying evil power. These

---

1. Note how most translations, completed by people who are worldview bound and therefore don't understand the spiritual side of the term *bless*, translate the word *thanksgiving* or some such word designed to capture the human meaning. However, they miss the spiritual side of it captured in the word *bless*.

objects are usually from non-Western societies and are bought or given as souvenirs. When God's authority was invoked to break that power, the strange things that were going on stopped.

When Meaning and Empowerment Interact

Spiritual warfare is as much a matter of dealing with meaning as it is dealing with power. We have repeatedly brought up the issue of the spiritual blindness inherent in our Western worldview. This blindness is a matter of the meaning we have been taught to assign to the events of life. If we do not see the spiritual dimension because of our worldview blindness, we will assign naturalistic meanings to spiritual events. We will not assign spiritual meaning, and we will not recognize the spiritual power that may be active in many of our life experiences. So we may have both a spiritual blindness and a meaning blindness.

The problems raised by inadequate handling of the meanings and empowerment of cultural forms can be very troublesome. The blindness of the people in our families or the congregations of pastors who have not awakened to the reality of spiritual power is one of these problems. In many of our families and churches, in addition to those who are blind to spiritual warfare, there are people who have been affected by occult involvements that they innocently became involved in. Among these are New Age, Freemasonry, Scientology, yoga, fortune-telling, Ouija boards, certain video games (e.g., *Dungeons & Dragons*) and even certain movies and books (e.g., the Harry Potter series). Our people are often quite unaware of the spiritual power behind these involvements. They, therefore, fall into the meaning problem of considering such activities harmless.

> **Spiritual warfare is as much a matter of dealing with meaning as it is dealing with power.**

Whether we are dealing with family members or friends who are in positions of Christian leadership, then, it is important for us to learn how to handle both empowerment and meaning. Often the meaning problem is more difficult to deal with than the empowerment problem. However, the two problems regularly come at the same time.

Once we learn to work in the authority Christ has given us, we recognize that breaking the power of empowered objects is usually not difficult. Since we have infinitely more power stemming from our relationship with Jesus than such objects can convey, we simply have to claim Jesus' power to break the enemy's power in the object. I usually simply say, "I break any enemy power in this object in Jesus' name." Then I also bless it in His name. The problem with satanic empowerment is not that we do not have the power to break it. It is that we must overcome ignorance (which is a meaning problem) so that we recognize when spiritual power is there and know what to do to break it.[2]

In many non-Western societies, implements used for warfare, religious practices, seeking food and other necessary activities are routinely dedicated to the spirits or gods of the society. Temples, homes, workplaces and sometimes whole nations (e.g., Japan) also are dedicated by priests with the authority of their gods behind them. In the South Pacific, for example, those who made the large canoes used for fishing and/or for warfare regularly dedicated them to their gods. Since dual allegiance is prevalent, I suspect they still do this, even if they call themselves Christians. When such things are dedicated to satanic spirits, they are empowered by those spirits. Again, many missionaries or travelers who have brought dedicated cultural items home with them have unwittingly invited enemy spirits into their homes.

Here in the United States, I have been asked from time to time to advise people who have experienced strange things in certain places. In one case, a church was experiencing difficulties that most of the people interpreted naturalistically. These problems stopped, however, when it was discovered that the church had been built on an American Indian burial ground and the power of Christ was claimed by the pastor who, as pastor, had authority over the area to break the power of the Indian spirits.

In another situation, a missionary to American Indians observed that over a thirty-year period, everyone who lived in a certain house on their mission station had left that station in some sort of severe difficulty, such

2. For a more thorough discussion of these points, see Charles H. Kraft, *I Give You Authority: Practicing the Authority Jesus Gave Us*, rev. ed. (Minneapolis: Chosen, 2012).

98

as marital problems, problems with children or sickness. Though many of the missionaries attributed this fact to chance, the new leader of the mission decided to fast and do spiritual warfare praying over the house. Things are fine now.

When we suspect an object or place has been used for satanic purposes, it is important to disempower it before attempting to use it. Satanic power can and should be broken over rituals, buildings, carvings, songs and just about anything else people use. Those cultural forms should be captured for God's use. Despite the fact that many counsel us to refuse to use whatever the enemy has used,[3] I believe we are to capture most cultural forms, not reject them merely because our enemy uses them.[4] My rule of thumb is to capture anything except those items that have no other purpose than to honor false gods and spirits, such as idolatrous carvings and masks and other items used in religious rituals. Those things I destroy. But we should not try to use even the ones we can capture until the power is broken. That would be unwise in the extreme.

> I believe we are to capture most cultural forms, not reject them merely because our enemy uses them.

The world is felt by many traditional religionists to be a dangerous place, requiring that people protect themselves from spiritual interference in their lives. To do this, they often make use of amulets or other empowered items that are carried on their bodies or kept in their homes. Necklaces, rings or belts are frequently dedicated to provide protection for individuals. Small household shrines are used by many people to protect their homes.

On the Christian side, as well, there are both meaning and empowerment issues. We need to recognize the spiritual dangers of the world we live in, which is a meaning issue. We also need to protect ourselves by employing the spiritual power we have been given, which is an empowerment issue. We can bless our homes and other possessions with protection against enemy schemes. We should also protect our family members and any people we

3. One example would be David A. Hunt and T. A. McMahon, *The Seduction of Christianity* (Eugene, Ore.: Harvest House, 1985).
4. See my discussion of this position in Kraft, *Christianity with Power*, 211.

have authority over. We can claim protection when traveling or when staying in motels or other places that may have been used for evil purposes or even dedicated by previous occupants. Awareness of the activities of evil spirit beings in many areas of life should stimulate us to claim the power of Christ for protection continually.

How the Meaning Problem Continues

Converts to Christianity who have, in their pre-Christian days, experienced satanic power in items and techniques now in use within a Christian context may have a difficult time using those items and techniques (e.g., music, visualization) associated with their old life. They may agree that the power is broken, but their memories of past events in which these items or techniques were used may be a major hindrance to their being able to use them while living as Christians.

For people converted out of non-Christian religions or occult organizations, such as New Age, Freemasonry, Scientology or animism (see chapter 8), it may take years or a whole generation before the pre-Christian meanings associated with given objects are fully replaced in the converts' minds. Frequently, such people simply want to throw away every vestige of their old culture that reminds them of their involvement with shamans, rituals and evil spirits. In their place, they tend to borrow cultural forms from the West (e.g., music, monologue preaching) on the assumption—the meaning—that these Western forms carry more spiritual power than their traditional forms. The Bible, in fact, is often interpreted as a fetish, a more potent carrier of spiritual power than their former fetishes.

These borrowed items are interpreted to mean that God wants Christians in non-Western societies to Westernize and be foreigners in their own countries rather than to capture their own traditions for Christ. Since we Westerners understand so poorly the spiritual power dimensions of our movement, we often go along with and even encourage such a desire to disassociate from their traditional practices rather than capture them. This has caused converted foreigners to produce a Christianity that is as powerless as ours in the West. They might find the Western forms unattractive and reject them or attractive and adopt them for the wrong reasons.

The point is, people come into Christianity with their own meaning system—a system or worldview that will continue to interfere with whatever changes in interpretation they attempt to make. And this regularly causes problems for both those who lack understanding of the power issues and for those who have been into power and find it difficult to reinterpret customs and places that once conveyed evil power. In addition, the enemy, knowing the history, cleverly tempts people to continue assigning the old meanings.

People come into Christianity with their own meaning system.

For those who have been immersed in satanic activity, we can demonstrate the power of God and help them cross the bridge from working in satanic power (e.g., animism or New Age) to working in God's power. This bridge, then, is often a shorter bridge to empowered Christianity than that from secular naturalism (or powerless Christianity) to a Christianity with power, since most of the principles in the former are the same. The basic difference is not in the principles—both God and Satan obey the same rules—but, as I have mentioned before, in the fact that powerful Christianity is plugged into God as the source of power while animism and New Age are plugged into satanic power.

Whether at home or abroad, we can learn that a secularized Christianity—the usual form both in America and in most missionized lands—is a long way from the Bible in the area of spiritual power. This fact is as much a meaning problem as a power problem. When people have learned to depend on secular medicine, secular psychology and secular education without the power of God, they have not experienced the spirituality of the Scriptures either in the power dimension or in the meanings they attribute to Christianity. It is an important part of spiritual warfare to fight powerless Christianity on both the power front and the meaning front.

7

Toward a More Complete Christianity

Moving into warfare theology and practice may require numerous other worldview changes. Following are a series of theological propositions that attempt to integrate the warfare aspects of our faith with the more peaceful aspects. Many of these items reflect standard evangelical beliefs, but some will require a paradigm shift for many evangelicals. All are worldview issues.

1. **God created and sustains the universe.** The earth is the Lord's and the fullness thereof. He created the universe for Himself and sustains it according to His will.

2. **Something happened in heaven to upset things.** We believe it was a rebellion sponsored by Satan. The passages in Isaiah 14:12–17 and Ezekiel 28:11–19 are commonly interpreted as describing Satan's revolt.

3. **God created humans and put them in second place in the universe.** Previously, Lucifer/Satan had been in second place. But God created humans in His image and thus displaced him. Satan is jealous because he lost his position in second place.

4. **God gave humans dominion over everything.** We see this responsibility reflected in Psalm 5:8 and Genesis 1:26–30. Before his fall, Satan was probably in charge of all that God gave to Adam at Adam's creation.

5. **Satan sought to defeat God and be in charge of the universe.** However, he never did gain supremacy or even equality with God. He is still only an angel, though a very powerful one, and is still seeking to defeat God and to use humans in his quest to replace God.

6. **Satan tempted humans.** According to the rules of the universe, the plan was for humans to partner with God in running things. Satan, however, recruited Adam to be his partner. Through Adam's obedience to Satan, Satan gained the authority Adam had been given to rule over the earth (see John 14:30). Humans fell, and all creation with them.

7. **In the Fall, Satan gained power over human systems.** He claims in Luke 4:6 to have dominion over all the power and wealth of the world, since it was given to him at the Fall. According to 1 John 5:19, he is now known as the ruler of this world's systems.

8. **When Satan and his angels rebelled, God never redeemed them.** Apparently, they do not get a second chance.

9. **In contrast to the way God treated fallen angels, He set in motion the plan of redemption for humans after they rebelled.** God worked with Jesus, His partner, to redeem us. He now works with human partners in human affairs to bring about His plan to rescue us from the continuing activity of Satan.

10. **Human history functions in a context of warfare between God and His human partners against Satan and his human partners.** The battles take place in the human context as well as in the heavenlies. We do not know much about the warfare in the heavenlies, but we are becoming increasingly aware of what the warfare looks like here on earth. Daniel 10:13 and Job 1 give us a glimpse of what God is doing "in the air."

11. **Satan has gained rights to humans and, through them, to human systems and human territory.** For example, in the Scriptures we see that he has gained rights over systems (see Luke 4:6), gained rights over territory (see Daniel 10:13, 20), gained influence in human affairs (see 1 John 5:19; John 12:31; 14:30; 16:11; Luke 4:6; 2 Corinthians 4:4) and is called "the god of this age" (2 Corinthians 4:4 NIV).

12. **God partnered with Mary to create the Man, Jesus, who would partner with God to redeem humans.** Since Adam, not Eve, bears responsibility for our sin nature, Jesus could be born sin-free if He had no earthly father to pass on to Him the sin nature.

13. **Jesus lived, died and rose again to defeat Satan.** He lived totally as a human, never using His divinity. He was filled with the Holy Spirit (see Luke 3:22) and worked entirely under His Father's authority (see John 5:19) in obedience to the Father.

14. **Jesus planted His Kingdom in the middle of Satan's kingdom.** The context in which God's Kingdom emerges is the physical and spiritual realm that we call the universe. This is what Satan was able to steal from Adam. Satan is called the god of this age (see 2 Corinthians 4:4).

15. **Jesus was the inaugurator of a new age that starts now and continues forever.** The manifestations of this new age include the empowering presence of the Holy Spirit in our lives, a close relationship with Jesus, the gifts of the Spirit, the ability to break free from sin bondages and the authority over evil spirits.[1]

16. **While on earth, Jesus showed us the importance of fighting Satan.** We are to do Jesus' works (see John 14:12). His ministry was full of confrontations with demons (see Mark 1:21–28, 39). Deliverance is a major sign that the Kingdom is here (see Matthew 12:28; Luke 11:20).

17. **For reasons we do not understand, God has allowed Satan to continue to exist and fight.** Even after his defeat at the crucifixion and resurrection and his humiliation in Jesus' victory parade (see Colossians 2:15), Satan still exists and fights. The battle continues to rage in the human context even though Satan cannot win. But he is allowed to cause problems for humans.

18. **Christians are called to participate in this war.** We are to be filled with the Holy Spirit as Jesus was (see Acts 1:8). Our aim is to join Jesus in taking captives back from Satan (see Luke 4:18–19). We are to put on spiritual armor to fight spiritual battles (see Ephesians 6:10–12). We are to tear down strongholds (see 2 Corinthians 10:1–5), both in individuals and at higher levels.

1. Clinton E. Arnold, *Three Crucial Questions about Spiritual Warfare* (Grand Rapids, Mich.: Baker Academic, 1997), 21.

A Threefold Christianity

A basic problem in evangelical Christianity is that our focus tends to be primarily on knowledge *about* things (e.g., theology), with our having a lot to think and say about those things without much doing of them. We have learned in our schools that we can pretty much control our life through learning and knowledge and even create an escape from reality into a world of thought and theory. Our schools are known for the theoretical knowledge they pass on, not for the practical application of that knowledge. This leads, I believe, to a certain sterility and lack of "boots on the ground" in our lives.

For example, in 1982, some of us at Fuller Seminary began learning about spiritual power. This was acceptable to the theologians on our faculty as long as we stayed at the theoretical level. We were allowed to discuss and even debate the issues involved. But when we began to apply the principles and actually *do* something, like pray for healing and see people set free, things changed. This turned them against us, and we had to discontinue the course. Theory was all right; practice was not. Unfortunately, this is the mood alive in institutions of higher learning throughout our nation.

> **We need a worldview shift from a knowledge orientation to an experiential focus.**

Where is the life that we see in the Bible? Where is the life in Christ that we see modeled in the New Testament? Do we have a complete Christianity?

I believe we need a worldview shift from a knowledge orientation to what I will call an experiential focus, centered on our relationship with Jesus. The essence of our faith is relationship with Jesus. All the rest is there to support that relationship and to take it to others.

As evangelicals, we have known that relationship with God is core, but often our tendency has been to focus on knowledge *about* that relationship more than the growth of that relationship. There are, however, three major dimensions to a complete Christianity: allegiance leading to relationship, truth/knowledge leading to understanding and spiritual power leading to freedom. As evangelicals, we have shown great concern for the first two of these but have largely ignored the third.

Jesus, of course, majored in relationship—His relationship with the Father and our relationship with Him. But the thing that enabled those relationships was not knowledge. It was His use of power to free people from the grip of Satan. People listened to Jesus and learned about the Kingdom. But it was the experience of freedom that Jesus provided that enabled people to truly participate in the Kingdom.

Jesus spoke truth (knowledge) with power. The healing part of Jesus' ministry was not peripheral to the teaching part. It was central to it, a demonstration of the love (a form of relationship) that He and His Father have toward their creatures. But in our Christian experience as evangelicals, the power part is usually neglected. Ours, then, is a twofold rather than a threefold Christianity that easily becomes secular.

I see a complete, threefold Christianity as one that has all three of the dimensions in focus. We can picture it as a table named Relationship, supported by Truth and Spiritual Power.

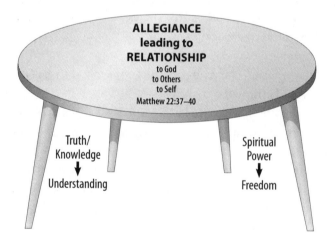

Dimension 1: Allegiance Leading to Relationship

The most important of the three dimensions is our relationship with Christ. This is the defining activity of Christians. This dimension starts with allegiance to Christ, without which one is not a Christian. It is supported by the other two dimensions.

Allegiance is the entrance requirement. We come to Jesus and pledge allegiance to Him. This makes us a part of the Christian community. From that point, then, we are in a relationship with Christ and His people. This relationship is to grow as we participate in life with Jesus. That life is the basic and most precious thing in our existence. Thus, this dimension is the most important of the three dimensions.

This aspect starts with our conversion, issuing in a commitment that is to replace every other commitment as our primary allegiance. There can be other allegiances in our lives, but none is to be above our allegiance to Jesus. This allegiance is expected to grow and to be expressed as loving God with our whole heart and our neighbor as ourself, as Jesus commanded (see Matthew 22:37–40). The word *love* is the primary relationship word in the Bible.

This dimension includes practicing all that the Bible teaches on subjects like love, faith, faithfulness, fellowship, the fruits of the Spirit, intimacy with Christ, forgiveness, repentance, reconciliation, obedience and salvation—indeed, all the major doctrines. This, again, is what James Kallas calls the Godward aspect of our faith, which we will discuss in further detail in chapter 8.

Under this dimension, the church is to be experienced as family. Witness to one's personal experience is key to communicating this dimension. Discipleship is the way to teach it. Relationship is learned through relating. Theology is experienced in discipleship and fellowship in which people experience being true to each other and to God in worship and submission to God (see Romans 12:2).

Allegiance, or relationship, is an extremely important part of our faith. All of our cardinal doctrines are relational. The love relationship, of course, is the cornerstone. We are to love God supremely and our neighbors as ourselves (see Matthew 22:37–40). Faith is basic to our relationship with God and is to produce faithfulness to Him and to our relationship with Him. The intimacy with Christ spoken of in John 15 is foundational and often referred to as "life in Christ," and the fruits of the Spirit flow from that intimacy. Forgiveness is relational. So are repentance and reconciliation.

Evangelicals have done well in this area, especially when it comes to the need for people to come to Christ for salvation. But virtually the only support we have given to that relationship is the focus on truth/knowledge. Only one of the two supporting dimensions is in play for most evangelicals.

Dimension 2: Truth/Knowledge Leading to Understanding

Truth and knowledge, though secondary to relationship, are extremely important. Jesus taught truth whenever and wherever possible but always in support of relationship, with love and faith in primary focus. Evangelicals, however, tend to overdose on knowledge. Our sermons and teaching institutions tend to be almost entirely knowledge- and information-oriented. We are good at talking about important subjects, but the amount of our time and energy put into talking about things tends to be disturbingly greater than the amount of time and energy we put into doing what we talk about. Jesus was an activist. His words were backed by actions.

This dimension involves teaching led by the Holy Spirit. Jesus promised that He would lead us into truth (see John 16:13). And He commanded His followers to teach those that follow them (see Matthew 28:20). Scripturally, both truth and knowledge are experiential, not simply cognitive. The Greek word for *knowledge* implies knowledge by experience. John 8:32 should be translated, "You'll *experience* the truth, and the truth will set you free" (emphasis mine). The Greek also implies that knowing will lead to obedience to what is known, not simply the storing of information.

Truth and knowledge are learned by doing what is believed, not simply by thinking about it. Truth provides antidotes for ignorance and error. We can fight ignorance or error with truth, but the other two dimensions (relationship and power) need to be dealt with on their own terms. That is, wrong relationships can only be countered by right relationships, never by knowledge or even spiritual power. And evil spiritual power can only be fought with good spiritual power, never simply by right relationships. Relationship and power have their place but function in different dimensions than does truth. Truth, for its part, needs to be rooted in behavior, not simply in the collecting of information. It is to be applied information, not a collection of true ideas.

We need understanding (truth/knowledge) to support relationships and the use of power. We lose a lot, though, if we try to substitute knowledge *about* for either of these other dimensions. This dimension embodies truth and knowledge of all aspects of Christian experience. We need to know as much as possible about all three dimensions, but as a means, not an end in itself. The three dimensions are intended to relate tightly to each other, with the relationship of truth/knowledge to the other dimensions especially important. Our relationships and spiritual power are to be based on accurate information.

In this dimension, we are to gain insight into the contents of the other two dimensions. We are expected to grow in this knowledge/truth dimension as in all other dimensions of Christian experience. Lies are to be countered with God's truths. The enemy seeks to deceive us. The antidote is truth.

Under this dimension, the church is to be experienced as a teaching place. Not all teaching is to be done in classrooms, however. We are to be mentored and discipled, learning information that equips us to live and minister. We should be learning in a relational context, not just in classrooms. Jesus' teaching of truth happened through practicing it in ministry, not through thinking about it in a classroom.

Theology should be primarily experiential with an important cognitive component. But our views of theology are often restricted to informational theology. There are other valid approaches to theology appropriate to the other two dimensions. And theology in practice involves us in relating and ministering, practicing what we believe.

We need understanding. Understanding is a product of the teaching of truth and knowledge. The problem is that we are immersed in much more cognitive knowledge than we need. This focus on cognitive knowledge detracts from the fact that true Christianity is to be played out in experience rather than just in talk.

We honor theological thinking and writing as if these are the essence of our faith, when the essence should be in how we live it out. Mere thinking, with a focus on information, is not what Christianity is supposed to be about. With the support of truth and knowledge, however, relationship has half the support it needs.

Dimension 3: Spiritual Power Leading to Freedom

The other half of support for relationship needs to come from evangelical Christianity's weakest area: spiritual power. This is the dimension that brings to people the freedom Jesus promised. For a relationship with Jesus is intended to include freedom as well as salvation. Indeed, entering into Christianity involves two major steps—a salvation step and a freedom step. And many wonderfully saved Christians never get to take the freedom step. The purpose of spiritual power is to bring and nurture *freedom*.

With regard to this third dimension, spiritual power, though, evangelicals have largely neglected anything but passing references to Satan and his activities. This fact leaves our Christianity incomplete and limping along, theologically and practically. We are left with a powerless, secular Christianity as the spiritual power dimension of our faith goes underrepresented in our teaching, writing and preaching. The spiritual power dimension, so prominent in Scripture, is largely ignored. Of the three dimensions in focus, then, this is the missing dimension.

> **The spiritual power dimension of our faith is underrepresented in our teaching, writing and preaching.**

The power in focus here is *spiritual* power, not political or personal. This dimension recognizes that humans are held captive by Satan. Jesus recognized this (see Luke 4:18) and spent His ministry freeing people from the enemy. He worked in the authority and power of the Holy Spirit to set captives free (see Luke 4:18–19). He did nothing under the power of His own divinity (see Philippians 2:5–8). Since we have the same Holy Spirit that Jesus had, He is not asking the impossible for us to do what He did.

Jesus passed this authority and power on to His followers, saying, "Whoever believes in me will do the works I have been doing" (John 14:12 NIV; see also Luke 9:1; Acts 1:4–8). This being so, He commissioned us to use His authority and power to free people from the enemy.

Satanic power can be defeated only by God's power. Neither truth nor a correct allegiance can overcome spiritual power, though these help. The power and the freedom it can be used to bring are necessary components to a complete Christianity.

Under this dimension, the Church is experienced as both a hospital where wounds are healed, thus freeing people, and an army that attacks the enemy, defeating him both at the ground level and at the cosmic level. Awareness of the power dimensions of Christianity needs to be taught, both cognitively and, especially, experientially (as Jesus did).

Working in Jesus' power is learned through working in Jesus' power. We cannot learn warfare by sitting and talking. We can only learn by doing. Theology is experienced as confronting and defeating the enemy in warfare, resulting in freedom to grow in relationships and understanding.

A Fourfold Church

These considerations highlight certain features of a complete, balanced Christianity. Each of the three features includes an important focus of the Church. Additionally, there are embedded in these dimensions four characteristics of the Church.

1. A Learning Place

The knowledge/truth dimension highlights the Church as a learning place. Much of what we do is like school, but the way Jesus did school was to focus on apprenticeship or discipleship, where we learn by doing and analyzing our experience. Analysis without experience, as much of our schooling devolves into, leads to the escape from reality that I mentioned above. Training is a legitimate function of the Church. Its members need to learn Christian truth. But we learn what we do, and often the major thing learned is little more than how to go to school rather than how to practice the threefold Christianity I am advocating. The truth and knowledge taught and learned need to cover all three of the dimensions we are dealing with, however. The teaching should not be limited to the non-warfare topics (as it is now in most institutions) and should not be limited to all head learning.

2. A Family

The allegiance/relationship dimension highlights the Church as family. As humans, we are made for relationships. And where better to practice and cultivate relationships than in the Church? The first concern should be our relationship with God. Secondly, fellowship and worship with people we love produces relational growth and health. Experiencing freedom through the application of spiritual power, then, maximizes our ability to relate both to God and to fellow believers.

3. A Hospital

The spiritual power dimension showcases the Church as a hospital, where people experience freedom through the application of spiritual power. It is to be a healing place to which people can retreat and receive healing away from the hustle of normal life. People who have hurts should be able to find emotional, spiritual and physical healing in the Church. There should be people in each congregation exercising gifts of healing and prayer, putting the same emphasis on healing that Jesus did and taking from Satan those he has wounded.

4. An Army

In addition, the spiritual power dimension makes us, the Church, an army that goes on the offensive against the enemy. We should be training for warfare and attacking enemy spirits that are disrupting our lives. We need churches that are dealing with demonization among church members. We need those who will cleanse homes spiritually and do prayer walking to cleanse neighborhoods. This view of the Church sees it as active in taking territory from the enemy, just as Jesus did.

A Threefold Theology

Though we have been exposed primarily to a knowledge-oriented approach to theologizing, that is not the only kind there is. Seeing Christianity from this threefold perspective gives us three kinds of theology.

1. Knowledge-Oriented Theology

The knowledge-oriented theologizing is the most obvious kind, where truth and doctrine are in focus. There is nothing wrong with theologizing this way unless it gets to be too much of a head trip. In our training institutions, especially, theology is often a head trip with little practical application outside the classroom, whether the focus is on systematic, biblical or missional theology. Wise instructors, however, find ways in which students can take at least some of their theological theories out into real life.

2. Relational Theology

The primary concern for relationship gives us what has been called relational theology. This is theologizing and theorizing that focus on relationships between God and humans and between humans and other humans. Among the emphases are worship, discipleship and fellowship in which people experience being true to each other. This theologizing is worked out, not just talked about. Human problems and solutions are in focus, and the application of spiritual power to solve human problems would be an important addition to the theology taught in our training institutions. Answers that are spiritual rather than secular need to be in focus in relational theologizing.

3. Warfare Theology

There is, in addition, a warfare theologizing that spins off from the focus on spiritual power. This type of theology is experienced as confronting and defeating the enemy in warfare, both defensively and offensively. It results in learning how to bring freedom to grow in relationships and understanding and working in that freedom to defeat the enemy.

Whether we are looking at the various functions of the Church or the various approaches to theologizing, we have a more complete Christianity if it functions in three dimensions rather than just one or two.

A Full-Fledged Christianity

Learning to work in all three dimensions could also counter the powerlessness of evangelicalism, both at home and abroad. We seek to help people.

But without spiritual power, the only answers we have are secular answers. The only recommendations we have for those who hurt are secular medicine and psychology. For the poor and homeless, we can only join and imitate secular approaches. Thus it is that Christianity has been a major secularizing force wherever it has been introduced.

It was Jesus' authority and power that set Him apart from the other religious teachers of His day. Most of what He said had been said before. The majority of His message, unlike ours, was in who He was and what He did. And He specifically taught that we are able, with the Holy Spirit, to follow His example (see John 14:12). It is this authority and power that proved His relationship with the Father. He did nothing on His own authority (see John 5:19, 30). And His works were endorsed by and empowered not by Himself but by the Father and Holy Spirit.

It is this authority and power that made His relationship with His followers life-transforming. They went out fearless, taking on the whole Roman Empire, because of the transforming power of that relationship. An important concomitant of that relationship, then, was that Jesus gave them the same Holy Spirit who had empowered Him. A Christianity without this authority and power has little to offer a world that Satan claims is his (see Luke 4:6). We cannot fight Satan's power with rational, theoretical truth. You can fight error and ignorance with truth/knowledge. But you have to fight power with power.

We know and practice a good bit of the power of love but often with little spiritual dimension to it. But Jesus used spiritual power as an exciting way to demonstrate God's love. A lack of such demonstration makes most of our evangelical Christianity spiritually lifeless and unable to deal with the spiritual realities of which Jesus, Paul, Peter and the rest of our New Testament authors were so conscious.

We act as if Satan is a toothless lion—not the roaring lion Peter speaks of (see 1 Peter 5:8). We treat those who take seriously Ephesians 6:12 as if they are off balance. We act as if demonization, so common in Jesus' day, is a thing of the past, and we regard those who deal with demons as simple-minded, weird or hyperemotional. This in spite of an incredible amount of evidence that demons are alive and very active today in American society as well as overseas.

114

We may criticize liberals for leaving out certain sections of the Scriptures, but we evangelicals do the same thing when it comes to issues of spiritual power. If we are going to be scriptural and realistic about our Christianity, we are going to have to join Jesus, Paul, Peter and the others on the lunatic fringe. As I have heard Jack Hayford say in lectures at Fuller Seminary, we should regard as strange those who *do not* deal with such spiritual realities, not those who do.

> **We act as if demonization is a thing of the past and regard those who deal with demons as weird or hyperemotional.**

Our enemy does not go away simply because we do not take his activity seriously enough to learn how to deal with it. And he rejoices that we have neglected, both in seminary and in church, to learn how to deal with him. We claim we are biblical but leave out of our theologies the recognition so prominent in the Bible that Satan and his demons are alive and very active today.

8

Issues and Insights

There are a couple of miscellaneous issues and insights that I want to highlight here. Each deals with an aspect of reality that does not fit neatly into the flow of our topic. First we will look at the accusation that dealing with spiritual power is a kind of "Christian animism." Then we will turn to the insight of Lutheran theologian James Kallas, who, if he is right, has uncovered a regrettable deficiency in our evangelical theologizing. As mentioned previously, Kallas estimates that no less than 80 percent of the Synoptics and Pauline epistles are devoted to spiritual warfare (what he calls the "Satanward view") and only 20 percent to what he calls the "Godward view," yet our preaching and teaching are nearly 100 percent Godward.

But first, let's consider the charge of "Christian animism."

Are We Animists?

One of the more sophisticated attacks on power Christianity comes from those who feel that we are embracing a satanic counterfeit called *animism*. These people are accustomed to a rational, non-warfare type of Christianity and assume that Jesus was working out of His divinity while on earth, using a power not available to us. They then see any use of spiritual power today as satanic since they know that Satan works in power.

Robert Priest and associates,[1] for example, seem to assume that we who are involved in power ministry could not be on God's side. They criticize us harshly and accuse us of practicing Christian animism.

It is true that Satan acts in power, and this fact can deceive the inexperienced into attributing his exercise of power to God. For this reason, we must be discerning. Spiritual power is not always satanic. Our God is a God of power, even though there are counterfeits. The counterfeits, then, must be challenged and defeated with God's power.

Animism is Satan's cleverest counterfeit, and it is worldwide. Animism assumes that the world is populated with spirits, most of which are capricious and unpredictable. These spirits are very much a part of daily life and can reward humans if treated well but may take revenge if not treated well or neglected. Keeping the spirits happy is, then, a major concern for animists. If things go wrong, animists assume the reason is that the spirits have not been treated well. Techniques such as divination and magic are employed to activate spiritual power. Worship is assumed to keep the spirits happy. So is providing them with food and performing rituals that honor them.

To share an example with you, a hotel in which I once stayed while teaching in Thailand had a replica of a large building set high on a post in the parking area. Each morning, food was placed on the spirit house platform to keep the spirits fed. It is likely that when the hotel was built, a ritual was performed to ensure that the spirits knew which house was theirs so they could reside there rather than bothering the people in the hotel.

Many whole religions can be considered animistic. Among them are Hinduism, Shintoism, folk Buddhism (as opposed to book Buddhism, which is atheistic), folk Islam, most of the tribal religions of the world, Korean shamanism, Latin American Christopaganism, New Age, satanism, Scientology, spiritism and most other religions. Given this worldwide spread, animism can be considered the majority religion of the world.

1. See Priest, Campbell, and Mullen, "Missiological Syncretism."

Animism and Christianity Share Similarities

Though there are varieties of animism, most varieties of animistic belief are very similar in many ways to biblical faith. Both animism and Christianity see reality divided into three parts: God, spirits, humans. Christianity says, "Focus on God and He will look after whatever the spirits try to do to us." Animism says, "God will be good to us; therefore, ignore Him. The spirits can hurt us, so focus on them."

Most of the animists of the world know that there is a supreme God who lives above the capricious spirits and is more powerful than they are. God, to them, though, is usually seen as benign and to be ignored unless there is a big crisis. Most animists agree, however, that spirits—especially evil spirits—are capricious and therefore dangerous, so they need to be watched and appeased.

Animists believe that material items, buildings and geographical territory and features can be inhabited by evil spirits. So do Christians. And we both believe such things and places can be empowered by God. For the animist, spirit power can reside in these and can take the form of certain mountains (e.g., the Old Testament "high places"), trees, statues (e.g., idols), rocks (e.g., the Kaaba in Mecca), rivers (e.g., the Ganges), dedicated territories, fetishes, charms and any other thing or place that is dedicated to the spirits. Animists also believe in magic, divination and the ability of at least certain people to convey power via curses, blessings, spells and the like.

In Scripture, we see God's power conveyed through material items, too, such as Paul's handkerchiefs and aprons (see Acts 19:12), the Ark of the Covenant, Jesus' robe (see Matthew 9:20; 14:36), the Temple, Communion elements ("the cup of blessing which we bless," 1 Corinthians 10:16 NASB) and anointing oil (see James 5:14), not to mention the flow of spiritual power through our words of blessing and healing.

One of Satan's deceits, however, is to lead people to believe that items and places are powerful in and of themselves. For example, animists believe that objects such as idols or implements used in religious rituals that are dedicated to gods or spirits *contain* spiritual power in and of themselves. Christians believe that objects and places can be dedicated to our God to *convey* His power. On the surface, containing and conveying power look the same, especially since what animists believe to be power contained in objects is, in reality, satanic power conveyed by those objects.

The importance of ritual and sacrifice is also similar in both Christianity and animism. Within Christianity, worship and sacrifice and other acts of devotion are important and when directed toward God please and empower Him. The Old Testament sacrificial system, for example, centers on sacrifices to God. So was the ultimate sacrifice that ended all blood sacrifices—the completed sacrificial work of Jesus on our behalf. Such worship and sacrifice enables God and His spirits to exercise more of their power among humans.

Similarly, within animism, specialist priests, shamans or gurus usually play an important role in the relationships between people and the spirit world in the animistic view. These specialists preside over many, if not all, of the rituals and are consulted whenever difficulties arise that are perceived to be the result of spirit interference in the lives of people. Animists believe that such acts of devotion please and empower their spirits. They quiet, or appease, their spirits when their spirits are angry, deterring them from vengeance.

As another example of similarity, animist diviners, shamans and priests can heal. So can God. The fact that satanic healing leads sooner or later to captivity and misery is often not immediately apparent to the one healed. Nor is the fact that God's healing leads to freedom and peace. On the surface, both types of healing look the same, and people who seek the healing rather than the Healer are easily deceived, especially since satanic spirits seem often to work faster in bringing about results than the true God does.

God Created the Principles

The principles and practices employed by animists are there because God put them there. They are intended by God to be used under Him for good as the basis on which both humans and spirits are to relate to Him and to each other. Animism has, however, hijacked these principles and practices, using them under the power of Satan rather than under the power of God. But the rules are the same for both sides. The major differences between animism and Christianity stem from the different power source, whether God or Satan. Many of the outward forms are similar or even the same, but the power source is not. It is as if there are two electrical outlets: one is God, the other Satan. Humans can plug a religious system into either outlet. The wires leading to the plugs may look very similar, but the source of the power flowing through the wires is different.

> When we work in the power and authority Jesus gives us, we are not animists.

Our authority as Christians versus the authority Satan can give his followers is an important issue at this point. Again, some of those who do not know the difference between God-given authority to work in spiritual power and what animists do accuse us of practicing "Christian animism." But when we work in the power and authority Jesus gives us to do such things as healing, casting out demons, blessing people and objects, dedicating buildings and praying for rain or against floods—some of which animists can do—we are not animists. We are working not in the power of Satan but in the power of God. We are simply exercising the authority Jesus gave His disciples (see Luke 9:1) and told them to teach their followers (see Matthew 28:19–20). We also are emulating the example set for us by Jesus Himself.

The Bible teaches that the spirit world is real, encompassing both good angels who serve God and evil demons who serve Satan. As Christians, the way to approach the spirit world is to submit to the God who has power over it, not to try to manipulate either the spirits or God Himself for our purposes. The animistic approach, however, is to pay attention to the spirits but to ignore the God who is over all, since they believe He is no threat to harm them. The animist view of how to deal with the spirits is a magical one, aimed at manipulating the spirits by precisely performing certain prescribed activities.

In God's dealings in the Old Testament, we see the constant tendency of Israel to return to animism. God's message in the Old Testament was that people should focus on God, using the principles He has put into creation to honor and obey the true God, not Satan. God, then, would take care of their fear of the capricious spirits and would protect His people from them. For He has greater power than the spirits, can be counted on for support and blessing, is worldwide in His authority and will be good and trustworthy.

The position of animists, though logical, embodies a serious misunderstanding of how God intended humans to respond to the very real interference of evil spirits in human life. Understanding the differences between how God wants us to respond to Him and the way animists behave helps us understand the approach of modern cults. The way they approach spiritual issues is animistic rather than according to God's plan.

In recognizing this difference, we must remember that the enemy specializes in counterfeiting and confusing. For example, in the case of animists who worship gods and spirits or New Age channelers, it may be clear whom they serve. But what about counselors and even some pastors who use techniques reminiscent of "guided imagery" and the use of spirit guides to help themselves and their clients? They, too, are plugged into the wrong power source. Recognizing this difference is crucial, then, whether we are trying to communicate the Gospel to animists in other societies or trying to evaluate the ministries of those who claim to work in the power of God here at home.

Unlike animists, we do not try to manipulate God and His power. We, like Jesus, submit to Him (see John 5:19). Then we assert our position in Christ—a position that He gave us. This authorizes us to use the authority He delegates to us to convey His power. The power is in Jesus, not simply in certain objects and places or words.

We need to distinguish between animistic practices and true Christianity. The counterfeits are abundant and are luring more and more of those people who feel powerless in today's world, including, sadly, many pastors and psychologists.

To summarize and amplify my points, I present the following chart designed to highlight many of the contrasts between animism (including New Age) and God-given authority. Note again that the primary expressions of each of these areas looks very similar on the surface. They differ in the underlying power and motivations.

	Animism	God-Given Authority
Power	Power is believed to be *contained* in people and objects.	God *conveys* His power through people and objects.
Need (in order to utilize spiritual power)	Animists feel a need to learn how to manipulate spirit power through magic or authority over spirits.	We must submit to God and learn to work with Him in the exercise of power and authority.
Ontology (what is really going on)	Power is from Satan. He is the one who manipulates.	Power comes from God. He empowers and uses us.
God	God is good but distant; therefore, ignore Him.	God is good; therefore, relate to Him. He is close and involved with us.
Spirits	Spirits are fearful and can hurt us; therefore, appease them.	Spirits are defeated; therefore, assert God's authority over them.
People	People are victims of capricious spirits and never escape from being victims.	People are captives, but we can work in Jesus' authority to free them.
Result	Those who receive power from Satan suffer great tragedy later.	Those who work with God experience love and power throughout life.
Hope	No hope.	We win.

What about the Godward and Satanward Views?

One of the questions that evangelicals often raise is what to think about the issues of spiritual power in Jesus' ministry. Are the healings and deliverances just for Jesus' time and ministry? Or are these parts of Jesus' ministry to be imitated today?

It is obvious by now that I believe Jesus expected us to follow His example in healing and deliverance as we follow His example in faith and love. Jesus used His power to show His love. Jesus was involved in both love activities and power activities. He was a practitioner, not merely a theoretician. I believe we are to be practitioners as well.

In an enormously important book for evangelicals titled *The Satanward View*, Lutheran theologian and pastor James Kallas has given a name to these two aspects of Jesus' ministry. He calls the love, faith and relationship part of Scripture the "Godward view" and the power and spiritual warfare emphasis the "Satanward view." He observes that both of these perspectives are thoroughly scriptural but that the Satanward perspective has been neglected in our teaching and preaching.

In the Godward view, Kallas says, God holds people responsible for their sinful choices. Nowhere in Scripture are we released from this responsibility. Therefore, we need the intervention of a loving God to solve our problem. The need to deal with the human responsibility part of the New Testament perspective is totally there in the Scriptures, even though we often get the impression that Jesus felt we are victims of a power too great for us to handle. Though Jesus held people responsible for their choices, He did not condemn those who, under pressure from Satan, made poor choices, except for the arrogant Pharisees. The way He treated the woman caught in adultery or the various demonized persons He healed are cases in point.

Dealing with this power, then, is what Kallas calls the Satanward view. And he claims that this Satanward view is even more prominent in Scripture than the Godward view. This view, according to Kallas, presents humans not as those in control of their lives but as tormented and harassed by spiritual enemies they cannot control.

The presence in Scripture of these two perspectives side by side is perhaps the greatest paradox of Scripture and the Christian life.

The presence in Scripture of these two perspectives side by side, Kallas claims, is perhaps the greatest paradox of Scripture and the Christian life. The Godward perspective requires full responsibility on our part for what we do about our sinfulness, while the Satanward view, to a large extent, represents humans as victims of an active and powerful enemy they cannot control.

Both perspectives are present in Jesus' words and works. Though He held people responsible for their own choices—especially those who, like the Pharisees, had studied the Scriptures—He never condemned anyone for being demonized or ill. He simply rescued them as if they were helpless victims.

As traditional evangelicals, we have learned well the Godward perspective. We have, however, largely remained ignorant of and puzzled over the part Satan plays in the universe.

As I said in chapter 5, the Scriptures portray the Satanward side as governed by an enemy committed to "steal, kill, and destroy" everything good (John 10:10). Jesus came, then, to defeat Satan (see 1 John 3:8) and to release people whom He saw as captives and oppressed (Luke 4:18–19) from Satan, "the ruler of this world" (John 14:30).

Satan's presence and activities are very much in the consciousness of Jesus and the authors of the New Testament. For example, Satan is named "the ruler of the spiritual powers in space" (Ephesians 2:2). Furthermore, we are depicted to be at war not merely against humans but "against the wicked spiritual forces in the heavenly world" (Ephesians 6:12). And Peter pictures Satan as "roam[ing] around like a roaring lion, looking for someone to devour" (1 Peter 5:8).

> **Paul sees people not as supremely evil but as supremely unfortunate, victims of tyrannical forces.**

With regard to sin, Paul defines it as "bondage under Satan. Sin can be personified, written with a capital S, the Sin, a tyrant who enters into us and holds us helpless against our will."[2] Like the demoniacs in the gospels on whom Jesus had compassion, Paul sees people not "as supremely evil people who had sold their souls to evil and thus merit their fate, but . . . as supremely unfortunate people, victims, against their will, of tyrannical forces."[3] The answer for Paul, then, is salvation, defined as a rescue from the evil one by God's power, resulting in freedom.

It is the superiority of God that counts. He is stronger than Satan and able to set man free. It is not that God's love is unimportant. If He were not love, He would not attempt our rescue.[4] But if He did not have the power, He would not be able to rescue us and His love would be meaningless. For both Jesus and Paul, the cornerstones of their message are power and hope. There is a limited dualism. God has ultimate control, but Satan also has real influence and real power.

Satan's power is indicated by the titles he carries. The following Scriptures label the status of Satan in the world. In 1 John 5:19, we are told that the

2. Kallas, 55.
3. Ibid.
4. Ibid., 56.

world is under the power of the evil one. He is called in John 12:31 and 16:11 the prince of this world (NIV) and in 2 Corinthians 4:4 the god of this world. In Ephesians 6:12, we are told that we are at war with wicked spiritual forces in the heavenly world and that we need to be freed from this present evil age.

But there is hope. Jesus spoke of the passing away of heaven and earth (see Matthew 24:3, 35). Paul spoke of freedom for the creation from "bondage to decay" (Romans 8:21 NIV), which is hope for newness, for power and for freedom.

The miracle stories show God in action, demonstrating Jesus' power to free people by taking them out of the hands of the enemy. Ultimately, then, He confronts the devil's greatest weapon: death. He wades into and defeats that greatest of enemies that "through his death he might destroy the Devil, who has the power over death" (Hebrews 2:14) and set free those who have been living under Satan's tyranny. Thus, Jesus defines His own ministry, a ministry of setting captives free (see Mark 3:26–27; Luke 4:18–21).

This attack, leading to victory and freedom on Jesus' part, ties Him to Paul's emphasis on the cross, the resurrection and the Second Coming. These, too, are demonstrations of God's power and the defeat of the enemy.

The Satanward and Godward Views Compared

The Satanward perspective takes seriously the power focus. This perspective, Kallas says, sees "the work of Christ [as] a battle with Satan, aimed at Satan, *Satanward*."[5] The Godward perspective, on the other hand, sees Jesus involved in a transaction between God the Father and Jesus in which Jesus is obedient to the Father, taking on Himself the sins of humanity. In doing so, He makes it possible for rebellious mankind to be saved. This activity is aimed at God and is, therefore, *Godward*.

The Scriptures support both perspectives. Both are valid. Biblical truth is not totally on one side or the other. That truth is, however, discovered by holding the two in tension.

Kallas holds that "the Satanward view is the fundamental view of the Synoptics, and . . . dominates Paul."[6] Kallas then makes what seems to be

5. Ibid., 24.
6. Ibid., 32.

an astounding claim, saying, "Translated into mathematical terms, although both views are valid, *the Satanward view comprises about 80 percent of Paul and the Synoptics, and the Godward view about 20 percent.*"[7]

Yet the Satanward view is largely ignored in our churches and training institutions. Theologians largely ignore this perspective and have not accepted the dominance of the Satanward view in Scripture. This fact, plus the preaching and teaching built on it, keeps the focus on the minority position of Scripture, the Godward view. Though focusing on the Godward view is valid, it is only part of the story, and it is the lesser part. This imbalance has affected the view of evangelicals on man, sin, salvation, eschatology and the nature and work of Jesus.

Seeing the Satanward view enables us to be aware of a number of things evangelicals have ignored. These are articulated by Kallas on pages 24–28 of *The Satanward View*:

1. First, that "the devil has a measure of real control in this world" and must be taken seriously even though he is less powerful than God.

2. Sin is seen "not as an act of man, but rather, as a condition of man— man enslaved by forces too potent for him to resist successfully."

3. Humans are seen as "not self-determining but helpless, exposed to the interference of supernatural powers outside of [them]."

4. Salvation is seen as "a cosmic or physical act, the cleansing of an enslaved world now subject to an evil head."

5. Our hope, then, is in "a real end to the world as we know it."

6. "The resurrection and the return of Jesus must be interpreted within the context of victory, a victory in the past at the empty tomb," signaling a final victory "when Satan's activity will be finally ended."

7. The Kingdom of God is to be seen as involving "a liberation of a total world complex at the moment under the hand of Satan."

8. Jesus' suffering, and indeed all suffering of believers, is not seen as fulfilling some desire of God. "Suffering in and of itself is not redemptive or cleansing," Kallas says. He sees "no moral quality to it." Suffering is simply an expected consequence of war.

7. Ibid., emphasis mine.

9. The Satanward perspective has implications for both our doctrine of Satan and our doctrine of the Holy Spirit, for both doctrines see "man as open to the interference of external powers."

With regard to the Holy Spirit, Kallas does not hold the same position as I do on the nature of Jesus. I see Jesus as the Holy Spirit–filled human Jesus who never used His deity while here on earth. Kallas attributes Jesus' miracles to His divinity rather than to His Holy Spirit–filled humanity. The conquest of Satan by Jesus is, however, the same whether or not He used His deity while on earth.

In contrast to the Satanward perspective, the Godward view results in a different set of implications. They are as follows, again on pages 24–28:

1. Salvation is seen not as release from satanic domination but as reconciliation with God by eliminating guilt over the sin problem—"not freedom from a foreign foe, but instead, the setting aside of one's own hostility and the pardoning of one's guilt."

2. Our hope is seen not as the victory hour when our enemy is destroyed but as the fulfillment of our desire to enter into our spiritual inheritance.

3. The Kingdom of God is seen "not as a new cosmic entity but as entry into a right religious relationship with God earlier ruptured by hostility and consequent guilt."

4. Suffering is seen not as battlefield wounding but, in Jesus' case, an expression of God's judgment on the One who represents sinful humanity. The suffering of believers, then, "must be seen as in some way a supplement to the work of Christ."

5. The resurrection is seen not as a victory over Satan but as "a sign of God's approval of or acceptance of the work of Christ, already completed in his suffering on the cross." The focus of the Godward view then moves from the resurrection to the crucifixion. The cross becomes central, where Jesus was truly obedient and paid the price for our sin.

6. Sin is seen not as something that enslaves us but "as [a] wrong and perverse abuse of man's freedom—his refusal to bow before his Creator."

127

7. A human "is by definition free and responsible, and his sin is that he has misused that freedom."

8. Jesus is seen not as our hero against Satan but as subordinate to God the Father, offering His perfect humanity to God to pay for the sins of humans, obedient in passive submission to God's will and plan.

Following is a summary chart showing what has been said above.

Summary Chart of the Satanward and Godward Views[8]

	Satanward	Godward
Jesus		
His nature	Divine	Human
Type of person	Liberator or Savior	Model or good example
His obedience	Active	Passive
His crucifixion	Attack by Satan	Judgment of God
His resurrection	Victory over Satan	Corroborative sign
His return	Final destruction of Satan	Symbolic, not literally seen
Sin		
Its nature	Enslaving power	Rebellion and consequent guilt
Man		
His nature	Helpless, open to external powers	Free, self-determining
Salvation (Kingdom of God)		
When	Future	Now
Its nature	Objective, cosmic in scope	Subjective, internal religious experience
Man's entry	Predestination	Personal decision
This World		
Its ruler	Satan	God
Source of suffering	Satan	God
Nature of suffering	Evil, nonredemptive work of Satan	Good, purgative act of God

Kallas makes his case quite convincingly with several further examples. The following chart is an example of his perspective on sin.

Kallas then goes into a word study, quite convincingly making his case that Paul's primary focus is Satanward. He sees Paul as using sparingly such Godward concepts as forgiveness, sin as rebellion, sin as guilt or

8. Ibid., 30–31.

Godward and Satanward Perspectives on Sin

	Sin	Man	Answer to Sin	Nature of God
GODWARD	Rebellion	Free, responsible, enemy of God	Repentance, reconciliation	Love
	Guilt	Free, guilty, unclean	Forgiveness, atonement	Love
SATANWARD	Bondage, a tyrant	A slave	Salvation, freedom, rescue	Power

uncleanness, repentance, reconciliation, enmity toward God, man as responsible and more. The terms Paul uses for the Satanward focus, however, are abundant. Kallas sees the "floodgates boom open"[9] with respect to the vocabulary Paul uses. He says, "We find ourselves in the full current of Pauline vocabulary. All of a sudden, where this or that word was used sparingly before, we find ourselves in a veritable torrent of warfare words verifying the centrality of this motif."[10]

Kallas then lists the specific words and the number of their occurrences to prove his point, found on pages 61–70 of his book:

1. Paul uses words for *slavery* or *enslavement* no less than 44 times. Humans are seen as slaves to Satan. "Whereas the terms of reconciliation and forgiveness were sparse," he says, "the terms of liberation, of rescue and freedom, abound."

2. The words for *save* or *rescue* occur 47 times, for *ransom* 7 times and for *freedom* 11 times. Paul sees sin "as power and the answer as being a saving intervention of an even more powerful God who sets man free."

3. With regard to the nature of God, Paul definitely focuses on God's power. Paul does use *agapao* (love) with reference to God, but not

9. Ibid., 61.
10. Ibid.

often. Romans 5:8ff and 8:35ff are the only places that Paul portrays God as love. And in the first of these contexts, the reference to the love of God is not the main thought. It is no accident of expression, then, that in precisely those places where Paul would emphasize the fullest meaning of God's action in Christ, he speaks not of God's love but of God's power—"'the power of God for salvation' (Romans 1:16); 'the word of the cross . . . is the power of God' (1 Corinthians 1:18); 'Christ the power of God.'"[11]

4. The early sermons in the book of Acts focus not on the love of God but on His power and His ability to overcome Satan's power by bringing Jesus back from death. Kallas says, "God's love is valuable because it is backed by power."

5. Seeing sin as a "tyrannical, enslaving force" that takes over humans even when unwanted is sharpened when we examine closely *hamartia*, the main word for sin. Paul uses it 59 times, 45 times in Romans. Only ten times does it represent sin as rebellion or guilt. In all but three places in Romans, sin—or, better, *the Sin*—is seen as an enslaving tyrant, an objective force personified that "enters a man and rules against man's will." Kallas continues, "In Rom 7:8 and 11, the parallel between Sin and the depiction of Satan is quite remarkable. For Paul, sin seems to = Satan."

6. Paul sees Jesus' overcoming sin as overcoming slavery, which correlates to the Satanward view.

7. Paul sees sin as one "member of a gigantic cosmic host of evil powers that holds man enslaved." Some of the others are suffering, death, Satan, the Law and the elemental spirits of the universe (see 2 Thessalonians 2:9).

8. Paul sees the blame for Jesus' death as belonging to "the rulers of this age, headed by Satan" (1 Corinthians 2:8), the "god of this world" (2 Corinthians 4:4).

9. Kallas says, "Paul flatly insists that the major or last or greatest enemy is not sin, but *death* (1 Corinthians 15:26). It is because death is the greatest of all enemies that the resurrection is the vital center of his thought (vs. 14, 17). The resurrection is important because it is historical proof that the greatest of the enemy arsenal, death, is no match for Christ's power."

11. Ibid., 24.

Kallas then goes on to deal with the Church, creation, salvation, baptism, the Holy Spirit and Christology in the same exhaustive way.

I have gone into detail in dealing with Kallas because I believe he has hit on something very important to our subject and much neglected. We preach and teach endlessly on the Godward aspects of Scripture and life and neglect what turns out to be the majority perspective in the Bible that we claim as our guidebook.

Of all the paradigm shifts and worldview changes we evangelicals need to go through in developing a spiritual warfare mentality, this one may be the greatest. I would like, therefore, to cement in our minds the above discussion to help us recognize the scriptural importance of spiritual warfare thinking in contrast to the absence of such thinking in our churches and training institutions.

Part 4

Ground-Level
SPIRITUAL
WARFARE

9

Eight Controversial Issues

We now turn a corner from worldview issues to dealing with demonization and related topics. In this area, there are several issues that engender controversy, especially among those who are just waking up to the reality of spiritual conflict.

1. Can Demons Live in Christians?

One topic that often engenders heated discussion is the question of whether demons can live inside Christians. Considerable discussion has taken place in the Church as to whether or not this is possible. As you will see as you read, I and just about everyone who has experience with demonization believe Christians can, and often do, carry demons.

Confusion about the topic stems from two sources: the term *demon possession*, which we will discuss again in chapter 11, and the lack of experience within the Christian community in delivering people from demons. Prominent Christian leaders with no experience perpetuate the myth that Christians cannot be demonized. At least one whole denomination holds to this belief.[1] Their doctrine assumes that since the Holy Spirit lives within

1. See Opal Reddin, ed., *Power Encounter* (Springfield, Mo.: Central Bible College, 1989).

a Christian, a demon cannot also live there. They usually point to 1 John 4:4—"Greater is He who is in you than he who is in the world" (NASB)—as proof that demons cannot live in Christians.

This assumption is unconsciously employed when interpreting both the Bible and human experience. Though those who believe this myth may claim it is founded on biblical truth, it is, in reality, based on a prior assumption (stated above), and that assumption, without experience, is governing their interpretation of this and all other Bible verses that seem to apply.

Such an unexamined assumption is very dangerous because it keeps those who believe it from investigating other possibilities. They, therefore, never consider the possibility of a demon in a Christian, no matter how obvious it may be. Should the evidence of a demon become clear even to them, then, their assumption forces them to deny that the demonized person is a Christian. So the person feels doubly condemned—for having a demon and for not truly having accepted Christ.

The lack of experience in dealing with demonization within our churches, then, leads to the idealistic belief that Christians cannot be demonized. Though all of us wish that Christians were impervious to demonic inhabitation, experience contradicts such belief. I often wish people with such a view could follow me around for a few weeks and listen to the testimonies of Christians before we get their demons out and then listen to them again after they have been delivered! Those in ministry who have honestly looked at the evidence have changed their assumption.[2]

In the face of the overwhelming evidence that Christians can carry demons, then, the burden for proving that Christians cannot have demons rests again on the skeptics. They will have to take seriously the evidence in a way not done in supposedly definitive works like Opal Reddin's *Power Encounter*. Once they have taken that evidence seriously, they will have to either agree that Christians can be demonized or develop some pretty sophisticated theory to explain away the phenomenon of demonization in Christians' lives.

All of us who work in deliverance frequently have to cast demons out of Christians. C. Fred Dickason, whose book *Demon Possession and the Christian* treats the subject exhaustively, speaks for all of us when he says:

2. Merrill Unger and Ed Murphy are two such examples, though there are many others.

I have encountered from 1974 to 1987 at least 400 cases of those who were genuine Christians who were also demonized. . . . I would not claim infallible judgment, but I know the marks of a Christian and the marks of a demonized person. I might have been wrong in a case or so, but I cannot conceive that I would be wrong in more than 400 cases.[3]

Personally, I can attest to several hundred Christians whom I have been able to free from demons. My experience and that of countless others who have delivered Christians from demons proves conclusively that Christians can be demonized. We can, therefore, be dogmatic about asserting it. Only those who draw their conclusions theoretically, without experience, deny this fact. To quote Dickason again:

The burden of proof lies with those who deny that Christians can be demonized. They must adduce clinical evidence that clearly eliminates any possibility in any case, past or present, that a believer can have a demon. . . . We must note that those who deny that Christians can be demonized generally are those who have not had counseling experience with the demonized. Their stance is largely theoretical.[4]

Most of us started with the assumption that Christians cannot be demonized. But we soon discovered that we, like Jesus, have to evict demons even from people of faith. Though the demons in a Christian may be weaker than those in a non-Christian due to the spiritual growth of the Christian, they usually remain there until cast out.

However, those who assume that Christians cannot be demonized are partly right. A demon cannot live in the Christian's spirit. This is the person's central core, the part that died when Adam sinned and the part that became the new nature when they came to Christ. The Holy Spirit now lives there, and demons have to leave. Demons can, however, still live in the body, mind, emotions and will of a Christian, the parts where sin also can still dwell. For some, the process of battling the enemy as they grow in Christ involves battling indwelling demons as well as overcoming sinfulness within.

3. C. Fred Dickason, *Demon Possession and the Christian* (Chicago: Moody, 1987), 175.
4. Ibid., 175–176.

As Christians, our spirit, the central part of us, has become sinless. We call this change in our spirit our new nature (see 1 John 3:9). If, then, a person is carrying demons when he or she comes to Christ, the demons cannot any longer inhabit his or her spirit or new nature.

> **We, like Jesus, have to evict demons even from people of faith.**

I have tested this theory scores of times by commanding demons—under strong pressure from the Holy Spirit to tell the truth—to tell me if they live in the person's spirit. I ask, "Did you used to live in the person's spirit?" They usually answer yes. Then I ask, "Do you live there now?" They consistently answer no. So I ask, "When did you have to get out?" They reply something like, "When Jesus came in." Or they give the date of the person's conversion.

I conclude, therefore, that demons cannot live in that innermost part of a Christian, the spirit, since it is filled with the Holy Spirit (see Romans 8:16). That part of us becomes spiritually alive with the life of Christ and is inviolable by the representatives of the enemy. As I have said, sin and demons can live in a Christian's mind, emotions, body and will. We regularly have to evict them from those parts of Christians. I suspect, then, that the reason a demon can have greater control of an unbeliever is because it can invade the unbeliever's spirit.

But there is still another support for my position. To test the theory that Christians can carry demons, we need go no further than the New Testament. We define *Christian* as "one who has faith in Jesus." If we look at those whom Jesus healed and delivered from demons, we can ask the question, Did they or did they not come to Jesus in faith? I think we have to conclude that they came to Jesus in faith—faith that probably needs to be seen as saving faith. Why else would Jesus say to some, "Your faith has made you well" (Luke 8:48)?

When Jesus said that, He was certainly not saying that there is some magic in faith. He would not have said that faith in Buddha made them well. He was saying that they had come in faith to the right person—namely, Himself. It was people of faith who came to Jesus for deliverance. Coming to Jesus in faith, then, puts those individuals in the category we call Christian.

I conclude, then, that Jesus was casting demons out of people that we would call Christians. It was not unbelievers, or people of negative faith, that Jesus ministered to and freed. It was believers—people of faith in Jesus. If even Jesus cast demons out of believers, so can we.[5]

2. Should We Interview Demons?

Many of us who deal with demons are criticized, largely by the inexperienced,[6] for asking demons for information to use in expelling them. The theory of such critics is that since demons are liars, they never can tell the truth and, therefore, can never be of help to us—even under pressure from the Holy Spirit.

Due to the pressure of the Holy Spirit, however, those of us in this ministry find that God gives us a lot of useful information by forcing the demons to reveal their secrets to us. And this is the point: The information is coming under pressure by the Holy Spirit through His enemies! Just as God often gets His work done through His enemies, so He often gets the information we need to us through His enemies. But we need to be careful.

Though our critics claim that demons cannot tell the truth, notice that whenever Satan or demons speak in the New Testament, they always speak truthfully, though usually at the wrong time. Demons often do try to lie. But when they do, the Holy Spirit usually reveals it to us right away.

Our experience in getting helpful information from demons convinces us that the Holy Spirit uses even demons to provide the information we need. Hundreds of times I have received information from God through demons that was accurate and helpful in casting them out.

We have in Scripture a record of Satan himself telling the truth when tempting Jesus (see Luke 4:1–13). Though he was trying to deceive Jesus, he was not lying when he pointed out that Jesus had the power to turn stones into bread and that God would send angels to protect Jesus if He

5. For a more detailed treatment of this issue and the complications that arise in understanding it due to the serious mistranslation of *demon possession*, see Charles H. Kraft, *Defeating Dark Angels* (Minneapolis: Chosen, 2011). (Originally published Ventura, Calif.: Regal, 1992, 2011.)

6. For example, Priest, Campbell, and Mullen, "Missiological Syncretism."

jumped from the temple (see Matthew 4:1–7). Jesus, of course, under the guidance of the Holy Spirit, was wise enough to call Satan's bluff, since Jesus knew that if He used His divine power, He would have broken His agreement with the Father to never use His deity. The Holy Spirit still is able to give such guidance to us, enabling us to defeat the enemy by using against him the very information he gives us.

Since the primary problem in demonization is not the demons but the emotional and spiritual garbage in the person's life that gives the rats, or demons, a legal right to live there, the information we seek when we interview them concerns those root problems. I do not simply converse with demons for the fun of it or to obtain general information—though a good bit of such information, whether accurate or inaccurate, comes along the way. The whole purpose of talking to demons is to use them to obtain the information we need to get people healed and, in the process, to get rid of the demons. If the demons reveal something that, when we use it, enables us to defeat them—often when healing people with whom others, using other methods, have failed—we are grateful for the way God uses this technique.

Though getting information from demons does not fit the theory of those who criticize us, they need to take seriously our record. We have found that the Holy Spirit is the one in charge when we seek to get information from demons (as well as in the rest of the ministry session). So we are careful to never simply quiz demons to get esoteric insight, thus giving them a kind of control by letting our curiosity carry us away. We do note, however, that most of the things the demons say under pressure from the Holy Spirit prove out. In addition, the demons seem to get weaker because they are forced to go against their nature when they tell us the truth. And people get free. Once again, our critics must deal not only with a practice they do not approve of, but also with the results we gain from using that practice.

Another worthy result of forcing demons to give us information is the fact that receiving this information usually speeds things up. In comparison with ministries that refuse to interview demons, we get more done in a shorter time. I have heard of one such ministry in which the usual time to expel demons is four to five hours, probably in part because they do not deal as much as they should with inner healing. We usually accomplish at least as much as they do in one-fourth to one-half the time, even though we spend about three-quarters of our time on inner healing and much less time than they expend on deliverance. Perhaps one reason we derive so much help from demons is because we spend so much time weakening them through inner healing. (We will discuss the inner healing aspect in chapter 12.)

Those who tackle demons when the demons are strong find that the demons are able to lie and deceive very effectively. That ability dissipates, however, when we do inner healing first, focusing on getting rid of the garbage, as it weakens the demons and diminishes their ability to lie.

Using demons to help us is somewhat parallel to what happens in court when a hostile witness is put on the stand. By definition, hostile witnesses try to support the side opposite to that of the attorney who called them to the stand. Thus, the aim of the attorney who questions a hostile witness is to entrap the witness into revealing information that will help the attorney's case, not that of the witness. Nobody has suggested that our judicial system not make use of hostile witnesses simply because we cannot trust them. Everybody knows that they and their statements should be handled carefully. An important difference between using a human hostile witness and using a demon, though, is that the power of the Holy Spirit adds to the pressure on demons in remarkable ways, even greater than the pressure derived from the oath the witness on the stand in court has taken to speak the truth.

Our critics contend that God can tell us all we need to know about demons so we should depend entirely on Him. God can, indeed, reveal all we need to know. But experience teaches us that He often does not do things according to our rules and expectations.

Furthermore, our critics believe that Satan and his helpers are too much for God because they assume that even God does not have the ability to make demons tell the truth—ever! Our critics must learn that when we extract information from demons under the influence of the Holy Spirit and that information checks out as the truth—as it usually does—the source of the revelation is not, as they contend, demonic. The demons are only the means. The source of the truth is God.

When we command demons to give us information, then, we put them completely under the authority of the Holy Spirit. A typical question I ask is, "Does this person still need to forgive anyone?" When the answer is yes, I command the demons to tell me who it is. The demon usually tells us the name. When, then, the person forgives the one named, the demon's power is obviously lessened and we are able to free the person both from the kind of garbage that gave the demon its rights and from the demon itself.

If we can get this kind of information in any other way, we do. Often God reveals such information to the person or to a ministry member through a word of knowledge. But if not, getting it from the Holy Spirit through His pressure on the demon is a good second choice. And it has so far enabled at least several hundred people in my ministry to be freed from demons who probably would not have been freed if we refused to use this method.

I am reminded of the story of someone who criticized evangelist D. L. Moody for some of the methods he used in evangelism. His reply was something like, "I don't always like my methods, either, but I like the way I'm doing it better than the way you're not doing it!"

Is getting information from demons the way Jesus did it? Not as far as we can tell from the scriptural accounts. But Jesus did ask the Gerasene demon his name and did converse with Satan himself in the wilderness temptations. Though the way I obtain information from demons is not strictly parallel to what went on in Jesus' conversation with Satan, the latter shows at least two things that we have found true—demons can tell the truth, and we, under the authority and power of the Holy Spirit, can, like Jesus, control the situation. What I have found consistently is that the Holy Spirit forces demons to reveal to me information concerning what we need to deal with to weaken and get rid of them.

Do we naïvely trust everything these hostile witnesses say? Of course not. But do we believe the power of the Holy Spirit is great enough to get liars and deceivers to help us? Yes. And we have seen it happen over and over again. Risky? Yes. But there are an awful lot of people now free of demonic interference in their lives because we risked it, trusting not the demons but the Holy Spirit.

Sometimes people ask me if I enjoy talking to demons. The answer is that I guess I do a bit, since in that way I can use what they say to defeat them. But I do not trust them without checking up on them. And I am not confident that I can always keep them from lying. It is important, though, to control things in the power of the Holy Spirit and not to allow them to do what they want to do.

A further effect of interviewing demons is that those, like me, who do not have spectacular spiritual gifts have been able to learn how to use enemy spirits in this way to obtain the information they need in order to bring freedom and healing to many. Other methods of deliverance, though they may work reasonably well for those who have the gifting to get their information directly from God, are not as effective in the hands of those of us who do not have such gifts. But note that our aim in getting such information is not simply deliverance. My aim is to get the person free from the spiritual and emotional garbage that gives the demons rights and then, usually as a second step, to cast out the demons.

3. Should We Use Visualization?

Some of our opponents criticize us for the fact that we use visualization. They claim that this is a New Age technique, a tool of Satan, and should not be used by Christians.[7] They associate visualization with New Age "guided imagery," where a person imagines something that is not real and uses it to motivate a position or activity that he or she wants. Since what is imagined is not real and therefore not truthful, guided imagery plays right into Satan's hands and is to be avoided.

> I do not trust demons without checking up on them.

"Faith picturing," on the other hand, which we use, is based in truth. In this practice, we are not merely conjuring up something that is a figment of our imagination or our wishes. We are picturing the truth by tapping into memories of things that actually happened under the guidance of the Holy Spirit—and our God is a God of truth. So, though the two things may look similar on the surface, one is not factual and taps into satanic power while the other is based in truth and taps into the Holy Spirit's guidance and power.

7. See, for example, Hunt and McMahon, *The Seduction of Christianity*.

We are seeking to deal with memories. Memory experts tell us that we store our memories in pictures. Thus, we are looking for a way to get at memories to get them healed. We invite the Holy Spirit to guide us into parts of the truth that may have been forgotten or damaged in order to get them healed. The primary fact that we ask people to picture is the truth of the presence of Jesus in the events of the client's past.

Faith picturing is simply the practice of going back in the mind to picture events, people and places and to feel again the emotions associated with those memories. Faith picturing is, for many of us who work in deep-level healing, our most useful technique.

The most effective way for people to experience Jesus in their memories is through faith picturing. Most people can quickly picture the events in the memory we invite them to remember. When they have it in view, I usually ask, "Where is Jesus, and what's He doing?" Some see Him immediately. Others have to look around a bit. If they say they just cannot see Him, I ask them to look behind them in the picture, and He is usually there. I do not know why He likes to stand behind people, but He does!

Some have difficulty with faith picturing because they are afraid of the imagination. They fear they may simply be imagining what they want to have happen rather than letting Jesus bring healing. This is, indeed, a risk. However, I have worked with hundreds of people who have taken this risk and found that Holy Spirit–guided imagination is very effective in enabling healing. Whenever we ask the Holy Spirit to guide us in the use of picturing, He really does. Since our experience with picturing in the ministry process is so often positive, then, we make no apologies for using it.

A more serious problem is that a certain number of people find it impossible to picture memories. It is not a large number of people who find this to be the case, but it includes many who have achieved high academic levels. Some of these, though not able to picture the memories, are able to feel Jesus' presence. Others may be able to achieve most of the value of picturing by simply thinking the process.

Throughout the Bible, God has revealed Himself and His messages in pictures, whether through visions and dreams or in word pictures and analogies. He spoke through visions and dreams to just about all of the heroes of the Bible, including Jacob, Joseph, Samuel, Isaiah, Peter, Paul and John (see Genesis 28:10–17; 37:5–11; 1 Samuel 3:1–15; Isaiah 6; Acts 10:10–16; 16:9; Revelation 1:10–22:5). In addition, as Gary Smalley and John Trent point out:

> Jesus' primary method to teach, challenge, and motivate others was word pictures. When discussing love, He launched into a word picture about a good Samaritan. . . . To describe the forgiving heart of a father, He shared a story about a prodigal son.
>   . . . Word pictures are also the most frequent biblical means of describing who Jesus is.[8]

With all the pictures in Scripture plus the insights of science into how we use picturing to store personal information, we should not think it strange that when God seeks to free people, He uses pictures to reveal the memories that bind them. Just as He speaks through and empowers words, so He speaks through and empowers pictures to lead people to truth. Faith picturing, then, is the use of our God-given ability to picture under the leading and power of God. This recall under the direction and empowerment of God is a function of our spirit, not just a product of our imagination.

We rationalistic Western Christians are often suspicious of this technique because we are captured by our left-brain orientation. Unlike Jesus and the Hebrew world of which He was a part, we often fear anything emotional or picture-oriented. Dave Hunt, in his book *The Seduction of Christianity*, points out that visualization is used heavily by psychologists (whom he considers anti-Christian) and those in New Age and other occult groups. He judges that since the technique is used by such groups, any use of it by Christians will necessarily draw us into their errors. His conclusion is that the method itself is evil.

This viewpoint fails to take into account the fact that few, if any, techniques, activities or created things are completely sacred or profane in and of themselves. Satan can use even the most sacred things, including prayer, the Bible (see Luke 4:1–13), worship, spiritual gifts and the Church to serve his purposes. Are these things therefore evil and therefore unusable? No.

8. Gary Smalley and John Trent, Ph.D., *The Language of Love* (New York: Pocket Books, 1991), 29–30.

Very few things should be labeled evil in and of themselves simply because the enemy finds a way to make use of them.

In fact, a focus on whether cultural forms, such as words and rituals, are good or evil obscures the real issue. The crucial aspect of the argument should not be the nature of the techniques but the way they are used and the source of the power behind them. Within New Age and other occult organizations, the power source behind such techniques is not Jesus but Satan. Whether knowingly or not, practitioners of such faiths are receiving their power from demonic sources, and, as such, any benefits they receive or bestow will ultimately do more harm than good.

Hunt rightly warns us to be careful when we see people using visualization techniques. But he warns us against the technique rather than pointing to the real problem: the source of the power. Our power source is Jesus. When we begin each ministry session, we ask the Holy Spirit to be in charge of what takes place, and He honors that request. Thus, our use of faith picturing is submitted to the Lord's control, as is every other practice we employ, like prayer, anointing with oil and blessing.

However, even when we use faith picturing under God's power, I would raise a caution. When we are dealing with memories, we are dealing with events that actually happened, not events as we wish they had happened. Some who minister are in the habit of guiding the imagery in such a way as to change what actually happened. Such re-creation of history is, I believe, ultimately harmful because it is a kind of deceit. God never condones lying and distortion. In the long run, such an approach will not help the person. We cannot deny or rewrite the past to suit our desires. Our aim is to heal the damage to emotions that resulted from actual events.

The way we use faith picturing is to ask people to close their eyes and go back in their minds to an event in which emotional damage was done. We point out that Jesus was there when the event happened. This is fact. David Seamands puts it helpfully: "Remember that Christ is alive. He is here now. And because He transcends time, He is also back at that painful experience. Confess to Him, turn over to Him each experience, each emotion, each attitude."[9]

9. David Seamands, *Putting Away Childish Things* (Wheaton, Ill.: Victor Books, 1993), 28.

We try not to suggest what people ought to see but ask the Holy Spirit to lead. When they are able to go back into the memory, we ask them to allow themselves to experience the feelings associated with that memory. This is often difficult, since avoiding these feelings has usually been the person's method of coping and is the reason they are now in need of help. At this time, preferably without having them leave the memory, it is often necessary to give lots of encouragement or even to ask questions concerning how they felt about the situation, the other person(s) involved, themselves and God.

The process of feeling the emotions again plus the realization (usually pictured) that Jesus was there protecting them from greater harm usually results in turning the painful wound into a painless scar. The true emotions have been felt and the truth of the Lord's presence made clear, paving the way for healing.

> **Often the results are surprising and the healing spectacular.**

With a little experience, we can often predict at least part of what will happen as the person sees Jesus in the painful events. Sometimes, too, God reveals part or all of what is going on through words of knowledge. Often, however, the results are surprising and the healing spectacular. Usually at least some of the things that happen are new to even the most experienced ministry leader.

We need to be on our guard as we lead people through faith picturing because Satan may try to interfere with the process. He has a lot to lose if the person becomes aware of the Lord's presence in the painful events of their memory and gains healing. Demons will sometimes pose as Jesus in the picture, in fact. At times this is evident, as when one of my clients saw a fake Jesus holding a knife behind his back. Another time a woman reported being kissed by a false Jesus in an unwholesome fashion. These uncharacteristic behaviors tipped us off to the fact that we were dealing with an impersonator, not the real Jesus.

At other times it is not so clear that an imposter has appeared. Frequently, though, when this has happened, the Holy Spirit has alerted me and I have challenged the being the person is seeing in their imagination. My challenge is simply to command any false Jesus to disappear or to turn black. If the being is an imposter, it will usually disappear or turn black immediately.

Precautions can be taken against this type of interference by forbidding it at the beginning of the session, though occasionally it still occurs.

Sin in a person's life or an unforgiving attitude can block faith picturing, and especially the picturing of Jesus in the event; likewise with feelings of shame, guilt, unworthiness, rejection, fear, anger or other negative emotions. Not infrequently, a person will feel shame over the thought of Jesus seeing her or him in the situation. Feeling that people have always rejected him or her, the person believes that Jesus is no more accepting than others have been. Often such attitudes need to be dealt with before the faith picturing can be effective.

There are quite a number of possible variations in faith picturing. Often when we are focusing on one memory, the Lord will bring a quick succession of related memories to the person. In this way, God may bring healing to several memories at the same time. On one occasion, when the emotions aroused by the memory were so intense that a woman pleaded with me not to make her relive it, God enabled her to see the event as a still picture on which Jesus poured His blood, turning the picture white as He healed her emotional hurt. Once people have experienced this type of ministry, they can often work through other memories on their own with the Lord.

Some people are unable to visualize or may object to doing so for personal reasons. Some have been exposed extensively to visualization and guided imagery as members of occult groups. It may be unwise to use visualization with them. With such people, it may be just as effective for them to recall the events in their minds without feeling them again. Techniques such as covering the event with the cross, planting the cross between the person and the event or claiming the blood of Christ over the event can be used. The healing that takes place through these methods can be just as great as that gained through faith picturing.

4. Can Objects Be Infested?

Though we covered this topic in chapter 6, it bears mentioning again that some people are skeptical about the contention by those of us committed to spiritual warfare that objects can carry spiritual power. However, we have a lot of before-and-after data that suggests this. And when we work on this assumption, take the appropriate action and find that the demonic activity stops, we become believers. The major activity we engage in is to take authority in Jesus' name over the object and cancel satanic power. The result is to conclude that the objects were infested with demons.

As an example, one time I was ministering to a man during a seminar on the island of Cyprus. We dealt with several demons and felt that the ministry was successful. Indeed, the man was elated over what felt to him like a new experience of freedom. But he came to me the day following his ministry experience and described an "unfree" feeling related to three rings he was wearing. My suggestion was that he dispose of the rings. His response, though, was to let me know that if he followed my advice, he would be in big trouble. For, he pointed out, one of the rings had come from his wife, the second one from his mother and the third from his mother-in-law.

Not wanting to risk problems with these close relatives, I asked him to let me hold the first ring. I took authority over it and commanded any enemy spirit in the ring to be gone. I then asked how he felt. He felt free. So we did the same with the other two rings and the result was the same. The man felt totally free. The unfree feeling was completely gone.

An experience of my former colleague Peter Wagner and his wife is another illustration of material forms carrying demonic power. The Wagners were experiencing satanic activity in their home. This activity was traced to several lamps and masks the Wagners had brought home from their years in Bolivia. Peter and the students he had called to help took authority over the objects, cast the demons out of them and were able to spiritually cleanse the house. And the Wagners had no such problems for the last ten or more years that they lived in that house.[10]

Probably all of us who deal with demonized persons have had the experience I have had a few times of getting nowhere with a demon until the person removes some object. Often this is a necklace or a ring, and sometimes it is a Masonic ring or one with satanic symbolism. I once worked with a man who had a satanic ring on his finger. We were not able to release him from the demon until after he got rid of the ring. As soon as

10. C. Peter Wagner, *The Third Wave of the Holy Spirit* (Ann Arbor, Mich.: Servant, 1988), 63ff.

the ring was removed, our ability to deal with the demon was immediately improved. Usually when we ask the person about the item, we find that it has been blessed with satanic power and given to him or her by someone in an occult organization or religion.

In many societies, implements used for food-getting, warfare, religious practices and other necessary activities are routinely dedicated to clan or tribal spirits when they are made. Temples, homes, workplaces and whole nations are dedicated by priests with the authority of their gods behind them. The items are thereby empowered and thus enabled as conveyances for spiritual power. And the ability of cultural forms to carry spiritual power is not limited to material items. It also applies to immaterial things, such as music, rituals and words.

As I have written in chapter 6, even Western Christians recognize the need to dedicate church buildings, the elements of Communion, anointing oil and babies to our God to call God's blessing on them. In addition, we bless individuals and, in benedictions, whole congregations in the name of Jesus Christ, invoking God's presence and power. Though people with a man-centered worldview believe such dedications and blessings are merely rituals, those aware of Satan's activities see both meaning and power in such dedications.

Empowered objects are frequently mentioned in Scripture. Those on God's side, like the Ark of the Covenant, are empowered by God. They convey God's power and are dangerous. They are not to be handled carelessly. The pagan shrines, on the other hand, are also empowered but are no threat to God's people when they are being faithful to God. These are animistic items, thought by animists (and the Israelites) to contain power. In reality, though, as I have said before, they merely convey power that comes from outside the object, from spirit beings. That power, then, flows through the object. It is not a part of the object, coming from the object itself, even when animists think it is.

Though there is much more that could be said on this topic, it should be clear from this discussion and that in chapter 6 that objects do indeed convey spiritual power. This is true on both God's side and Satan's. The imparting of power to such objects, then, is a matter of blessing and cursing, to which we will now turn.

5. Are Curses and Blessings Powerful?

Though some people bless as a form of greeting or gratitude, they may not understand that spiritual power is conveyed when we bless. Likewise, negative spiritual power is conveyed through cursing. Neither of these activities is really neutral. And either can be very spiritually powerful.

The authority to bless is one of the most precious gifts God has given us (see Matthew 5:44; Romans 12:14). Genuine spiritual transactions take place when we speak blessing in Jesus' name. Jesus modeled this privilege for us. In the Beatitudes, He blessed people for specific behavior and attitudes (see Matthew 5:3–12).

When Jesus sent His followers out to minister in Luke 9 and 10, He told them to bless those who cared for them (see Luke 10:5). Blessing is especially noticeable after His resurrection (see John 20:19, 21, 26). Then, when Jesus left the earth, He commanded His followers to teach their followers "to obey everything [he had] commanded [them]" (Matthew 28:20). And the command that His followers be taught to minister as Jesus did comes down to us. So, just as Jesus blessed, we are to bless.

The Bible is full of blessing. Jacob and other Old Testament fathers pronounced blessings on their sons in the belief that God would really empower their words (see, for example, Genesis 48–49). The apostle Paul starts each of his letters with a blessing (see Romans 1:7; 1 Corinthians 1:3; 2 Corinthians 1:2; Galatians 1:3). Jesus was blessed before He was born (see Luke 1:42) and afterward (see Luke 2:34–35). Jesus blessed children (see Mark 10:16), people who lived Kingdom values (see Matthew 5:3–12), His disciples after His resurrection (see John 20:19, 21, 26) and those present at His ascension (see Luke 24:50–51). Further, He commands us to bless those who curse us (see Luke 6:28).

I have had multiple experiences of blessing or anointing a person that produced an immediate and unexpected spiritual reaction. Such events have convinced me that we are also dealing here with God's empowerment of our words.

The effect of blessing and dedication on buildings and babies is more difficult to demonstrate, but enough anecdotes can be collected in this area to point strongly in that direction, at least for those open to believing in such a possibility. We have the authority of Jesus Christ Himself to speak God's power through blessing and dedication. When we bless, we are not practicing animism, in spite of the view of some of our critics. We are simply employing an inestimable privilege given us by our Lord.

A curse, on the other hand, is the invocation of the power of Satan or of God to affect negatively the person or thing at which the curse is directed. The invocation may be given through words or things that have been cursed or dedicated. The words used may be as mild as "I hate . . ." or "You'll never amount to anything," said to others or to oneself. Or they may be more forceful: "I wish . . . were dead" or "May . . . never succeed in . . ." or "God damn you" or "I curse you with . . ." The power of the curse may be increased through the use of a ritual. In addition, cursed or dedicated objects in a person's possession can provide enemy forces the opportunity to afflict the person, even if the person is not demonized.

Scriptural examples of curses empowered by God are those directed against the serpent (see Genesis 3:14), the ground (see Genesis 3:17–19), Cain (see Genesis 4:11–12), those guilty of certain sins (see Deuteronomy 27:15–26; 28:15–68), those cheating God (see Malachi 1:14; 2:2; 3:9), whoever hangs on a tree (see Deuteronomy 21:23; Galatians 3:13), those who ridiculed Elisha (see 2 Kings 2:23–24), anyone who rebuilds Jericho (see Joshua 6:26) and a fig tree (see Matthew 21:18–19). As Christians, we have God's power to back up curses. But we must be careful with our words, lest we invoke that power wrongly. We are to bless, not curse (see Luke 6:28; Romans 12:14).

Curses and blessings are nonmaterial forms that convey—not contain—spiritual power. When we speak of cursing or blessing, then, we are not speaking of a kind of "verbal magic," as Priest and his colleagues assert. These are, rather, expressions based on authority. Those working under God's authority have the privilege of conveying His power through blessing or cursing. Those working under Satan's power, likewise, can invoke his power through satanic blessing or cursing. For those of us on God's side, there is the danger that we may employ the power of God under the authority God gives us to hurt others through words that curse rather than help others through words that bless.

People own blessings or curses. When Jesus sent out the 72 into the villages where He was about to minister, He gave them interesting instructions. In Luke 10:5–6, He says, "Whenever you go into a house, first say, 'Peace be with this house.' If someone who is peace-loving lives there, let your greeting of peace remain on that person; if not, take back your greeting of peace." Here we learn that a blessing is given to another person but that if the person receiving it rejects it, the blesser is to withdraw the blessing and take it away. The same ownership applies to curses.

The fact that we own our blessings and curses means that we can renounce them. Those who have cursed people can renounce the curses and bring freedom. I find that many who come to me have cursed themselves or some parts of themselves, most often their bodies. We can claim the power of Jesus to break the power of those curses if we renounce them.

It appears that a fair number of God's servants have used the authority He has given them to serve ends other than His. So, indeed, it is with Satan, who was given a certain amount of authority and power as one of God's highest angels but then chose to use that power to oppose God, the Source. It looks to me as though Satan has been able to keep the power he used to have as an archangel, even though he is using it against God.

> **We must be careful with our words, lest we invoke that power wrongly.**

God uses His people, to whom He has delegated authority, to assert power in Jesus' name by using Jesus' methods, including blessing and, I am afraid, cursing. Paul commands us to bless rather than to curse (see Romans 12:14), and James warns us against the fact that blessing and cursing can come from the same tongue (see James 3:9). Jesus has delegated to us authority over demons and diseases (see Luke 9:1), authority to bless and its inverse authority to curse (see Luke 10:5–6) and authority to forgive (see John 20:23).

The same kind of authority we have with God, then, is given by Satan to his followers, since the rules are the same for Satan as for God. Demons, therefore, also have the ability to bless, curse, heal and do miraculous works in the power of their master (see Matthew 24:24). Perhaps the clearest scriptural indication of the power Satan's followers can wield is given in the record of Moses challenging Pharaoh in the early chapters of Exodus, where sticks turned into snakes, the Nile water became blood and frogs came up onto land (see Exodus 7:12, 20–22; 8:7).

Many are troubled by the suggestion that even Christians can be affected by curses. But since curses are the inverse of blessings and people can be affected by blessings, it seems we must believe in this possibility. The only question is, Under what conditions? We take Proverbs 26:2 to indicate that for a curse to affect a person, it must connect with some vulnerability inside him or her, such as sin or another spiritual problem, like demonization. Those we have ministered to who suspected they had been cursed, with a few puzzling exceptions, met this condition. I do not know what to do about the exceptions except to suggest either that they are really not exceptions, meaning there was something in the situation we did not know that put them in the above category, or that God gave permission, as He did with Job, for a curse to get through.

The ideal would seem to be what Jesus was able to say of Himself in John 14:30—that the ruler of this world is coming but finds nothing within us to connect with. However, it may have been a curse that God let through that occasioned Paul's thorn in the flesh, a problem that he referred to as "a messenger of Satan" (2 Corinthians 12:7 NIV).

I believe blessings and cursings are very common in our lives. I have mentioned some of the things we do in church, such as invocations, benedictions and baby dedications. House dedications and car dedications also are blessings. I like to bless the people I write to, so I frequently put blessings at the end of my letters. I believe the Holy Spirit empowers such activities.

Curses, too, are very common. I work often with missionaries. They are frequently in situations where they are not wanted and are cursed. There are stories of missionaries who were given or bought property that had been cursed and experienced difficulties as long as they lived on the property. I suspect that some who beg by the side of the road regularly curse those who pass by without giving anything. The lesson here is that we should regularly cleanse ourselves spiritually and return both known and unknown curses to their senders as blessings (see Romans 12:14).

6. Can Demons be Transmitted Generationally?

I have been involved in casting out too many demons of Freemasonry and other occult and non-Christian religious involvements from people who themselves have had nothing to do with those organizations or religions to avoid the reality of this issue. Those affected by it are people whose fathers, grandfathers, mothers or grandmothers—or sometimes a lineal relative even farther back—were members of the organization or religion.

In this area, I have had the most experience with Freemasonry. As part of the rituals they undergo to become members, Freemasons take vows—often unconsciously—that dedicate themselves and their descendants to Lucifer.[11] These dedications result in the demonization of the ones who dedicate themselves. But that dedication also applies to families and those of succeeding generations who inherit the demons at conception.

When, then, we take authority over the person's ancestry, using the power of Jesus to break generational curses, vows, dedications and rights given to the enemy through sin by the person's ancestors, the demon's power is broken. This frequent experience suggests either that the demon was inherited and has power through the family connection or that some tendency was inherited that gave rights to the demons.

On one occasion, I was attempting to get a lady free from a spirit of Freemasonry. The demon taunted me, saying, "Ha, ha, you can't get me out. You don't even know the curses she is under." I simply said, "I don't have to know the curses. I cover them all with the blood of Jesus to break your power." Next there was silence for a moment. Then the demon remarked, "I don't have any more power!" And we kicked him out. In Christ, we have enormous power to break the hold of these occult spirits, even though they have been there for a long time and are held in place through generational curses.

When a person inherits demons, there are likely to also be additional demons that have attached themselves either to the inherited demons or

11. Ed Decker, *What You Need to Know about Masons* (Eugene, Ore.: Harvest House, 1992); James D. Shaw and Tom C. McKenney, *The Deadly Deception: Freemasonry Exposed by One of Its Top Leaders* (Lafayette, La.: Huntington House, 1988).

to the person's own emotional and/or spiritual garbage. The presence of one or more demons coming by inheritance seems to make persons more vulnerable to becoming inhabited by additional spirits, such as those that can come through curses (see Proverbs 26:2) or through contact with infested objects.

As throughout Scripture, we are finding we have to deal with the fact that spiritual and moral issues may be a part of a person's heritage, inherited just as physical features are inherited. Though such problems as demonization are indeed the result of personal choice, the choice that gave the enemy his rights may have been that of an ancestor rather than that of the individual. And this may be a lineal relative who has long since passed away.

As with sin in the case of the man born blind (see John 9), the demonized person may not be personally to blame. Many of the demonized who have come to me are not in their condition because of their own moral or spiritual rebellion. They have already, through confession, taken care of their individual sin problems but, through no fault of their own, still carry demons that entered from some other cause.

Even when the original source of the demonization is inheritance, though, there is usually emotional and/or spiritual garbage for us to deal with also. The person may have added garbage to their life that brought additional demons beyond those that were inherited. It was, however, the inherited demons that gave opportunity for other demons to empower curses (see Proverbs 26:2).

Satan has the ability to attack based on factors other than our doctrinal, spiritual or moral response. We certainly see this ability demonstrated in Job's life, with the attacks on Jesus and with Paul's thorn in the flesh. We live in a world where Satan is called the ruler (see John 14:30; 1 John 5:19; 2 Corinthians 4:4). This understanding and the laws of the universe that give Satan the right to attack us, however, cannot simply be dismissed as magical and animistic thinking, as Priest and his co-authors dismiss them. In the face of spirit-world realities, whatever they are, we need to seek to live lives worthy of the God who called us and also give attention to trying to figure out whatever the conditions might be that allow satanic interference in our lives.

7. Do Territorial Spirits Exist?

Given the spiritual realities we have been discussing, it does not seem to me too farfetched to speak of a satanic "force field" influence over people who live in given territories. Note that when we refer to territories, we are referring to the people living in those territories more than to the geography. As we see throughout the Old Testament, starting with Adam's sin and continuing through the murder of Abel and on throughout Israel's history, the sinful acts of humans brought curses on the geography in which those sins were committed (see Genesis 3:17; 4:10; and frequent references thereafter to spiritual damage brought upon the land).

So the geography is affected by the behavior of people, both past and present. In keeping with the spiritual warfare theme of Scripture, then, we hold that such sinful behavior gives Satan rights over the land. As with Adam and Eve, human disobedience to God gives the satanic kingdom certain rights to territory. The Fall gave the enemy general rights, as Satan pointed out to Jesus in Luke 4:6, saying that the kingdoms of the world and all their power and wealth have "all been handed over to me, and I can give [them] to anyone I choose." This is a territorial outcome even though it was people who handed over the territory. And it is continuous, affecting generation after generation until either we take it back in Jesus' name or He comes to take it back personally.

Recognizing the fact of Satan's authority over the world plus the fact of the organization of his kingdom into something like the Ephesians 6:12 hierarchy leads many of those who ponder the situation to postulate satanic rulers over territories, especially over the people who inhabit the territories. This theory gains support from the observation that there are particular groups of people committed to particular types of evil and that there seem to be concentrations of sinful institutions and/or organizations in particular localities.

For example, I think we can assume that Satan is smart enough to be behind the curious tendency for businesses that promote sinful behavior, such as drugs, pornography, prostitution, gambling, occult bookshops and the like, to often be found congregating in the same locales. And as John

Dawson[12] and others[13] point out, a look at the history of many of these places draws attention to the fact that these very locales have usually been specifically committed, often formally dedicated, to satanic influence in earlier generations. There are also experiments in Argentina, Guatemala, Colombia, Kenya and other places in which both Satan's power over a territory or group of people and the ground-level human sins are dealt with and a great response to the Gospel results.[14] We will deal more with the reality of these territorial spirits in later chapters.

8. What about Multiple Personalities?

Though I will deal with multiple personality disorder (MPD) in more detail in chapter 11, I am introducing it here as one of the important controversial issues because many inexperienced people confuse MPD with demonization. This disorder, now known as dissociative identity disorder (DID), is usually a reaction to severe abuse. The typical DID person is a female survivor of early childhood sexual abuse. Under such abuse, a certain number of people "split." They create one or more "person parts" that we call "alters" to protect the core person by taking the abuse. In some cases, the person creates personalities that do not know each other; we call this *amnesic DID*. If the parts know each other and each other's stories, we call them *co-conscious*.

MPD/DID emerges for some of the parts as a way to survive. In that sense, it is a good thing, keeping the person from falling apart. When working with a person with DID, it may be like working with more than one person in the same body. This can be confusing both for the victim and for those who work with him or her.

DID is different from demonization, but the reaction to the abuse that results in dissociative identity disorder usually invites demons in. Both

12. John Dawson, *Taking Our Cities for God: How to Break Spiritual Strongholds*, rev. ed. (Lake Mary, Fla.: Charisma House, 2002).

13. C. Peter Wagner, ed., *Engaging the Enemy: How to Fight and Defeat Territorial Spirits* (Grand Rapids, Mich.: Baker, 1995).

14. George Otis Jr., *Transformations* (Lynwood, Wash.: Sentinel Group, 1999), videocassette (VHS), 60 min.; Otis, *Transformations II* (Lynwood, Wash.; Sentinel Group, 2001), videocassette (VHS), 60 min.; Ed Silvoso, "Argentina: Evangelizing in a Context of Spiritual Warfare," in Kraft, *Behind Enemy Lines*, 263–283.

alters and demons can talk to you. Demons, however, tend to be less co-operative than alters and less reasonable. Though it may not be apparent at first, the job of the alters is to keep order. Demons, though they may try to fool you into thinking they are person parts, are not interested in keeping order or helping.

If there is DID at play with a person, look for demons as well. But do inner healing first with each of the personalities individually to break the power of the demons. It is like working with more than one person in the same body as you do the inner healing. With the demons, you may also be able to command them to be bound together and to respond as one. We will come back to this issue in chapter 11.[15]

15. For a more complete treatment of this topic, see Charles H. Kraft, *Deep Wounds, Deep Healing: An Introduction to Deep-Level Healing*, rev. ed. (Minneapolis: Chosen, 2010). (Originally published Ventura, Calif.: Regal, 1993, 2010.)

10

Demons and Their Activities

N ow that we have established that spiritual warfare exists and that even Christians are affected by it, let's turn to the beings that bring warfare against us and how they do so.

The first thing I want to address on this point is that Satan needs helpers, since he can only be in one place at a time. He is not like God, who can be everywhere at the same time. Members of Satan's hierarchy carry out his schemes throughout the universe. And a major assignment of evil spirits is to bother humans, especially Christians.

Here is what we know about demons, which are also called evil spirits or unclean spirits (I use the terms interchangeably). Most Christians believe they are angels who followed Satan in his revolt against God. The passages in Isaiah 14:12–17 and Ezekiel 28:12–19 are believed to refer to that satanic revolt, when a large number of angels chose to follow Satan. These angels are or became what we now call demons.

Demons are the "ground level" troops that fight against us, as opposed to the "cosmic level" principalities, powers and rulers of Ephesians 6:12 that we will deal with in later chapters. They are the ones we encounter most often during spiritual warfare.

There are certain things we can say about demons. For one, they seek people to inhabit (see Matthew 12:43–45). They apparently envy us our bodies. They have different personalities—some beg, some are arrogant, some give in easily. They can be destructive, seeking to impress people with their power (see Mark 9:17–29). They differ in power—some with more power, some with less. Some seem more wicked than others (see Mark 5:4; Matthew 12:45).

Demons are especially interested in disrupting and/or crippling anything or anyone who might be a threat to Satan's domination over the world. They aim their guns at individuals, groups and organizations that in any way seek to serve God's purposes, especially Christian ministries. They produce strongholds in people's minds (see 2 Corinthians 10:4) and in places as well. They are agents of doctrinal aberrations (see 1 Timothy 4:1). They may affect health (see Luke 13:11). They perhaps affect weather (see Luke 8:22–25). They may even have "the power over death" (Hebrews 2:14). But they have no power except that allowed them by God.

Satanic beings are probably involved in every kind of disruptive activity in human life. They can hinder earthly activities. They can even delay answers to prayer (see Daniel 10:13). They exercise authority over places and territories, such as buildings, cities and temples. They appear to have authority over certain social groups, organizations and people groups. They influence sinful behavior, such as homosexuality, drug addiction, adultery, incest, rape, murder and prostitution.

As I have said before, they are like rats, feeding on garbage. Rats are attracted to trash and garbage. If we find rats in our houses, the most important thing is to deal with what has attracted them. So it is with demons.

Inside a person, emotional and/or spiritual garbage provides a congenial setting for demonic rats. So do curses and vows. Wherever such garbage exists, demonic rats seek and often find entrance. If, however, the garbage is disposed of, the rats have nothing to attach themselves to and lose their power. With people as with homes, the solution to the rat problem is not simply to chase away the rats but to first deal with the garbage, then dispose of the rats. The biggest problem is not the demons, then; it is the garbage. The demons are important but secondary.

Demons are most frequently attached to curses, damaged emotions and/or sin. They usually have names appropriate to what they are attached to, which we call their "function" names. A demon attached to a person's anger, for example, may be called a demon of anger. Likewise with fear, shame, rejection and hundreds of other functions. Demons may also have personal names. For example, I once had to deal with three demons named Fear, Worry and Louey. But in dealing with demons through inner healing as I do, it is more useful to know their function names than their personal names, since it is this name that indicates which emotion or attitude needs to be dealt with in getting the demon weakened and out.

> **Demons are most frequently attached to curses, damaged emotions and/or sin.**

Demons seldom come singly. They are most often found in groups. They are arranged hierarchically, with a leader demon in charge of a whole group. My practice is to discover which demon is the head "rat" and to bind to him, by the power of the Holy Spirit, all others under his control. This enables me to deal with the whole group at the same time. The head, or controlling, spirit then speaks for the whole group.

There usually is more than one group of spirits in any given person, with a head spirit over each group that has roughly equal status with the other head spirits. It is usually possible, once the demons have been weakened through inner healing, to tackle them group by group and to lock each group in a box, where they wait to be cast out.

These evil beings seem to respond only to those over them or to a greater power. Only their supervisor or a power greater than them, such as God, can release them from their assignment and break their power.

Three Types of Ground-Level Spirits

Spiritual warfare is waged on at least two levels. The lower level is what I call *ground-level warfare*. This type of warfare deals with the spirits that are assigned by the demonic kingdom to live and work within people. The higher level is what I call *cosmic-level warfare* and is tied to principalities, powers, territories, groups and even whole nations. We will address this higher level in later chapters.

On the ground level, demons take at least three forms: family spirits, occult spirits and, for lack of a better name, ordinary spirits. Family spirits are stronger than occult spirits, and occult spirits usually are stronger than ordinary spirits.

Type 1: Family Spirits

Family spirits are those that are inherited from generation to generation within families. In societies that routinely dedicate their children to gods and spirits, these are given rights through the dedication of newborn children to them. They can be found living in large numbers of Asians; in the tribal peoples of places like Africa, Melanesia and Latin America; and in indigenous peoples, such as American Indians, Australian aborigines, gypsies and the like.

Unfortunately, these spirits can be passed down from generation to generation, even to people who have not been dedicated personally. I do not know how many generations such demons can affect, but I have found them in people two generations after the ancestor who was dedicated. I have found family spirits representing both the father's line and the mother's when ministering to Koreans, Chinese and Africans. I have also found, on occasion, that people with European backgrounds may have family spirits, especially if their ancestry goes back to European royalty or they have parents who were demonized.

Family spirits gain and keep their power through the dedication of each generation of children to them. They may be worshiped or honored as gods or as ancestors. They may be addressed by the father's family name or the mother's family name or simply as the father's or mother's "family spirit."

To give you an example of what this can look like, I will share with you a recent story. I was working to bring inner healing and freedom from some demons to a female Chinese Christian missionary of about fifty years of age. In addition to the fairly normal problems to which demons are attached, such as shame and anger, she carried family demons that she had inherited from her parents. Some demons also entered her when her parents dedicated her at a temple soon after her birth and when they took her to a temple as a child for healing. She also carried demons that entered when she practiced Chinese martial arts under a "master" who, without her awareness, dedicated all he did to demonic spirits. This woman had no idea that these things that had happened long ago were responsible for the daily (and nightly) torment she experienced. She believed in demons but until recently had believed the lie that demons could not live in Christians, especially dedicated ones, such as those who served as missionaries.

I have found that just about every Asian, African or American Indian child born into non-Christian families—and even many born into Christian families—is dedicated in traditional ways to family spirits. Though many in these societies claim not to believe in spirits anymore, often the dedication is done "just in case."

Though these spirits may be strong and well hidden, the power of Jesus is so great that claiming it to break all power passed down to these individuals by their ancestors usually renders the spirits powerless. This involves canceling the rights given to the spirits through vows, curses, dedications, sins, violence and anything else the ancestors did. Any permission given by the person or anyone in authority over the person, such as having appealed to those spirits for healing or blessing, also needs to be canceled.

Type 2: Occult Spirits

Occult spirits are those that come from membership in religions, cults or occult organizations. Like family spirits, these can be passed down to succeeding generations, even to children and grandchildren who are not dedicated. I have worked with perhaps a hundred people who carried spirits of Freemasonry passed on to them by parents or grandparents, even though they themselves were never part of that organization.

To deal with occult spirits, one must cancel the rights given to demons through dedications, vows and curses a person has brought on himself or herself through membership in an occult group. The initiatory rites of religions and secret societies (even some university fraternities and sororities) give demons the right to live in those who experience them, whether they know it or not. And most do not know the spiritual price they pay to belong to such groups. People automatically give demons rights to inhabit them when they follow non-Christian religions, such as Islam, Buddhism, Mormonism, Christian Science, Scientology and Jehovah's Witnesses. They also give demons those rights when they join secret societies, such as Freemasonry or certain college fraternities and sororities, where they take oaths.

When a person renounces his or her association with a religion or cult, the person leading the ministry session then simply cancels all rights that had been given by covering every word or ritual with the power of the blood of Christ. In most cases, this is all that is necessary. But in some cases, the person may need to renounce specifically each oath that he or she took.

Type 3: Ordinary Spirits

Ordinary spirits are those that gain a legal right to people because the people hang on to unforgiveness, anger, hatred, fear, shame, feelings of rejection, hurt and the like. These are the kinds of problems we see most in deep-level healing. A rule of the universe seems to exist that when such human problems are not dealt with, the enemy has a legal right to enter the person.

Ordinary demons gain rights through a person's wallowing in some negative emotion or sin. Or someone in authority over the person can give a demon permission to live in that person. As with the other ground-level demons, the person is usually quite unconscious of the presence of these spirits since they masquerade as the person's own thoughts or voice.

Many acquire such demons at conception, due to the fact that their parents did not want them or did not want a child of their sex. Spirits of shame, fear, abuse, unwantedness, anger and just about any other emotion can enter at conception. Spirits like fear, anger, rebellion and a host of others often enter during childhood, attaching to negative experiences. Dealing with such spirits is a function of inner healing, since the presence and strength of demons is calibrated to the amount and kind of inner garbage the person carries.

Six Ways Demonization Happens

Two conditions are necessary for demonization to happen. First, demons must find an entry point, such as an invitation or an emotional and/or spiritual problem in a person. Second, demons must have a legal right to stay—a right that accords with the laws of the spiritual universe. A legal right is given in one or more of the following ways.

1. Through Conscious Invitation

Demons can enter a person by invitation, conscious or unconscious. A conscious invitation happens whenever there is deliberate involvement with or worship of gods, spirits or powers other than the true God. Though the invitation is conscious, a person may not be aware of the fact that he or she is inviting demons to take over.

The organization of the spirit world seems to be such that cosmic-level demons assign ground-level demons to live in people. Leaders of occult groups seem to be able to call upon cosmic-level spirits to make the assignments.

Such occult leaders as shamans, leaders of New Age groups, fortune-tellers, psychics or witches may know very well that they are inviting demons to take over at certain times. But ordinary members of such groups may or may not know that they have opened themselves up to satanic influence since they may be unaware of the existence of the spirit world.

Following is a listing of some of those groups that invite demons in, whether consciously or unconsciously, and are, therefore, very much influenced by them. These groups are governed by cosmic-level spirits, but their working out is done at both ground and cosmic levels.

Religions	Occult Organizations
Islam	New Age
Buddhism	Freemasonry
Hinduism	Scientology
Shintoism	Witchcraft
Religious knowledge	Satanism
Mormonism	Yoga
Liberal Christianity	Tae kwon do
Christian Science	Other Eastern philosophies
Jehovah's Witnesses	

There are also a variety of practices that people who may or may not be a part of such organizations engage in. Young girls at sleepovers, for example, may play games such as "Bloody Mary," during which they look into a mirror and invite spirits to come out. Another "game" is "Light as a Feather, Stiff as a Board," in which people put their hands or fingers under a person who is lying on the floor and see him or her lift off the floor.

Some may engage in séances or play with Ouija boards or go to fortune-tellers or use tarot cards or engage in table-tilting or levitation. And then there are computer games that are satanic. One of the older ones is called *Dungeons & Dragons*. I am told there are worse ones than that. The Harry Potter books and movies are another source of demonization, as are Eastern practices such as yoga and tae kwon do.

Our society has been invaded by occult practices such as these, giving Satan ample opportunity to infest millions. He takes advantage of our ignorance to make captives out of unsuspecting Westerners, even Christians who have no idea that some of these things are dangerous.

We classify such activities as conscious invitations in spite of the fact that such persons, given their worldview blindness to spirit-world activities, often do not actually know they are inviting demons into their lives. Few involved in Freemasonry know, for example, the risk at which they are putting themselves and their families. The decision to be involved in any of these activities, however, was a conscious one, just as a decision to defy the law of gravity is a conscious decision, whether or not one knows the law.

2. Through Unconscious Invitation

Unconscious invitation is more subtle. Demons gain rights when a person wallows in some negative attitude, usually in reaction to some difficult experience. Physical or emotional mistreatment usually leads a person to get angry, and we may have a right to get angry, but if we keep the anger, demons gain a legal right to inhabit us. The anger itself is not a sin. Even Jesus got angry. But He did not sin by holding on to the anger, so He did not allow a demon in.

Ephesians 4:26 says, "[*When*] you become angry . . ." (the Greek word means either *if* or *when*). The implication is clearly that we will become angry. But when that happens, we are told to "not let [our] anger lead [us] into sin, and do not stay angry all day" so that we "don't give the Devil a chance" (verse 27). Wallowing in anger and its accompanying unforgiveness gives the enemy, by a rule of the universe, the right to enter us.

The same is true of a large number of normal reactions that we have to the circumstances of our lives. Among them are shame, guilt, bitterness, resentment, rage, depression, fear, worry, hatred, rebellion, rejection, abandonment, control, sexual sins, misuse of power and another hundred or more such reactions. Holding on to these rather than giving them to Jesus is a very common form of unconscious invitation for demons to enter us. The reactions make up the major part of the garbage that is addressed when ministering inner healing and deliverance.

3. Through Addictive Behavior

A third category that gives demons rights is addictive behavior. Many people repeatedly give in to temptations of various kinds so that these activities control them. Among these addictions are pornography, alcohol, drugs, gambling and lustful thoughts. These addictions are well-known.

There are some other addictions that may not be so identified but are just as powerful. Among these are self-rejection, self-hatred, self-condemnation and envy or jealousy. These are the things that contribute to a low self-image, and they are some of the enemy's favorite attitudes and habits to use for his purposes.

Such behavior weakens one's spiritual defenses, providing what John Wimber has pictured as an airport with "a runway with all the lights on, showing the way for demons to enter." And Satan is very accomplished in taking advantage of such weaknesses.

4. Through Invitation of Someone in Authority

People can also be demonized through the invitation of someone in authority over them. A child dedicated by a parent or grandparent gets demonized at birth. I know a woman who was raised in a satanist family and dedicated by her mother to Satan at birth. At that point, one or more demons entered the girl, having been invited by a person in authority over her.

Such dedication of children to spirits or gods is a common practice worldwide. Adults who submit to the authority of others in cults can become demonized through such dedication or satanically empowered "blessings" uttered by those in authority over them. Parents can also demonize their children through cursing. Such cursing can also result in the demonization of wives by husbands and vice versa.

5. *Through Inheritance*

A fifth way people can be demonized is through inheritance. Children may be born demonized (see Exodus 20:5). We call this the passing on of generational or bloodline spirits or power. Inherited spirits gain entrance through some vow, commitment or self-curse that was made by an ancestor or through some curse that was put on descendants by an ancestor.

Demons live in people whose parents and/or grandparents were in non-Christian religions, witchcraft or occult organizations, such as satanism, Freemasonry, Mormonism, Christian Science, Scientology and the like. The spirits get passed down through spiritual inheritance.

Such generational spirits may cause similar emotional problems, sins, illnesses and/or compulsions to exist in family members from generation to generation. Generational demons may be operating if we see in several generations of a family such problems as alcoholism, depression, sexual perversion, hypercriticism, extreme fearfulness, cancer, diabetes or any other emotional or physical problem or besetting sin. I once ministered to a woman, for example, who needed a hysterectomy at age 43. Interestingly, both her mother and her grandmother had hysterectomies at the same age. I suspect demonic activity was at work in that family.

6. *Through Cursing*

A curse is often a major factor in the power a demon has over a person. Curse spirits are often released through hateful words aimed at a person or spoken by the person against himself or herself. Sometimes, though, the curse is more formal, involving a ritual performed by someone practicing witchcraft. Such curses can be very powerful, especially if they involve the shedding of blood.

Many people have cursed themselves, especially their bodies. This often happens at puberty, but many who have a low self-image continue such self-cursing throughout their lives. Cursing and its siblings—vows, oaths, pact-making, spells, hexes and the like—are more likely to bring about demonization in combination with other spiritual activity.

> **Many people have cursed themselves, especially their bodies.**

Some entry point and/or giving of authority probably also needs to be there for a curse to enable a demon to enter. As pointed out in Proverbs 26:2, without something in a person for them to "hook onto," a curse is like a bird that flutters around but cannot find a place to land. Curses that do "land" probably carry demons with them. As an example of the kind of freedom that can come to a person freed from a curse, a prominent Jewish Christian leader once described for me the total newness that came into his life when he was delivered from a demon hooked to the curse the Jewish people put on themselves at the time of Jesus' crucifixion: "Let the responsibility for his death fall on us and on our children!" (Matthew 27:25).

Nine Activities Demons Promote

Demons encourage several kinds of activity. They prefer to do these things from inside of people, if possible, since they can do more damage that way. If they cannot get in, however, they attempt to do the same sorts of things from the outside, often trying to fool people into believing the activities are coming from inside them.

1. Disruption

A major activity of demons is to disrupt. Though they cannot create problems out of nothing, demons can aggravate existing situations. They push, prod, tempt and entice people to make poor or unwise decisions. They work to make bad things worse and to get people to overdo good things so that the once-good things are no longer positive.

2. *Temptation*

Demons are the primary agents of temptation. They do Satan's bidding at his command (see Genesis 3:1–7; Matthew 16:21–23; 26:69–75; Acts 5:3). They apparently can put thoughts in people's minds, though we are responsible for what we do with those thoughts. They tempt primarily in areas of a person's greatest vulnerability. They tailor-make the particular thoughts they put in a person's mind to be appropriate for that person. It is their job to hammer away at a person. They will do whatever it takes to tempt them into action, in hopes that they can contribute to the person's failure.

3. *Hiddenness*

Demons do their best to keep people ignorant of their presence and activity. This is a particularly successful strategy in Western societies, as we have already learned. They love it when people do not believe they exist. Demons repeatedly have told us this during ministry sessions. And during one session observed by a psychologist who was learning about demonization, a demon became so angry during the ministry that it yelled (through its host), "I hate it that she [the psychologist] is learning about us! For years, we have been hiding and making them think we are psychological problems!"[1]

Because demons can only piggyback on problems that already exist, they hide quite effectively from many people. Westerners reason that if they can explain a problem as resulting from natural causes, they do not need to look further. Thus, the demon escapes blame and the person becomes discouraged, stops fighting the problem and blames himself or herself for it. Many give up hope, thinking they were crazy or that nothing could be done about the problem.

4. *Fear*

Demons often resort to persuading people to fear them. They do this in several ways. People have come to me fearing they had a demon and that

1. Rita Cabezas, *Struggling Against Demonic Principalities* (San Jose, Costa Rica: n.p., 1992).

there was something very wrong with them spiritually. They did not know that the presence or absence of a demon usually has little to do with their present spiritual condition, except to hinder it. Christians are often very good at suppressing demonic activity. They usually have become demonized through inheritance, some kind of abuse or pre-Christian activities, rather than through spiritual failure or rebellion. But the demons have pushed them to fear the worst.

Conversely, a certain number of people are afraid they do *not* have a demon! These are often people who want to avoid responsibility for their problems. They hope to blame them on demons. On the other hand, some have been accused of being crazy or otherwise permanently disabled, and so they genuinely hope that a major part of the problem is demonic and can be eradicated. It usually can.

> **Some try to blame all their problems on demons.**

Many people fear the power of demons. They have heard stories, seen movies or talked to people who became involved in fear-inspiring physical battles with demonized people. They have not learned that most physical battles can be avoided through inner healing and by exercising the spiritual power we have through empowered words—not the power of muscles.

5. Deceit

In all that demons do, deceit is a major weapon. Demons lie, and their lies often show up in our self-talk about who we are, who God is, who they are and what they do. As in Eden, demons deceive sometimes through direct contradiction and sometimes through indirect questioning of truth. Then they lead people to think the false concept or idea is their own thought.

6. Hindrance

By whatever means possible, the job of demons is to hinder anything good. They try to keep people from God or from doing anything God wants. They hinder unbelievers from believing (see 2 Corinthians 4:4). They also influence Christians in the belief area. In addition, such things as worship, prayer, Bible study and acts of love and compassion are high on the demonic hit list. They specialize in discovering and attacking weaknesses. The greater the weakness, the more often a person is likely to be attacked in that area.

Ground-level demons, often supported by cosmic spirits, attack Christians on Sundays, often from outside. They encourage conflict within families on Sunday mornings as they are preparing for or traveling to church. Demons like to push people's minds to wander during worship or the sermon. Headaches, crying babies or other means of breaking concentration in church are additional demonic tactics.

In addition, demons like to influence pastors to run churches as clubs rather than as hospitals, to focus on preaching and programs rather than on ministering to people and focusing on relationship, to preach theoretically rather than practically, and to perform rather than to communicate. They push musicians to show off, prompt those who give announcements to interrupt the flow of worship and press ushers to be too obvious—all to weaken what God wants to do in church.

7. Accusation

Demons specialize in accusing. In fact, the name *Satan* originally meant "accuser." Many such accusations that demons bring against us are negative statements or thoughts about ourselves or others. One of the enemy's favorite devices is to entice people to accuse themselves, others and God of disrupting truth, health, life, love, relationships and anything else that comes from God.

The self-rejection so characteristic of many in our society provides especially fertile ground for this aspect of demonic activity. In addition to self-accusation, demons plant in our minds thoughts that persuade us to accuse others or God. They encourage such things as rumors, anger at God and disrupted relationships based on misunderstandings, and they further encourage us to blame God for things He allows in our lives. They push people to retain guilt even after they receive God's forgiveness, convince people that something is incurably wrong with them, entice people into blaming themselves for abuse they received from others and strongly suggest that the troubles a person experiences are from God and are deserved because of that person's failures.

8. Enablement

Demons like to enable compulsions. They delight in helping people to develop a compulsive approach to both good and bad behavior. They reinforce compulsions relating to lust, drugs, alcohol, tobacco, overeating, undereating, pornography, gambling, materialism, competitiveness and the need to be in control. They also encourage overdoing attention to "good" things such as work, study, attractive dress, religion, doctrinal purity, family, achievement, success and so forth. They delight in pushing people to build on weaknesses and exaggerate strengths. The roots of such compulsions often lie in such attitudes as fear, insecurity and feelings of unworthiness. Knowing this, demons are quick to push their victims toward compulsivity.

9. Harassment

Demons are adept at harassment. They nip at our heels like angry dogs. Satan is referred to as "the ruler of this world" (John 14:30) and does not like it that those who belong to another King are wandering around in his territory. So he harasses us whenever and however he can. Demons can disrupt our lives in whatever ways God allows, influencing such things as traffic, weather, health, stress, relationships, worship, sleep, diet, mechanical objects (especially cars and computers) and anything else that affects us.

I believe harassment was Satan's aim when he ordered demons to manifest themselves when Jesus was teaching in the synagogue (see Luke 4:33–34). Satan probably also ordered demons to stir up the storm while Jesus was in a boat on Lake Galilee (see Luke 8:23–24) and to influence the Pharisees to continually bother Him.

To counter such influences in my own life if it looks like things are going wrong, I am in the habit of saying, "If this is the enemy, stop it!" It is amazing to me how many things stop when I take that approach.

Demons do not seem to harass every Christian equally. They pay more attention to those who are the greatest threat to them and to those who do not have enough prayer support. Many Christians, in fact, are so passive about their Christianity that they are no threat to the enemy. They get off with very little attention from him. But those who threaten the enemy without having enough prayer support are harassed regularly and sometimes effectively.

Whether or not a person is a threat to the enemy, no strategy enables us Christians to live completely free from demonic attention as long as we are in his territory. I have had numerous encounters with ground-level demons living in others and can testify that they are real and are in the world in abundance. Though I have seldom been able to simply command them to leave, as the gospels portray Jesus doing, I have been successful in freeing hundreds of people from demons by doing inner healing first, then confronting the demons in Jesus' name.

As I have said before, demons are able to live in people because they have "legal rights"—rights that are theirs by laws of the universe and that stay in a person until someone with more power comes along to evict them. These rights are granted to them by virtue of spiritual garbage. Such garbage consists of rights given through inheritance, invitation, wallowing in sin, curses and a few other methods.[2]

As we have already mentioned, demons are like rats, and rats live where there is garbage. Dealing with the garbage, then, is the most important aspect of the process of fighting demons at ground level. Thus, we will recommend an approach in chapter 12 that frees demonized people from the garbage first, thereby making it possible to then deal with the demons easily and effectively without violence.

2. For more information, see Kraft, *Defeating Dark Angels*.

11

Ten Myths Concerning Demonization

I was sitting in a restaurant with a couple of evangelical pastors one afternoon when the discussion turned to demonization. This topic was quite unfamiliar to them. One of them, whom I will call George, began to share with us a lifelong problem he had with fear. Though George had been meeting with a professional counselor for some time, his fear had not been overcome. Indeed, he said, he was highly anxious at that very moment. After a silent prayer, I looked straight at George and said, "Fear, I command you to leave, in the name of Jesus."

Shock registered on George's face as I looked directly at him but talked past him to the demon inside. For a pastor who was not sure he believed in such things, the approach seemed awfully direct, and I seemed overly confident in my diagnosis of what lay behind his problem. Then amazement filled George's face as he said over and over, "The fear is gone! The fear is gone!"

Though psychologists and others may try to explain what happened naturalistically, my interpretation is that an alien being inside George responded to my command to leave. What had not happened in counseling, when psychological principles were applied, happened immediately in response to a single command. That is, when I treated the problem as if an evil being was behind it and commanded that being to leave, in Jesus' name, the fear vanished. And it has not returned.

Not long ago, I would only have been able to offer George my sympathy and recommend he continue getting psychological help. However, I have since had so many experiences similar to this that I have come to believe that demons do exist, that they live in people and that they frequently are responsible for harassment not unlike what George had been experiencing for years.

My theory is that a fairly weak demon was living within George whose assignment was to use fear to hamper George's effectiveness as a servant of Christ. My analysis, however, is that the demon did not cause the fear. Talking with this pastor, I discovered that he had experiences in early childhood that predisposed him to fearfulness. This weakness allowed the demon to enter the scene during his early life. It provided the "food" on which the demon fed to keep George off balance. I think the demon was greatly weakened as George grew in his spiritual life and dealt with the problem through counseling. All that remained, then, was for the demon to be banished once and for all. And that seemed to happen that day at lunch (in no less than a public restaurant, by the way).

As a footnote to this story, it is interesting to note the reaction of the other pastor who was with us that day. He first indicated surprise and then what I will call *fearful skepticism*. He was not used to being in situations he could not explain. So he attempted to find a naturalistic explanation—in this case, a psychological explanation—that would restore his composure and give him a sense of control over what he had just witnessed.

George's description of how he felt inside, however, would not allow the second pastor to explain things away. But once the second pastor accepted the validity of George's experience, he became fearful that if his friend was carrying a demon—and was a pastor, no less—perhaps demons were all around us and inside some of the rest of us as well.

Why do many of us respond negatively to any suggestion that demons are alive and active? These men were pastors well acquainted with the Scriptures. But they were also Westerners who had imbibed with their "mother's milk" a naturalistic understanding of reality. They found it easy to regard accounts of demonization as biblical events that used to happen. But they assumed these events do not happen where we live since we in the West have an explanation for most things that occur that do not require belief in invisible spiritual beings. Or they believed that if such beings do exist and such events do happen, they occur only overseas, not in "Christian" America. We need not concern ourselves with them, they think, since "He who is in [us] is greater than he who is in the world" (1 John 4:4 NKJV). One way or the other, most of the people we interact with remain ignorant of the enemy, his helpers and their schemes (see 2 Corinthians 2:11).

When confronted with the possibility that demons are indeed all around us, a typical evangelical response is that of the pastor I mentioned in chapter 1 who said he would rather not know demons exist. In the first place, we may fear the possibility that there is some major part of reality we cannot control, as we are used to being in control. But second, if demons do reveal their presence, we fear that we will not know what to do about it. Usually mixed into all this is a heavy dose of misconceptions—encouraged by the enemy—about how to deal with this area of reality. One thing that confused the pastor who said he would rather not know if there are demons, for instance, was the matter-of-fact way I said I dealt with these problems. *If you are really dealing with demons, wouldn't they create a scene?* he wondered. *And don't you have to go through a lot of religious ritual, such as prayer and fasting, before you challenge them?*

Most evangelicals live in profound ignorance and fear in this regard. Neither is necessary. We do not know everything, but enough understanding is available for us to make a good start. Let's begin by dispelling ten myths that surround the subject of demonization. Many of these myths are among Satan's favorite lies!

Myth 1: People Are Possessed by Demons

The term *demon-possessed* is commonly used to describe a person with demons living inside him or her. This comes from the mistaken rendering in many Bible translations of the Greek word *daimonizomai*. In older translations and even in the New International Version, this word is rendered *demon-possessed*.

Please bear with the technicalities included in the following paragraphs. It is important that we not be sloppy in translation, especially when the issue is the amount of credit given to Satan—and what Satan is able to do to people is seriously overestimated by the use of the word *possession*.

The word *daimonizomai* occurs seven times in Matthew, four times in Mark, once in Luke and once in John. It means "have a demon," nothing more. A parallel expression, *echein daimonion*, also meaning "have a demon," occurs once in Matthew, three times in Luke and five times in John. Luke uses the latter phrase interchangeably with *daimonizomai*. Though the scriptural authors may have intended that *daimonizomai* signify a slightly greater degree of demonic control than *echein daimonion*, translators simply are not justified in rendering either term *demon-possessed*. This rendering signifies too much control given to Satan and his demons. Both wordings are better translated "have a demon." (See, for example, Matthew 4:24; 8:16, 28, 33; 9:32; 12:22; 15:22.)

It is critical that the relationship between demons and those in whom they reside be stated accurately. The word *possessed* greatly overstates the influence wielded by the vast majority of demons. One might argue for using that word to describe extreme cases (for example, that of the Gerasene demoniac of Matthew 8:28–34). But it is misleading and harmful to so label the many people battling the lesser influence demons more commonly have.

It is far better to use a more neutral term such as *have a demon* or *demonized*. Both are more true to the original Greek and also run less risk of frightening people. To quote Unger:

> The term "demon possession" does not appear in the Bible. Apparently it originated with the Jewish historian, Flavius Josephus, in the first century A.D. and then passed into ecclesiastical language. The New Testament, however, frequently mentions demoniacs. They are said to "have a spirit," "a demon," "demons," or "an unclean spirit." Usually such unhappy victims of evil personalities are said to be "demonized" (*daimonizomenoi*), i.e., they are subject to periodic attacks by one or more inhabiting demons, who derange them physically and mentally during the seizure![1]

1. Merrill F. Unger, *Demons in the World Today* (Wheaton, Ill.: Tyndale, 1971), 101.

The more neutral terms do not give more credit to Satan than his due. They also enable us to recognize the differing levels of demonic influence and indicate demonic strength more accurately. For example, if we say that George was demonized but that the strength of his demon was about a 1 or a 2 on a scale from 1–10, we get a very different picture than if we say he was demon-possessed. As a matter of fact, he was far from possessed by what was a very weak spirit of fear—a spirit that may have been stronger earlier in his life but had lost a lot of power through his Christian growth. George was constantly troubled but not possessed because his demon did not have the strength to take complete control, or possession, of him. The demon was indeed at about a level 1 or 2 on the scale.

Nearly all contemporary writers on demonization prefer the terms *demonized* and *demonization* in place of *demon-possessed* and *demon possession*.[2] I also prefer to avoid imprecise terms such as *affliction*, *oppression* or *bondage* to describe the condition of persons inhabited by demons, though they may be useful labels for demonic influence operating from outside a person.

Experience leads me to believe that demons cannot totally control a person all the time, though in severe demonization nearly total control may occur for shorter or longer periods of time. In such cases, however, *severe demonization* is a more accurate label than *demon-possession*. In Scripture, the Gerasene demoniac would be one I would say was experiencing severe demonization—at a level 10 on a ten-point scale. Probably other scriptural examples could also be labeled this way. As noted earlier, a demon can never completely control a Christian, and this is because it cannot live where Jesus is.

Myth 2: Deliverance Always Entails a Big Fight

I often have people come for ministry who have previously participated in one or more deliverance sessions in which the demons threw them around

2. See, for example, Unger, *Demons in the World Today*; Unger, *What Demons Can Do to Saints* (Chicago: Moody, 1991); Dickason, *Demon Possession and the Christian* (despite the misleading title); Tom White, *The Believer's Guide to Spiritual Warfare*, rev. ed. (Minneapolis: Chosen, 2011) (Originally published Ventura, Calif.: Regal, 2011.); Wagner, *Engaging the Enemy*; John Wimber and Kevin Springer, *Power Healing*, reprint ed. (San Francisco: HarperOne, 2009); and Kraft, *Defeating Dark Angels*.

and thoroughly embarrassed them. In spite of this, sometimes the person was not even freed from the demon and comes to me in fear and trembling, lest the violence happen again. Such persons are usually happy to hear that with the hundreds of people I have helped, hardly any violence has occurred. They are delighted to learn that deliverance does not have to include violence. They learn that we have the authority in Christ to forbid violence and that when we deal first with the emotional and spiritual garbage the demons are attached to, the demons get weak and cannot cause violence.

Sensational stories of knock-down, drag-out fighting with demons have created the myth that the enemy is so strong that every deliverance is a battle. Media presentations (for example, the Hollywood film *The Exorcist*) and church testimonies also tend to focus on the sensational. "Great physical strength" is sometimes listed on diagnostic forms designed to help discern whether a demon is present in a person. And we all probably have heard of the need for five burly men to hold down a ninety-pound woman because of the strength of the demons in her!

The belief that deliverance always involves demonic strength, eyes rolling to the back of a person's head or other manifestations needs to be countered. Many people who suspect they have demons refrain from seeking help because they fear the battle they think is coming. One pastor told me he turned away from deliverance after a lady threw up all over his office. Now that he realizes he can forbid such manifestations, he is once more delivering people.

It is true that many who have attempted or sought deliverance have found themselves in violent situations. The enemy loves to use this tactic in ministry sessions led by people who have not had much experience or who think the violence is necessary. When demons are approached in the name of Jesus, they become desperate and will try any strategy they think will work to try to escape. They know their power is nowhere near as great as that of Jesus, so they resort to bluffing. As a demon I uncovered recently said to me, "Ooh, I'm in trouble now!" Another remarked, "You really know what you're doing!"

Demons know that many people believe the myth of inevitable violence, and they try to exploit the ignorance of such people. If demons think they can get away with it, they will stage violence, cause vomiting, arouse fear and use any diversionary tactic they can find. You might, too, if you were as desperate as they are!

In the heat of the contest, demons will do whatever they are allowed to do. But the key is *what they are allowed to do*. In the name of Jesus, we have power over them. They know this. We need to know it, too. They can do only what Jesus allows them to do. When we forbid them to cause violence, they can do little or none. We discover, as did the disciples, that when we minister in Jesus' name, "Lord, even the demons submit to us in your name" (Luke 10:17 NIV). The disciples simply exercised the authority Jesus had given them and were able to rejoice in experiencing God's power to banish demons. We can do the same.

> In the name of Jesus, we have power over demons. They know this. We need to know it, too.

People often expect violence because they believe the only problem in the situation is the demons. They fight the demons, therefore, when the demons are strongest. They tackle the demons head-on, assuming that when the demons are gone, the person will be well. If they recognized instead that the basic problem is *not* the demons but the emotional and spiritual garbage present in the person, and if they worked on that garbage before challenging the demons, they would find the demons weakened, with little or no fight left.

Those who first deal with the emotional and spiritual garbage experience little, if any, violence. Though some of my colleagues have occasionally experienced violent reactions, to date, in more than two thousand cases, I have not encountered one instance of extreme physical violence—though sometimes there is some shaking. I believe there are at least four reasons for this:

1. **I work almost exclusively with Christians.** This means the Holy Spirit, who empowers the process, indwells them. If I am asked to work with a non-Christian, I attempt to lead the person to Jesus before working with him or her.
2. **I work only with persons who are willing and eager to be healed.** Both God and Satan honor the human will. It is, therefore, virtually

impossible to free someone who does not firmly choose to start and continue the process, no matter how difficult it may become.

3. **I start each session by forbidding any demons to cause violence or vomiting.** We have authority to order demons to obey us. This authority is real for us, as it was for Jesus. Out of love for the victim, then, we forbid things that will embarrass the victim.

4. **As I have already pointed out, I do whatever possible to weaken the demons before challenging them.** Weak demons often can hardly talk, much less create a ruckus! So they are much easier to deal with than when they are strong.

One of our primary concerns should be to lead the client into an experience of feeling loved. Allowing the person to experience violence is not loving. If we can keep that from happening, we should use the authority Jesus has given us to prevent violence, throwing up or any other embarrassing things.

Myth 3: Demonization Is Simply Psychological Illness

Liberal Christians assume that the biblical accounts of Jesus casting out demons simply record Jesus' way of dealing with psychological illness. They contend, "Jesus simply accommodated to the belief of the people of that day that demons caused problems. He knew then what we know now—that the so-called demonized were really heavy-duty psychological cases."

Unfortunately, variations of this myth are common among evangelicals as well. As we have already discussed at length, our naturalistic Western worldview makes it extremely difficult for us to believe that supernatural beings, such as Satan and demons, are real. We are taught as we grow up that seeing is believing and that if you cannot see it, it does not exist. We come to assume that invisible beings with power are all right in fairy tales but have no place in real life.[3]

Furthermore, we are so impressed with Western scientific thought, including psychology, that it seldom occurs to us that our scientists may not always have the correct explanation for such phenomena. Most Westerners

3. For a more extensive review of this perspective, see Kraft, *Christianity with Power.*

trust our scientists and assume they have a better understanding of demonization than the people of the first century. But remember, scientists today are only working with two hundred pieces of the Reality puzzle.

Additionally, when we come in contact with persons acting like the demonized people of the gospels, we take them to psychologists, even though recent studies question the ability of psychological counseling to bring healing. Counselors are very often helpful, especially in enabling people to cope with their problems, but their record for bringing healing is not good.

So it would seem that most Westerners question spiritual interpretations of the demonization passages rather than question the correctness of the Western worldview. Those of us who have been blasted out of our naturalistic worldview assumptions in this area, however, have no doubt that we cannot reduce demonic phenomena to psychological phenomena. Psychological problems, though sometimes strong, cannot talk to us, but demons can.

It should be mentioned here that it is also wrong to regard all psychological phenomena as demonic. Demons and psychological problems are distinct, and to consider them as one and the same is a myth. However, it is important to know that when a person has psychological or emotional illness, there is almost always demonization present as well. Remember, as we discussed in chapters 3 and 5, we are dealing with things that have two causes—what I call *dual causation*.

Myth 4: Those with Demons Are Guilty of Spiritual Rebellion

Much damage is done to a person suffering from demonization when well-meaning Christians suggest that they have become demonized because they are sinful and rebellious. Jesus never blamed people or accused them of rebellion for having demons. The belief that demonization comes about only through conscious choice is a lie. As we will see, rebellion and other conscious choices are possible reasons but comparatively rare among Christians.

As we often hear these days, we Christians are good at shooting our wounded. Those who are suffering from demonization are already in deep pain and confusion. To imply that their problem is their own fault makes their plight even worse. Many to whom I have ministered have come to me with great shame, fearing that their turmoil indicates a major, perhaps even unforgivable, problem in their relationship with God.

These demonized Christians are, almost without exception, anything but rebellious to Christ or wallowing in sin. Rather, they are usually sincere believers who deeply love Jesus but cannot free themselves from something that has a hold on their lives.

A woman I will call Teri was faced with a situation typical of many. Whenever she attended a worship service, an intense battle went on inside of her. The compulsion to get up and run was well-nigh overpowering.

It was obvious, both from observing Teri's life and hearing her descriptions of her quiet times with the Lord, that she was deeply committed to Jesus. Because I know that demons hate worship, I suspected that the interference she was experiencing might be demonic. After doing inner healing work that dealt with several "garbage" issues in Teri's life, largely related to self-esteem, Jesus used me to evict several fairly weak demons from her. Teri now worships wholeheartedly, without interference. (We will talk more about inner healing work in chapter 12.)

In another instance, a pastor I will call Paul came to me very hesitantly, admitting he had been hearing voices in his head since childhood. Paul's sense of guilt was high since he believed something was wrong with his spiritual life if the voices in his head came from demons. Indeed, he was convinced that if the voices *were* those of demons, he would be disqualified from continuing in the ministry. However, we were able to establish that the demons had come to him through inheritance and that, therefore, he need carry no guilt for their presence. Today, having experienced Jesus' power to deliver him, Paul is free from both the demons and the guilt.

Rebellious persons, on the other hand, seldom come for deliverance. Individuals who do come usually have been deeply wounded or abused. Their great pain, through little or no fault of their own, has opened the door to a demonic presence in their lives. Usually they were abused during their childhood, often by family members whom they trusted and wanted to please. Sometimes the abuse had a satanic or ritual dimension. When people become demonized through abuse or inheritance, it is totally un-Christian to suggest it was their fault. They were victims and, in accordance with some law of the universe, they became demonized.

185

Even persons who contracted demons during rebellious times in their lives do not need guilt added to their already heavy load. That is not Jesus' way. Over the years, I have worked with many people who invited in demons during times of rebellion—some consciously, some unconsciously. Usually the sweetness of their relationship with Jesus is so precious that they do not want to remain permanently under the influence of the demons. So they come, seeking deliverance.

When people become demonized through abuse or inheritance, it is totally un-Christian to suggest it was their fault.

Jesus' way is not to condemn even bad choices. Though their condition is the result of rebellion or some other collection of poor choices, they are not to be treated in terms of that rebellion but according to their desire to be free. And Jesus graciously frees them, without condemnation.

It is cruel to add to the wounds of demonized people. What they need is Jesus' love and power to bring freedom both from demons and any guilt coming from inside of them or from the Christian community. Besides deliverance, they need to experience the truth (see John 8:32) of Jesus' presence, forgiveness and acceptance. Whatever responsibility they may bear for their condition can be forgiven. "There is no condemnation now," Romans 8:1 tells us—even for those afflicted with demons.

Myth 5: Problems Are Either Demonic or Psychological

As I have mentioned previously, part of our worldview is an either-or mentality. We also tend to look for simple answers. This leads many to assume that symptoms of the kind we have been discussing are either demonic or psychological—not both. Those with a naturalistic mentality attempt to see such problems as psychological, while those who are more aware of the spirit world may want to blame the problems on demons.

To believe that such problems can be categorized into one or the other, however, is a myth. They cannot be neatly divided into exclusively psychological or exclusively demonic categories. Experience teaches us that demons have to have something human to attach themselves to, so there is a human cause that then created a spirit cause. Thus, most problems have both demonic and emotional causes.

Demons cannot create something from nothing. They can only take advantage of what already exists. Emotional or spiritual problems provide the garbage that attracts the demonic rats. But not all emotional garbage is sufficient to attract them. Thus, many people with symptoms of emotional illness may simply be emotionally ill. Others with similar symptoms may suffer from both emotional illness and demonization.

Since this is true, it is extremely important that we not simply look for demons or, when demons are discovered, deal with only the demonic problem. The aim is to bring healing at whatever level necessary—and usually there will be both an emotional cause and a demonic cause. We have to deal with both.

When there are human problems to which demons are attached, the demons are secondary. In fact, demonization is *always* secondary, just as rats are secondary to garbage. If we get rid of the rats and keep the garbage, the rats can come back. But if we get rid of the garbage, what we have done automatically affects the rats. Whether there are demons present or not, therefore, we go after the primary problem first—the emotional and spiritual garbage.

Unlike other deliverance ministries, then, I do not divide people into the "demonized group" and the "emotionally ill group" for the purpose of treating one group one way and the other another way. Instead, I assume that emotional problems are to be treated as emotional problems, whether or not there are also demons, and that we should deal with the emotional problems first. If, as is usually the case, the person turns out to also have demons, we deal with them after the demons' "food" (the emotional problems) has been greatly reduced. By that time, any demons still there will be much weaker than if we had challenged them at the beginning. This approach recognizes that the real problem facing demonized people is never the demons but the deep-level emotional problems to which they are attached.

Because of this approach, we do not consider our ministry simply a deliverance ministry. Deliverance is never a simple process, where we go after demons and that is the end of it. The important stuff to deal with is the reaction against emotional wounding that has allowed demons to enter a person. These emotional problems must be addressed through inner healing and sound Christian counseling. The combination of inner healing, deliverance and solid Christian therapy is often the key to wholeness for the demonized. This is especially true for the severely abused, such as satanic ritual abuse victims.

Myth 6: All Emotional Problems Are Caused by Demons

In reaction against the third myth—that demonization is simply psychological illness—many who discover that demons really do exist go to the opposite extreme. They begin to believe that all emotional problems (and most other problems as well) are caused by demons. This is the "lunatic fringe" position of many Pentecostals and charismatics. And it turns off large numbers of both Christians and non-Christians to even considering the possibility that demons exist and are active.

Though I contend that demonization is very common, it is clear to me that emotional problems are seldom, if ever, *caused* by demons. The origin of such difficulties lies elsewhere. When a child is abused, for example, though a demon may have pushed the abuser to do his or her work, it is the reaction to the abuse, not the demon, that becomes the central problem in the child. The child often becomes demonized in reaction to the abuse, but the reaction to the abuse needs to be dealt with first if we are to get at the demons.

As I pointed out in myth five, Satan and his demons cannot create something from nothing. They can only piggyback on what is there already. Though demons may be involved in any given problem, we cannot simply assume that every problem has been caused by demons. That is too simplistic.

I have no idea what percentage of problems involve demonization. My impression is that though problems are not initiated by demons, demons are involved at least indirectly in the vast majority of problems. Demons are opportunistic. They jump in wherever they see an opportunity and affect whatever they can in their hosts' lives, acting from either inside or outside of those hosts.

Their ability to cause problems is, I believe, limited to whatever influence they can gain on persons and events. If, for example, abuse occurs even without demons initiating it, they are eager to take over and make it worse if the spiritual rules of the universe allow. Or if things are going well for a person, demons will do whatever they are permitted to do by those rules of the universe to push the person to ignore, exaggerate or divert those good things.

We need to see demons, therefore, not only in terms of their presence, but also in terms of their strategies and limitations. Two major limitations are the power of God and the strength of the human will. Demons cannot stand against the power of God, when activated, or a strong human will. And when a strong human will is empowered by God and directed against demons, it is impossible for the demons to win. When, however, a Christian does not know how to use his or her authority to challenge the right of the demons to be there and to be in operation, the spirits can take advantage of their host.

In summary, to ignore the activities of demons is folly. But to give them more credit than they are due is also folly.

Myth 7: Only Those with Special Giftings Can Cast Out Demons

Many Christians believe that only those who are very spiritual and have special deliverance gifts or a special anointing can cast out demons. Satan loves this myth because when people believe it, they do not even attempt deliverance.

However, the Scriptures do not speak of a gift of deliverance! In none of the lists of spiritual gifts in the New Testament is deliverance included (see 1 Corinthians 12; 14; Romans 12:1–8; Ephesians 4:1–16; 1 Peter 4:7–11). I believe this is because all believers have the authority to cast out demons in obedience to Jesus. And, as I learned from John Wimber, obedience precedes gifting (see John 14:12).

On earth, Jesus worked in the power of the Holy Spirit to free people from demons. He then gave His disciples—first the twelve, then the 72—authority to cast out demons (see Luke 9–10). Later, He gave the disciples

189

the Holy Spirit (see John 20:22), the same power He worked under to do His mighty works, and commanded the disciples to teach their followers "to obey everything [He had] commanded [them]" (Matthew 28:20). I take this to mean that all of us who, like the disciples, have both received the Holy Spirit and been taught to obey Jesus' commands are to cast out demons, whether or not we are specially gifted for the task.

Since we have been given the Holy Spirit, we know the power is ours. And since we, like the disciples, have been given authority by Jesus, we know we have the right to cast out demons. All we need to do is use the power and authority that has already been given to each of us.

While all believers have authority and power, special gifting can still be extremely helpful. That is to say, while a specific deliverance gift is not required for deliverance ministry, God has given the listed spiritual gifts to enable His Church to bring freedom to the oppressed. It is very helpful, for example, to have on a ministry team those with gifts such as words of wisdom, words of knowledge, discernment, healing, miracles, mercy and prophecy.

We rejoice in God-given spiritual gifts to His Church and affirm that these gifts can and should be used to convey much insight and power in a deliverance ministry. In summary, God gives spiritual gifts to help set captives free, but specific gifts are not required to minister to the demonized. The only qualification for a Christian deliverance ministry is a humble, willing attitude and the boldness to work with Jesus to bring healing and freedom to the oppressed.

There is, however, the question of how people become proficient in deliverance ministry or any other healing ministry. As I have written elsewhere concerning my entrance into a healing ministry, "Perhaps the biggest surprise for me, once I got started, was the need for learning and experimenting. I had always assumed that people received the 'gift' of healing all at once. But what I have experienced is a gradual learning process that comes along with constant practice and a lot of risk-taking."[4]

People who watch me minister to demonized people often make statements like, "It seems so easy when you do it. I'm not sure I can now or will ever be able to do that." My reply is usually something like, "I understand.

4. Kraft, *Christianity with Power*, 134.

190

It was only a few years ago that I was in your place, struggling with discouragement as I watched the experts minister. 'Will I ever be able to work so smoothly and confidently?' I remember wondering. The answer, after a lot of practice, is yes."

Myth 8: Demonization Is Uncommon in the West

Church leaders often ask me why we in Euroamerica need to learn about deliverance. They believe that our countries have been so thoroughly influenced by Christianity that the enemy could not be a serious threat here. Unlike many other Americans, these people believe in the reality of demons but are deceived in several ways.

First, they assume that the Christian influence in Western culture has been sufficient to thwart demonization. Second, they assume that demonization will be obvious. Third, based on that assumption, they further assume that demonic activity occurs only where it is obvious, such as in other societies. It does not occur to them that Satan is clever enough to work evil in a less obvious manner than they have assumed is required.

The myth that demonization is rare in the United States is extremely damaging. The enemy is delighted to see so many Christians, including pastors, teachers and other leaders, buy into this lie. The truth is that the United States is far from free of demonic influence. For those whose eyes are open to seeing them, the enemy's fingerprints are all around. Let those who have eyes observe the following.

All American cities have a variety of occult establishments that often include open witchcraft. In them, satanic power is used and passed on by people called witches, palmists, fortune-tellers, psychics, tarot card readers, yoga masters and astrologers. Spiritists, Scientologists and psychics advertise openly. In addition, people can pick up demons in older establishments, such as Masonic temples, Christian Science churches and Mormon and Jehovah's Witnesses meeting places. Buddhist and Islamic temples are springing up. Yoga, karate, tae kwon do and tai chi instructors regularly commit themselves and their students to evil spirits as they lead and teach their movements.

The Christian world often seems less knowledgeable about the reality of spiritual evil than the secular. There are a large number of articles on the Internet on subjects such as witchcraft, the occult and demons. In addition, there are many articles on specific occult subjects, some written by Christians, many from other perspectives.

> **For those whose eyes are open to seeing them, the enemy's fingerprints are all around.**

The influence of the New Age movement, the Harry Potter books and movies, Transcendental Meditation and other occult practices is very great. So many health food shops are infected that we would be well advised to claim God's protection whenever we enter one. In addition, curricula in some elementary schools teach children to link up with spirit guides, which, whether those using the materials know it or not, are demons. Parapsychology programs in our universities provide another opportunity for satanic influence.

The print and electronic news media assault viewers with reports of ritual killings and abuse, such as the satanic symbols and language of serial killer Richard Ramirez ("The Night Stalker"), the satanic cult involvement of mass murderers David Berkowitz (Son of Sam) and Henry Lee Lucas, satanists and occultists on popular TV shows and alleged sexual abuse in child care centers.

These perk up our ears and make us wonder what else is going on that we do not hear about. Startling accounts of the activities of satanists[5] and devotees of New Age[6] should cause us to sit up, take notice and do something about the problems, for Americans are choosing to become demonized at what is probably a more rapid rate than ever before.

Demonic activities *are* occurring throughout the United States, much of it illegal. Most such crime, however, goes unpunished largely because good people will not believe it is happening and do something about it—which, again, is a worldview problem.

5. See Bob Larson, *Satanism: The Seduction of America's Youth* (Nashville: Thomas Nelson, 1989).

6. See Douglas R. Groothuis, *Unmasking the New Age* (Downers Grove, Ill.: InterVarsity, 1986); Russell Chandler, *Understanding the New Age*, rev. and updated ed. (Grand Rapids, Mich.: Zondervan, 1993).

Most people are shocked to learn that those involved in satanic and other occult activities are not stereotypical "gang-like" individuals. Most behave quite normally in ordinary life. Many are socially prominent and well respected, such as doctors, teachers and lawyers. They sometimes even use church facilities for their rituals.

There are at least three good reasons for reporting this information. First, because it is happening on a large scale in our country and we need to adjust our belief system to accept this fact. Second, because adults who participate in such rituals—and children who are abused in them—become demonized. Third, because the Church needs to wake up and put to work its unique power to free victims. Demonization is not simply a problem for missionaries working in other countries. "The whole world is under the rule of the Evil One" (1 John 5:19), including America. Evil will spread when good people do nothing.

Myth 9: The Demonized Speak in a Different Voice

Because there have been situations where a man's voice came out of a young girl's mouth, many people assume that a demonized person will always speak in a different voice. This characteristic is sometimes included on diagnostic lists that attempt to describe demonization. We can thank movies like *The Exorcist* and spectacular stories told by Christians for such stereotypes of how demons behave. Many people conclude that if the troubled person does not speak in a low, scary voice and have great, uncontrollable strength, the person is not demonized.

As with all these myths, the enemy delights that large numbers of people believe this lie as well. Demons are bluffers who like to influence people by frightening them. But in the vast majority of cases, demons speak through the natural, or nearly natural, voice of the person they inhabit, especially if inner healing has been done first and the demons' power is thus reduced. Or they simply speak to the person's mind.

Sometimes a demon will use another language. On one occasion, I dealt with a demon in the daughter of a missionary that would speak only Mandarin Chinese. Fortunately, the girl was herself able to understand most of what the demon was saying. On another occasion, I encountered a demon that would speak only Arabic. In fact, it used some words and phrases that the missionary woman in whom it was living did not understand. She had to depend on her husband to interpret the words coming out of her own mouth! In both of these cases, I commanded the demons to speak English but to no avail, for reasons I do not understand. However, since they understood my English and I could understand what they were saying through the interpreters, they had to submit to the power of Jesus, and we were able to soon cast them out.

Many demons seem to be bilingual. I have ministered to a number of Taiwanese and Mandarin-speaking Chinese people. As with the two demons mentioned above, I have often found it possible in these situations to speak to the demon in English and receive its response in Taiwanese or Mandarin. On one occasion, however, the Taiwanese woman in whom the demon lived spoke quite broken English. The demon, however, spoke much better English than the woman herself did!

My theory with regard to demons speaking in different voices or languages is that several factors, either alone or in combination, may enable them to behave in this way. First, demons with a stronger grip on a person may use an alternate voice or another language or demonstrate great strength either all the time or on occasion. This is especially true of persons who do not know Christ, which enables demons to inhabit their spirit. (I suspect deliverance ministers who work more with non-Christians than I do see this phenomenon often.) I once ministered to a Christian in the strong grip of a demon who used Spanish, German and English. The demon's host knew neither Spanish nor German, but that host responded to those who addressed the demon in each of these languages. Second, demons may use this tactic to fool their host into thinking they are the reincarnation of someone who has died. Third, demons with particular personality characteristics or a particular assignment from their demonic leaders may use a voice in keeping with their personality or assignment.

Myth 10: Inner Voices Are Sure Evidence of Demonization

Lastly, in ministering healing and deliverance, we need to continually remind ourselves that not every problem is demonic. We know this, but it is easy to forget, especially if the symptoms are exceptional—for example, when the person reports hearing voices or sometimes seems completely under the control of something angry and hateful. While it is true that demons can be responsible for such voices and personality changes, certain psychological conditions also could be the explanation.

The most frequent example of this occurs with multiple personality disorder (MPD), now called dissociative identity disorder (DID), defined as "the existence within an individual of two or more distinct personalities, each of which is dominant at a particular time."[7] Those in deliverance ministry need to learn to distinguish between demonization and MPD/DID.

Not only do some alternate personalities talk and behave in ways similar to demons, but these disorders are often developed in circumstances similar to those that allow demons to enter. I have worked with at least one hundred individuals with DID but have yet to meet a person with DID who is not also demonized. Even so, when both DID and demonization are present, they are not the same thing and need to be treated differently.

An alternate personality, or alter, is quite different from a demon and needs to be treated accordingly. Integration and healing can be hindered if attempts are made to cast out a personality on the mistaken assumption that it is a demon. One personality I encountered who had been treated as a demon exclaimed, "Everybody treats me as if I am a demon. I am *not* a demon! I'm a person!" And she was right—she *is* a person. But there were also demons in her (and in the other personalities inhabiting her body) who sought to block merging that personality with her core person. They also worked hard to keep all the personalities inside her at odds with each other.

It is easy to be fooled. For example, both demons and alternate personalities can speak in internal voices. They both can cause physical distress, such as headaches, dizziness and facial distortions. They both can express a range of emotions, such as anger, fear and resentment. However, though alters can easily express positive emotions, this is rare for demons.

Both alters and demons can exhibit differences in personality characteristics, though an alter can show a greater range of them. For example, I have met demons who whine or plead or are arrogant, proud, angry or fearful.

7. American Psychiatric Association, *The Diagnostic and Statistical Manual of Mental Disorders*, 3d ed. (Arlington, Va.: APA, 1980), 257.

Though their arrogance sometimes changed to fear and pleading as they were challenged, none showed as wide a range of personality characteristics as the alters I have met. A three-year-old alternate personality I worked with, for example, though very limited in life experience, exhibited much more personality than the demons of death and fear we cast out of her. So did the seven-year-old alter (living in the same body as the three-year-old alter) who had never been out of her hospital bed until Jesus freed her.

For insight into DID that is both Christian and cognizant of spiritual warfare, I highly recommend James Friesen's *Uncovering the Mystery of MPD*.[8] He explains the phenomenon in detail and demonstrates the close relationship between DID and satanic ritual abuse. Startlingly, 97 percent of DID patients have suffered severe childhood abuse. Furthermore, he estimates that possibly more than 50 percent of those with DID in North America have been subjected to satanic ritual abuse. He shows there is a high probability that children who suffer severe abuse then creatively produce another personality to enable them to survive the ordeal.

Friesen's observations carry much relevance for our ministry. Those who have undergone severe childhood abuse usually react in such a way that they become demonized, and the chance of developing DID is also a strong possibility. It is, however, important to recognize that treatment for demonization and treatment for multiple personalities differ. Indeed, Friesen warns, an alter accused of being a demon could grow frightened and become buried within the person for years.

So, inner voices and the switching of personalities are not always evidence of demonization, though both need to be taken seriously and dealt with in the love and power of Jesus. Though this reality complicates our approach, we can proceed with a minimum of fear if we inform ourselves. We also would do well to find a trained therapist with expertise in working with DID patients to advise and help us.

Where to From Here?

Now that we have looked at these ten myths, we need to look at the reality of demonization. There really are demons that influence human life. Jesus

8. James G. Friesen, *Uncovering the Mystery of MPD* (Eugene, Ore.: Wipf & Stock, 1997).

knew this and made His followers aware of this fact, giving them power and authority to cast them out (see Luke 9:1; see also Luke 9:2–9 and 10:1–20). We can either believe our worldview or believe Jesus.

The two pastors I mentioned at the beginning of the chapter were not different from the majority of Euroamerican pastors and their congregations. They allowed themselves to live and think under the influence of a lying worldview—a worldview that gives Westerners a pretty good grip on material and human reality but largely ignores spiritual reality, the missing hundred pieces of the puzzle.

This, until they saw a demon challenged and banished.

I myself was once where these pastors were. I lived what we would call a "normal" life, unaware of spiritual reality and its influence in the world. Oh, I read my Bible. And I knew that Jesus dealt with demons. But demons were not a part of my reality. I, too, had been duped—until I, too, had seen a demon challenged and banished.

I have been thinking lately about the definition of *normal*. Those two pastors and I considered life without demons as normal. But we read the Bible and see that Jesus and the other biblical characters had a different definition of normalcy. Whether Christ followers or Satan followers, they all believed in a very active spirit world. And Jesus followers were encouraged to take on the enemy spirits and to defeat them.

Perhaps you can see some of your own views and assumptions in some of the myths I outlined here. Furthermore, I hope you are able to see how very real the spirit world is in our lives today. Even in our Western experiences in the 21st century, demons are a factor. We need to be awake to the presence and power wielded by these dark spirit beings and know how to free people from them. Ultimately, I want to leave you with the truth that we have more power than most people realize, due to the presence of Christ in us. We need not be ignorant, fearful or powerless any longer.

12

Inner Healing Before Deliverance

When I hear people refer to my ministry as a deliverance ministry, I like to stop them to see what they understand by that term. What I and my colleagues have found is that what we do in delivering people from demons is different from what most people do. As I have shared in previous chapters, we consider demons to be a secondary problem, not the primary problem.

Many who do deliverance ministry go after the demons right away, assuming that the demon is the main problem. That approach presents at least two problems. First, it challenges the demons when they are at their strongest. This can result in a big fight that is not good for the deliverance team or for the person in whom the demons live. Second, the amount of what I am calling "garbage" may be so great that the person is a sitting duck for any banished demons to come back or for other demons like them to take advantage of the situation.

When the demons are dealt with first and banished, people often assume that all or most of the work is done, for what they consider to be the primary problem has been taken care of. Being freed from demons feels and looks so good that it is easy to neglect the number one problem: the need for inner healing. The demons may be gone, but the most important part of the healing has not taken place, and the person is at risk of being reinfested, perhaps by more demons than before (see Luke 11:26).

So I refuse to see our task as simply deliverance. I have found that the most important aspect of a deliverance ministry is never the casting out of the demons. Again, they are a secondary problem. The primary problem is dealing with what the demons are attached to. The aim is to get the person healed, not just delivered from the demons. And the heal-

> **The aim is to get the person healed, not just delivered from the demons.**

ing is not complete until the deep-level hurts and spiritual blockages that disrupt a person's relationship with God, self and others are healed under the power of the Holy Spirit. Such healing is commonly called inner healing. Other names for inner healing are the healing of memories, deep-level healing, prayer ministry or prayer counseling.

What Inner Healing Is

Inner healing, or, as I prefer to call it, deep-level healing, is a ministry in the power of the Holy Spirit aimed at bringing healing to the whole person. Since the majority of human ailments are closely tied to damage in the emotional and spiritual areas of a person's life, inner healing focuses on those areas. It seeks to bring the power of Christ to bear on healing the roots of the damage. Since those roots are often lodged in the memories carried unconsciously by the client, inner healing involves a special focus on what is sometimes called the *healing of memories*. Specific problems often encountered are shame, unforgiveness, anger, bitterness, rejection, low self-esteem, fear, worry, sexual issues and many more.

As we go through life, we get hurt. Indeed, most of us have been hurt so much that if we had a small bandage on our bodies for every time we have been hurt, we would look like mummies! When we are hurt, we do our best to keep from falling apart or reacting in such a way that our behavior is socially unacceptable. Either way, we suppress our honest (truthful) reactions.

Suppressing these reactions, with or without the help of a therapist, enables us to cope with the issues at the time. But these reactions become counterproductive later. When we suppress our true reactions, it is like putting bandages on open, unhealed wounds without first cleansing them and applying medicine. Those wounds, then, though bandaged, become infected and fester under the bandages. But the bandages leak, allowing the infection to affect our present lives long after the cause may have disappeared from our conscious memory.

Ideally, we would have dealt honestly with each hurt at the time it happened or soon afterward. We would do this by facing our true feelings, admitting them and allowing Jesus to take charge. He has invited us to come to Him with all of our heavy loads (see Matthew 11:28). We are further admonished by Paul to deal with our anger and, presumably, other such reactions before the end of each day (see Ephesians 4:26). Above all, as both Jesus and Paul made plain, we are to forgive anyone who has hurt us (see Matthew 6:14–15; Ephesians 4:32).

The fact that we have ordinarily not kept such "short accounts" with our hurts, leaving them to fester within us, results in mild to severe disruption in three relationships: with God, with ourselves and with others. Disruptions in these three relationships create most of the garbage the enemy takes advantage of. Bringing healing into those areas breaks the enemy's grip on us.

Our ideal relationship with God would see us as new and growing creatures (see 2 Corinthians 5:17), united with the Lord and one with Him in spirit (see 1 Corinthians 6:17), filled with the Holy Spirit (see Acts 2:4) and living as close to the Father as Jesus did (see John 5:19, 30).

Our ideal relationship with self would see us accepting, loving and forgiving ourselves as God accepts, loves and forgives us. We would then see ourselves as full-fledged children of God (see 1 John 3:1; Romans 8:14–17; Galatians 4:4–7), heirs with Jesus of all that God has for Him and holding our heads high as His princes and princesses. Such a relationship frees us to totally forgive any who have hurt us, including ourselves.

Our ideal relationship with others would see us accepting, loving and forgiving others as God accepts, loves and forgives them and as He has enabled us to accept, love and forgive ourselves. We would relate in a healthy, constructive manner with all others, and especially with Christians, free of envy, judgmental attitudes and other negative emotions. We would also relate properly to all God-ordained authority.

These are the ideals. The actual, however, is often far from these standards. So we find spiritual illness in all three areas of relationship. We find spiritual illness in our relationship with God as a result of sin, neglect of our relationship with God, wrong views of God and anger at God for what He has allowed to happen. In addition, we may have inherited a generational spirit or curse and be under satanic attack due to that spiritual inheritance. That inheritance, too, can cause spiritual illness.

There may be illness in our relationship with self due to feelings of unworthiness, inadequacy, shame, guilt, self-rejection and even self-hatred or self-loathing, usually stemming from reactions to childhood experiences. This may foster self-condemnation, anger and blame, leading to a refusal to accept and forgive ourself. In addition, intergenerational spirits and curses, including self-curses, or satanic attacks can damage our relationship with ourselves.

Lastly, there may be sickness in our relationships with others. Our individualism often keeps us from the right kind of closeness with others. Broken relationships, of course, bring relational illness. So do personal problems such as sin, an unhealthy self-image and attitudes such as pride, arrogance and a critical spirit. Intergenerational spirits and curses or satanic attacks also often play a role in disrupting our relationships with others.

Such relational illnesses tend to show up in emotional problems. Our reactions to what others have done or said to us or what we have done to ourselves often result in damaging attitudes, such as guilt, anger, bitterness, unforgiveness and fear. Improper family conditioning often ushers in certain responses, such as perfectionism, a performance orientation and a critical spirit.

Note that it is the reaction, not the hurt itself, that becomes the problem. Wallowing in even a legitimate reaction, then, results in the buildup of the emotional garbage on which demons feed. We often have the right to be angry or even to take revenge. But if we exercise that right, the inner infection will make us emotionally sick. So Jesus says, "Give it to Me."

Experiencing the feelings is not wrong, but holding on to them will ruin us and let demons in.

What Keeps Us from Seeking It

Such emotional illness is often signaled by a fear of facing the past. Our brains record nearly everything that happens in our lives from about two months of gestation on. However, our brains also hide and suppress the recall of the heavy stuff. This is helpful for immediate survival, but if our reactions to hurts are kept buried, the infection they produce infects the present. The trouble is that many of us have suppressed hurt for so long and know so little of what to expect if we let it surface that we respond with fear at the very suggestion of dealing with the past. And the enemy is very active in encouraging such fear.

> **Fear and the thought of possible embarrassment keep many from seeking healing.**

Instead of letting what is suppressed come to the surface and facing the stuff we fear, we may find ourselves overreacting to small irritations. We may experience depression or overt anger that seems unrelated to present circumstances. We may have weird dreams and experience strange sleep patterns. We often do not know what these things mean or what to do about them. Some people go to psychologists, and a percentage of those people gain control over such symptoms by dealing with the past. Yet, for many, it is frightening to think of exposing what is inside. *Maybe*, we reason, *it won't work anyway*. So fear and the thought of possible embarrassment keep many from seeking healing.

Hiding our inner hurt without dealing with it, however, affects our relationships with God, self and others. With God, we are uncomfortable, especially if He gets close, for we expect Him to punish and condemn us. We may be tormented by guilt, unworthiness and fear of His judgment. With self, we find ourselves mired in feelings of inadequacy and self-rejection, unable to accept love, forgiveness or acceptance from God or others. Nor can we love, forgive or accept ourselves. Instead, we blame ourselves for whatever bad things have happened to us, assuming they would not have happened if we did not deserve it. With others, we live in constant fear of discovery, assuming that if others or even God knew our past, they would reject us. We keep people at a distance and live in loneliness, envy and anger over the seeming differences between our situation and that of others. And often, physical problems develop along with these emotional difficulties. I have heard estimates by medical doctors asserting that as high as 80 percent of physical problems have emotional roots!

God's way, however, is honesty and truth. He wants us to face the past squarely and deal with it with His help. He says, as a northern Nigerian proverb puts it, "When it's time to bathe, don't try to hide your belly button!" When it is time to work toward healing, we must face and deal with everything. The good news, though, is that we can deal with our issues with Jesus and receive healing and freedom. Spiritual surgery, like physical surgery, is often painful. But it is also freeing, as stated by this man in a letter to me in 1997:

> Last Monday night, when you prayed for me, was a life-changing experience for me. I wish I could express how much better I feel now. I feel more liberated and freer than I can ever remember. I can now deal with things so much better, and I am able to think things out so much clearer. Now I feel like something has left me and at the same time I feel full inside. It is wonderful!

With Jesus, we can go back to the experiences in which we were hurt, both those we can recall and those that our brain has recorded but does not allow us to recall. We can re-experience them with Jesus there, enabling us to forgive those who hurt us and to give our pain to Jesus. The result is freedom from the bondage to the past that has crippled us and provided demons with the garbage they have been feeding on.

What a Ministry Session Looks Like

I would like to outline for you what a typical ministry session looks like, and I will use an example from a session I shared with a woman I will call Jeanie, who is a composite of typical people who come for ministry. Jeanie was in her mid-thirties, and her life had *dysfunctional* written all over it.

She described a marriage she hated, a relationship with her children that was meaningful but marred by her angry outbursts, and a childhood and earlier marriage marked by hurt, abuse, jealousy, resentment and fear.

From what Jeanie shared with me, I was pretty certain that she was demonized. She feared that she might be, though she had believed the myth that Christians could not be demonized. However, like many who believe that myth and also suspect they might have demons, she found it difficult to be sure she was saved.

Back to the Womb

As we started our time of ministry, I asked the Lord to guide us and to take over and do whatever He had planned for our session. Then I led Jeanie into an initial exercise that would take her back to the womb. What we expected to gain from this exercise was to uncover any pre-birth issues. This is based on the psychological theory that feelings and memories start in the womb at six to eight weeks of gestation and are greatly affected by what the mother is feeling and thinking during her pregnancy. We also assume that enemy forces are actively attempting to destroy or damage babies before birth.

I asked Jeanie to picture Jesus' hands, with a sperm in one hand and an egg in the other—the sperm and egg chosen before God made the world (see Ephesians 1:4). I then led her to agree with Jesus that her conception was a good idea by asking her to voluntarily put Jesus' hands together, picturing the fertilization of the egg by the sperm to produce an embryo with Jeanie's name on it.

Then I asked Jeanie, "Do you think God made a mistake in allowing you to be conceived? Or in assigning you your gender?" Many people know or suspect their parents did not want them or that they wanted them to be of the opposite sex. If the person can choose with God not only to exist, but also to be the sex God has assigned, great healing can come to the person's self-image.

As Jeanie contemplated her conception, I took authority over the father's bloodline and then the mother's to break the power of all curses and to cancel all dedications and other effects of sinful behavior. I also canceled any other satanic influences that may have been passed down through Jeanie's inheritance. Often people will not feel any response. Sometimes, though, there is a feeling of release, probably indicating that some satanic power was broken. Even if there is no felt response, not infrequently we find out later that some power was indeed broken.

Next, I took Jeanie through the months of gestation, blessing her in each of the months while looking for any uncomfortable reaction in her. Most people sail right through the months with no negative feelings. Sometimes, though, the person gets a feeling of discomfort, shame, fear, anger, loneliness, darkness or some other uncomfortable feeling. These feelings often relate to what was going on in the parents' life at that time in the child's development. One woman felt uncomfortable and had a feeling of not wanting to live, probably due to the fact that her parents were not getting along with each other and likely did not really want her to be there. I spoke against a spirit of unwantedness and asked her to give her feelings of not wanting to exist to Jesus. This she did and became very peaceful as she imagined herself giving these feelings to Jesus.

As we go from month to month, the Holy Spirit often leads us to speak against negative attitudes that may have been passed along from the person's mother. Typical attitudes are anger, fear, feelings of unworthiness, negative attitudes toward father or mother, and harmful reactions from trauma while the person was in the womb. Many such attitudes are passed on from mother to child. If the person was a twin, negative attitudes toward the other twin or issues of overdependence often have to be dealt with.

Again, we ask clients to forgive anyone who is perceived to have hurt them in the womb and to give all negative emotions to Jesus. We bless the child in each month of gestation with such things as joy, peace, excitement about coming into the world and the opposite of any negative emotions that come to their attention. If people feel they should not have been born, it is good to lead them to say something like, "I choose life."

Birth and Early Childhood

After blessing Jeanie's ninth month, I invited her to picture her birth and to note that she was born right into Jesus' arms. As Jeanie pictured

205

Jesus holding her as a baby, a feeling of pleasantness and security washed over her. She saw a pleased expression on Jesus' face.

Sometimes I ask if the umbilical cord is still connected. If it is still connected, this usually signals some unhealthy attachment (a soul tie) to mother or father that can be broken by inviting the person to enter the picture as an adult to cut and tie the cord.

I then asked Jeanie to take the baby from Jesus and to help the child to feel safe and secure in her own arms, just as she did when Jesus held her. She reported that it felt "really weird," but she soon got over that feeling and began enjoying a new bonding with herself and a love for herself.

Not infrequently, people experience some difficulty re-experiencing their birth. This usually indicates that some more inner healing needs to be done. Many find it difficult either to allow Jesus to hold them or to hold the baby themselves. A man once said to me, "I'm afraid I'll drop the baby." One man saw knives surrounding the picture of his birth. It turned out that he had a demon of hatred. Another man saw the baby disintegrate and fall through his hands. This related to guilt and anger over an abortion his wife had had without his permission.

When these things happen, it is good to stop and deal immediately with any unforgiveness, anger, unworthiness, self-curses, desire to die and the like. Most such problems relate to feelings of unworthiness or of not feeling they have a right to be alive. Sometimes it does not become immediately clear why the interference has happened. If it is not clear, those who minister should put it aside and look for clues later in the ministry session.

Inner Child

After Jeanie had re-experienced her birth and spent some time in Jesus' arms and her own arms, I invited her to grow the baby up. I asked her to search her mind for her earliest memories and to go to them with Jesus. Jeanie could recall many pleasant experiences, such as Christmases and birthdays. I helped her to see and experience Jesus in several of them. There were also several childhood sicknesses and accidents, plus some instances of verbal and physical abuse. She was able to see Jesus in each event and to forgive the perpetrators. We invited Jesus into every event that came to Jeanie's mind through her whole life.

There were also a number of fairly normal experiences, where Jeanie was hurt by people close to her, especially her father. There were things she experienced in childhood that she did not understand, such as times when she was sick and left in a hospital or with a caretaker and felt abandoned. She had been regularly left with her grandparents for several days at a time. In each case, she was able to experience Jesus in the events, to give her hurt to Him and to forgive those who had hurt or abandoned her.

> **Jesus was in each event and willing to take all of her pain on Himself.**

The big issue, however, was an involvement with a boyfriend when Jeanie was seventeen. She was romantically involved with him and doing fine until on a date he forced her to have sex with him. This hurt her so badly that she broke up with him. But she just could not forgive him or herself. When, however, she saw Jesus with her in the memory, with tears in His eyes, she was able to give her ex-boyfriend to Jesus and to release him from her anger and hatred.

Jeanie spent quite a bit of time seeing her inner children and Jesus through memory after memory in this way. The results were spectacular, both with respect to her inner healing and the weakening of the demons that were involved.

Jeanie learned that Jesus was in each event even though she was not aware of His presence at the time and that He was willing to take all of her pain on Himself. In the happy memories, she learned to enjoy them with Jesus. In the abusive and unpleasant memories, she was able to give Jesus her hurts and to forgive those who had hurt her. In this way, we probed and prayed through quite a number of the wounding events in her past. We worked on anger, resentment, jealousy and fear, and we also led her to forgive everyone she remembered who had hurt her throughout her life.

Working through the hurts year by year is the most effective way I have found to bring healing to the badly wounded parts of a person and to weaken any demons that might be present. This is typical of my approach to anyone who comes for ministry.

Kids in Seats

When we had worked through most of Jeanie's life and she had experienced Jesus in each event, I asked her to picture an auditorium with a lot of seats in it and each of her inner children sitting in the seats. She was able to picture around 25 of these inner children at various ages. I asked Jesus to join adult Jeanie in going from person to person, giving each one a long, loving hug. I asked if all these inner "selves" were happy, and if not, could they give their "stuff" to Jesus. Most of them were able to give Him what was left of their problems. Some, however, still looked sad. I asked any who needed our help to raise their hand so their "host" could see them.

Jeanie saw three hands go up. One was about 8 years old, who hurt badly when her father had slapped her. The others were approximately 13 and 22. Though we had to work a bit, we were able to help Jeanie's eight-year-old self to forgive by giving her father to Jesus, who has promised to pay back any who have hurt us (see Romans 12:19). Once the 8-year-old had settled this issue, Jeanie saw the child with a smile on her face. We did a similar thing with Jeanie's 13-year-old self and her 22-year-old self. The 17-year-old who had been raped was already happy.

When this was finished, Jeanie saw all of her inner children dancing with Jesus, happy and free, except for the demons.

What Inner Healing Is About

Perhaps the most important reason to use inner healing during deliverance is that the process enables us to really demonstrate the love of Jesus. I cannot emphasize enough the fact that the main goal of deliverance, or any healing ministry, is not simply to experience the power of Jesus or even to fight against and defeat the enemy. It is to minister the *love* of Jesus. For if what we do is not loving, it is not being done in Jesus' way. And it is not, therefore, as healing as He intended it to be. Jesus used His power to show His love. So should we.

That is one reason I am against "big shows" when doing deliverance. Allowing demons to inspire fear with violence, screaming and vomiting is not a loving thing to do to the demonized person. When this happens, it

208

is no wonder that many regret ever having let themselves in for the experience. Many shy away from deliverance, even when they are pretty sure they need it. Though in the biblical examples we sometimes see brief violence, it nowhere approximates the amount we see in some contemporary deliverance ministries. Instead, we see Jesus and His followers casting out demons calmly and showing love to the victims.

We practice inner healing not only because it is effective, but also because it provides a loving way to minister to the wounded. I am constantly in awe of what Jesus does when we simply invite Him to come and minister to those who hurt. Time and time again, He shows up in powerful yet tender ways—touching the deep wounds within people in ways we could never imagine. He alone knows the deep pain buried within the hearts of those to whom we minister. When we call upon the Holy Spirit to guide, He gently leads from painful event to painful event, healing each as He goes along.

13

Deliverance

We deal with the inner healing issues first because we are concerned about healing, not simply deliverance from the demons. As I have already mentioned, many who deal with demonization focus on deliverance, assuming that the object is to banish any demons that are there. But that is not our primary aim. *Our primary aim is healing.* So we need to give primary attention to dealing with the big problems, the human ones that the demons are attached to. When these are dealt with and the person is free emotionally and spiritually, it is usually fairly easy to kick out the demons.

Another reason for doing inner healing first is that we do not want a fight if we can avoid it. We can think of the strength of a demon on a scale from 1 to 10. If the demon is strong, say at a level 7, and we challenge him before the human garbage is dealt with, he will have the strength to cause a fight. A level-7 demon has a lot of power. But that power is calibrated to the amount and kind of garbage he is feeding on. If, though, the garbage is dealt with, the demon loses strength and he is usually easy to get rid of without any violence. If the demon is reduced to level 0, he will have no ability to cause a fight.

Attend to Pre-Deliverance Issues

The first thing to know is that deliverance sessions should be bathed in prayer. We are working in partnership with the Holy Spirit, and in prayer we are claiming His assistance. We cannot do this by ourselves. We need His guidance and empowerment. We do not have to be frantic, however. Jesus was serious about deliverance, but He never got frantic. Our dependence on the Holy Spirit should be a natural thing, based on the knowledge that He is with us and in favor of what we are doing.

It is good to enlist prayer partners who will intercede as we minister. But we should not have to wait for them if we are approached without warning. We should be ready at all times to minister in the love and power of Jesus, even if we do not have time for special preparation. If we have time to prepare or if we know that the session is likely to be a difficult one, it is a good idea to fast as well. However, neither fasting nor any other preparation is magic. This has nothing to do with magic or superstition; it is about partnership with Jesus to get people free. There is no magical power in fasting or worshiping, in and of themselves, though God is pleased to flow His power through such vehicles.

Additionally, it is best to minister in teams whenever possible. A team of three works well—a leader whose focus is on the client, a second person to pray and listen to the Lord for information that the lead person may not be hearing, and a third to pray and take notes. One important reason for working in teams is that each person has different gifts, especially gifts that the leader may not have, that can be utilized for the benefit of the person receiving ministry.

Let Them Know Your Authority

Next, it is crucial that the demons know that you know your authority. A major part of the demons' strategy has been to keep Christians from knowing who they are and the authority this gives them. So, assert your authority at the start. Jesus said we would do the works that He did (see John 14:12), and a major part of His ministry was to confront and defeat demons.

I often start by asking the demons if they recognize the name of Jesus Christ. They usually answer yes or may remain silent in acknowledgment of the fact that He is Lord. I then ask if they recognize that I come with His authority. They usually answer yes to that question as well. They know the authority is there. One of them asked me, "Where did you get all this power?" I simply said, "Remember who we serve."

I then like to say something like the following:

> I command all demons to attention. If you are here without rights, I command you to leave and not come back. If you are here with rights, I command you to step aside. I forbid you to interfere with whatever Jesus wants to do. We are in His presence, and you must obey Him.

Next, I claim protection for all of us in the group—myself, the client and all that we hold dear, such as family and possessions. I have had demons cause headaches, stomachaches or pain or in other ways attack members of our group. They have even caused problems with people's animals or plants to distract us from dealing with them. To prevent any such things, I say something like this:

> I claim protection in the name of Jesus Christ for each one of us, our families, our friends, our property, our finances, our health and everything else that pertains to us from any revenge or other dirty tricks from the enemy.

If I suspect that there might be interference from higher-level spirits or other spirits inside the person, I cut off any spirits inside the person from help by other spirits outside or inside the person, saying something like:

> In the name of Jesus, I cut off any spirits inside this person from any help they might receive from outside spirits or from any others inside the person.

I then forbid any violence, throwing up or other diversionary behavior, saying something like:

> I forbid any spirits inside this person to cause any violence, any throwing up or any other diversionary behavior. You are in the presence of Jesus Christ, and you must obey Him.

In addition, there are certain more general things to remember concerning the person being ministered to. Among them are:

1. Do everything in love.
2. Maintain the person's dignity at all times.
3. Strengthen the person's will at every opportunity.
4. Continually encourage the person before, during and after the session.

People often ask me why I do not allow the demons to manifest, as many deliverance ministers do. They point out that Jesus allowed demons to throw their victims on the ground (see Mark 9:26). I answer that I do not know why Jesus allowed these things, but if I can prevent them, I will. I believe love should be our primary goal. I want the person to experience God's love in getting free, and I do not think it is loving to allow the demons to cause violence, though I trust that Jesus had His own reasons for allowing this kind of behavior. I very seldom experience even a small amount of violence from the demons we expel.

Take Care of General Matters

When the inner healing is finished and all the emotional and spiritual problems dealt with, it is time to challenge the demons. The first order of business is to deal with some general things. First, I ask the client for permission to check to see if there are demons there. If I ask this permission and the person refuses, I go no further. It is not good to go beyond what a person is willing to do.

If permission is given, it is good to first tackle any general demonic activity, such as:

1. Family, intergenerational or bloodline demons
2. A curse of unwantedness
3. Other curses
4. Soul ties
5. Vows

Family, Intergenerational or Bloodline Demons

Many people, and perhaps most, are carrying one or more family, intergenerational or bloodline demons inherited from their parents. These are spirits invited in by an ancestor. If an ancestor was in an occult organization, such as Freemasonry, or a member of a society that dedicates each child to their gods, there will be family demons.

We can challenge these spirits and break their power by taking away all authority and power they have gained in this person's life. We claim the authority of Jesus and of the client to break the power of the demons. We can announce this to the family demons and send them to Jesus by saying something like:

> I challenge family spirit of [person's name]'s family and cancel all rights you claim. I break your power and send you to Jesus.

A Curse of Unwantedness

Frequently, there is a curse of unwantedness at work in a person. If a mother did not want to be pregnant for whatever reason or wanted a child of the opposite sex, the person was unwanted. Many parents want a boy and get a girl. The child feels this rejection in the womb. The person then grows up feeling unwanted or trying to be the opposite sex. The curse is usually easy to break, however, simply by claiming Jesus' power to cancel it.

Other Curses

Other curses need to be dealt with as well. Many people have cursed themselves, their bodies or something else about themselves, usually during adolescence. Because curses belong to those who put the curse on, they can be broken by that person or someone in authority over the person who renounces them and cancels them in the name of Jesus. Curses put on by other people can also be canceled and returned to their senders as blessings.

Soul Ties

I picture soul ties as pipes or thick wires carrying satanic power from someone who wields power over another person to that other person. The most frequent type of soul tie is created by sex outside of marriage. The sinful spiritual "material" resulting from all of the person's previous sexual relationships flows through the pipe into the sex partner.

Other dominating relationships also create soul ties. Among these are mother-daughter relationships where a daughter is dominated by her mother. Often when the mother is aged, she becomes dependent on the daughter so that the daughter "becomes" the mother and the mother "becomes" the daughter. Another example of a soul tie is when a church or other organization is dominated by its leader in such a way that all major decisions must be approved by that pastor. Soul ties, like curses, can be broken by speaking the power of Jesus to break them.

Vows

Vows are a kind of self-curse, where a person vows to never do something. Typical vows are "I will not be like my mother" or "I will never have children" or "I will never let a man near me again" or the like. These should be renounced and given to Jesus.

Know How Demons Talk

I am frequently asked how we can hear what demons are saying. "Does a demon have a special voice?" some ask. The answer is that sometimes, yes, it does. If the demon is strong, he may change the person's voice or at least make it sound more gruff or angry. Usually, however, it uses the same voice as the person the demon inhabits. An experience I had just the other day was typical. The person's face showed great anger and the voice was low and threatening as he said, "I hate you." But the demon's power was gone and he could not do anything about his hatred for me. I simply replied, "Thank you."

One reason the demon uses the normal voice of the person is that we have taken away his power by doing the inner healing. No more power, no voice change. So the demon uses the person's normal voice and the words come out as if it is the client speaking, but the demon has taken over the client's voice and can deceive the client into thinking it is his or her voice.

Another scenario that happens a lot is that the demon speaks to the person internally and then the person simply repeats what he or she is hearing. The hearing is not a physical hearing but more of an impression that the person gets. This impression comes in a way that is usually very familiar to the person since he or she has been hearing it all his or her life, often not recognizing until later that it has been the enemy's voice.

Still another way the enemy speaks is through an impression that the one ministering or sometimes someone else receives. This way is through words of knowledge coming as direct revelations from God to the one leading the ministry or to a team member.

Sometimes the voice is heard by someone other than the client. The first time I experienced this it confused me a lot. A person other than the one I was ministering to began answering the questions I was commanding the demon to answer. When I got over the shock, I learned that the answers were right on. I was grateful for the information and that the team member was able to use her spiritual gift to give us the information we needed to get rid of the demons.

Make a "Suspects" List

During the inner healing portion of ministry, I make a list of what I have learned to call "suspects."[1] This list is developed from what the person has told me about some feelings he or she has experienced or hurts or sin in his or her life. In my ministry, I have the client fill out a questionnaire that asks, among other things, what emotional or spiritual issues the client is aware of. This alerts me to many of the hurts and emotions to which demons are likely attached.

1. I learned this method from an Oklahoma City deliverance minister named Everett Cox.

For example, I have on the questionnaire a section called "Problems" where I have listed a number of emotional problems, such as anger, shame, fear, rejection, lust, pride, death wish and the like. Whatever the client has checked off from that list makes me suspicious that there is a demon attached to that function. I may not be 100 percent sure, but this gives me a place to start. And I have found that the percentage is high that there are demons attached to the emotions on the suspects list.

> The percentage is high that there are demons attached to the emotions on the suspects list.

Many people are struggling with anger or its associates—bitterness, resentment, depression, rage, disappointment, frustration or discouragement. If the person has checked these emotions on the questionnaire, I will write *anger* on my suspects list. When I write *anger* on the list, I know that this label stands for all or most of the other items listed above. The demons named in parentheses below are the "family members" of the lead demon in each group. So my suspects list may look like this:

Anger (bitterness, resentment, depression, rage, disappointment, discouragement, frustration)

Shame (guilt, deception, lying spirits)

Fear (worry, anxiety, panic)

Rejection (abandonment, neglect, self-rejection)

Death (death wish, suicide, abortion, murder, infirmity)

Lust (fantasy, adultery, pornography)

Homosexuality (lesbianism)

Performance (striving)

Pride (arrogance)

Control (domination)

Abuse (violence, rape)

Occult spirits (Ouija, yoga, tarot, fortune-telling, Freemasonry, Scientology, Islam, Buddhism, Mormonism, Jehovah's Witnesses)

Etc. (many other emotions, religions or occult organizations)

In people's stories, there are other clues as well. As the persons describe experiences they had and their reaction to them, we get a picture of the emotional and spiritual issues to which demons are attached. There may also be demons attached to such things as compulsive behavior, disturbing dreams or family spirits.

The spirits are arranged in groups, so I challenge the group leaders, break their power and lock them in boxes to send them to Jesus. I call for each head spirit in order to come to attention and to tell me what legal right, if any, he has to stay in this person. If he has no right, I bind him together with his helpers and command them to go into a locked box.

Once the spirit is in the locked box, his power is broken and he is safely out of the way as I deal with the next group. I can still talk to demons in the boxes if I need to in order to get more information, but they are no longer free to do their work. Their power is broken.

If it is difficult to get a spirit into the box, it is usually because more inner healing needs to be done. So we look for things we missed that the demon may still be attached to. We can command the demon to tell us what it is, and often he will. If so, we take care of the problem and then kick the demon out.

On one occasion, I was trying unsuccessfully to get a demon out. So I asked the demon if there was anyone else the person needed to forgive. The demon replied, "Her sister." The woman was surprised but agreed that she had not forgiven her sister. So, she forgave the sister. This broke the demon's power. We were then easily able to kick the demon out.

Frequently, the thing that has to be dealt with is a curse or an inter-generational problem. The person may have inherited one of the demonic problems on the above list, and it may not have gotten dealt with yet. If so, I command the demon to reveal how many generations ago he entered and then claim the power of Jesus to break his power in each generation. I may say something like this:

In the name of Jesus, I take authority over that curse [six] generations back through the [father/mother] and break your power in the [sixth, fifth, fourth, third, second and first] generations. And I cut off any power you have over [her/him] through your involvement in this family.

As soon as this is done, we usually see a noticeable change in the strength of the demon. If you suspect an intergenerational root but for some reason cannot get confirmation either by word of knowledge or from the demon, guess that there is one and say something like:

> In the name of Jesus, I take authority over you, intergenerational spirit of [depression], coming through the [father's/mother's] bloodline, and I break your power and cover whatever gives you the power with the blood of Jesus. I forbid you to have any more power over [person's name]. I break the power of the curse concerning [homosexuality] that has come through the [mother's/ father's] bloodline in the name of Jesus Christ.

Since things are invisible, we are not always sure what is happening. When in doubt, though, I feel it is better to go ahead and speak against a curse or intergenerational spirit, since breaking any power operative in this area can have a major effect on the strength of the demons.

Know Their Legal Rights

I have mentioned legal rights of demons several times, and this is because the spirit world works legalistically. So, whether Satan or God, their rights are granted according to the rules God has set up to govern the universe.

One of the rules God has set up is that if a person holds on to anger or any other negative emotional reaction, a demon has the legal right to live inside that person. This is spoken of in Ephesians 4:26–27, where we are told to not hold on to anger past sundown, which marks the end of the Jewish day, lest we give the devil an opportunity—a legal right—to cause us trouble, presumably from inside of us.

Other legal rights come from curses, vows, sin, witchcraft, involvement in occult organizations or the like. In short, whatever one gives to the enemy constitutes a legal right.

Positive legal rights stem from our relationship with and obedience to Jesus. Commitment to Him and His will in our lives gives Jesus rights. A relationship with Him gives us authority and power over all demons and all diseases (see Luke 9:1). Jesus has given us tremendous authority and power, and it is our legal right to use it in His service.

Feel Free to Discuss Strategy

Feel free to interrupt the process of getting demons out at any time to take care of whatever comes up. There is no magical spell that can be broken by interruption. Frequently, it is advisable to take a break to discuss strategy with your team. It can also be worth taking a break to stretch, go to the bathroom and seek more guidance and/or power in prayer.

When you take a break to discuss strategy, say, "In the name of Jesus, I forbid any spirits to hear what I am about to say." This blocks them from hearing what we are discussing. When you are finished with your discussion, do not forget to give the demons permission to hear again. I have had times when I forgot to allow them to hear again and they could not hear when I wanted to challenge them!

On one occasion, I was called on the telephone by a lady who clearly had demonic problems. Before I made an appointment with her to come see me, I forbade the demons to hear what we were plotting. When I met with the lady, I asked the demon if he knew we were getting together. The demon said, "No. She knew, but she wouldn't tell us." I asked, "Didn't you ask other demons about our plans?" The demon said, "I couldn't find out from them. You had forbidden us to hear."

Do Not Let Them Take Control

The demons may try to divert attention from your attempts to break their power by causing pain, shaking the person, bringing diversionary thoughts into his or her mind, telling the person lies or even making the person nauseous or making him or her throw up. If so, forbid them and continue to assert your authority, even if it does not work at first. Take their control away from them, and forbid them to exert any control at all.

You do not need to shout or do strange things when dealing with demons.

They are neither hard of hearing nor impressed with our doing strange things. Though this is a power game, their primary weapon is bluff. They cannot outpower us, but they may outbluff us if we let them. Keep control, even if you feel insecure inside.

One thing you can do that is often helpful is to ask Jesus to assign several large, powerful angels to assist in getting the person free. When this is done, often the demons will admit that they see both the angels and Jesus. The presence of the angels intimidates them. If they do not cooperate, you can even have the angels punish the demons by using their swords or by doing embarrassing things like covering their bodies with crosses or replacing their horns with crosses, which they really do not like.

Lock Them in Boxes

I use locked boxes in which to gather each group of demons before I send them to Jesus. For each one, I usually ask the angels to lower a box over the group and lock the demons in so they cannot escape. As I go along, I ask each group, "Are you all in the box?" They may or may not tell me. They are usually upset at what is happening and may not be in a mood to cooperate. But they seem proud if they can stay out of the box and usually let me know if they can stay out.

When those of one group are all in their box, I go ahead to the next group. If there are one or more demons who do not get into the box, we need to do more inner healing. Often the issue that has been forgotten is unforgiveness. When the issue is dealt with, the demons' rights are gone and they can be sent to Jesus.

Some people do not like the use of boxes. They seem to think that there is something wrong with collecting the demons that way. However, this is simply a way of organizing the capturing of the demons and the sending of them to Jesus. I see no spiritual problem in collecting them that way. If the person prefers some other mechanism, though, this is no problem for me. One of my disciples uses garbage cans for the same purpose. Others prefer to simply bind them with cords of the Holy Spirit.

Remind Them of Their Identity

Sometimes you can simply say, "Spirit of _____, I command you to come out in Jesus' name and go to the feet of Jesus." If they leave, well and good. Usually, however, this is not enough. If the head demon in a group refuses, command it to tell you what right it still has to live in the person. Command it in the name of Jesus to tell the truth and to tell everything.

> **Demons do not like to hear about the blood shed on the cross or about the tomb from which Jesus escaped.**

If the demon continues to resist, you may find it useful to remind him of who he is and how he and his kingdom have been defeated. You may want the angels to punish or torment the demons. Demons do not like the angels to use their swords on them or to have their limbs cut off. Colossians 2:15 is a good verse to quote, as it says, "On that cross Christ freed himself from the power of the spiritual rulers and authorities; he made a public spectacle of them by leading them as captives in his victory procession." They hate that reminder that their leader has been humiliated and led by Jesus in a victory parade. Remind them of the cross and the empty tomb. Demons do not like to hear about the blood shed on the cross or about the tomb from which Jesus escaped.

Know What Deliverance Looks Like

When the time has come to challenge the demons, I may not be sure whether or not there are demons present. I find out by challenging them directly, as if they are there. If they are, they answer. If there is no answer, either they are too weak to answer or they are not there.

Going back to the example of Jeanie from chapter 12, we spent about an hour with her, doing inner healing and dealing with her anger, unforgiveness and tangle of damaged emotions: fear, self-rejection, depression and discouragement. Having worked through her life, getting the hurts healed, I then asked her permission to challenge any demons that might be present.

Jeanie was carrying demons, mostly with the above names. Most people with deep-seated emotional problems are carrying demons, in fact. And they were running Jeanie on a merry chase as long as she had a lot of unresolved emotions on which they could piggyback. With those hard-to-handle emotions healed, however, it was fairly easy to kick out the demons.

Challenging the Demons

In challenging the demons, I started by calling all the spirits to attention and commanding them to line up in front of Jesus where Jeanie could see them. I forbade them to hide or to go to any other host. In some cases I may at this time forbid them again to cause any violence or throwing up.

I will then usually challenge the demons by using their "function name," the name of whatever emotional or spiritual problem I suspect may be reinforced by the demons. Though the demons may have other names, they respond to the label of their function. For example, I address the spirit of anger as "Anger," the spirit of shame as "Shame," the spirit of rejection as "Rejection" and so on.

I will typically choose one demon and say something like:

Spirit of [anger], I challenge you in the name of Jesus Christ. I command you to come to attention. I forbid you to hide or to go to any other host.

Sometimes the demons seem to be too weak to respond. They do not say anything, so I am not sure they are there. When this happens, I go through the process that I use on demons I know are there. I am sure that by doing this I have sometimes cast out demons that are not there! But this is a small price to pay to get the ones that are there.

Do not give up if they are not responding. I have had many cases where I was not sure if demons were there but cast them out anyway and have had reports later that the person is free and that there is evidence that we did indeed cast out demons.

Not infrequently, it is necessary to challenge several demons before you get a response from any. I often try several names from my suspects list in succession. I will frequently press hardest on those I feel may be weakest, especially if I am quite sure they are present, on the assumption that the weakest may be easier to make contact with than the stronger ones.

I do not try hard to get the demon's name. Some people teach that we have greater power over demons if we know their names. I have not found that to be true. If I do not already have an idea of what the spirit's name and function might be, I command it to tell me what it is or I simply address it by its function or simply as "spirit." Getting them to admit their names is often difficult. But sometimes the spirit has already done something by which it can be identified—for example, I might say, "Spirit that has caused that shaking, come to attention."

When the inner healing is finished, the demons' power is gone or nearly gone. There may, however, still be things that have not come out yet. Jeanie still had a couple of issues keeping us from getting the demons out. I frequently ask the head demon of the group I am challenging if he and his underlings are ready to go or if they still have anything on the person. They will usually claim they have nothing left, even if there is still stuff. Sometimes, though, they will volunteer that there is additional stuff to deal with. If so, I go back to the inner healing mode and deal with it. If not, I put them in locked boxes to be sent to Jesus later.

As at all other times, my commands are firm but not loud. Jesus did not shout or get emotional. Neither did He coax the demons out, as did the Pharisees of His day. He treated the demons roughly and then cast them out (see Mark 1:25). We should be forceful and authoritative but patient if it takes a while. Know who you are and the authority Jesus has given you. The demons know and tremble, lest you know how to use the power and authority Jesus has given you.

Calling Out the Spirits

Back to the story of Jeanie. I first called up a spirit of shame. (I like to start with Shame, Guilt, Deception and the Lying Spirits.) At the start, I may have to challenge the first demon several times before I get it to respond. Once I have made contact with the first demon, it seems to get easier to get responses from the others. I think this is because the client is not used to this process at first but gets more used to it as we go along.

224

Jeanie had been regularly shamed by her father and her husband and, in turn, was ashamed of them. So I had a strong suspicion that demons of shame were there. They usually answer unless they are too weak to speak because we have taken away their strength by getting the human problems healed. They will usually speak to the person's mind and then the person reports what he or she hears; sometimes they are able to take over the person's vocal cords and speak right out.

I asked if Shame had any legal right to stay. Jeanie's demon was silent, so I went on to Guilt. (I do not stay long if they do not answer.) Then I went on to Deceit and commanded him to tell us some of the lies he had been feeding her. This usually gets a response, even if the demon has not answered so far, and as each lie is stated, I ask Jesus to tell us the truth.

He said, "I tell her she's no good." So I asked Jeanie, "What is Jesus saying?" She reported that Jesus disagreed, saying, "She's My precious daughter. She's special." I made the demon confess to Jeanie that he had been behind the lies she had been believing about herself, her father, her husband and several other people. She was then able to give both the demons and the lies to Jesus. So I commanded Shame and his associates to be locked in a box until we would send them to Jesus later.

Then we called up the spirit of anger. Jeanie had told me that Anger had been very strong. As she dealt with her anger and gave it to Jesus, however, the demon of anger became much weaker. He headed a group that included rage, bitterness, resentment, depression, disappointment, discouragement and frustration. I commanded Anger, under the power of the Holy Spirit, to tell me if Jeanie still needed to forgive anyone. He said she still had something against her younger brother. I asked Jeanie to deal with that, and she did. Then I asked the demon if he still had any legal right to stay. He did not, so I commanded him, with his helpers, into another locked box.

We then dealt with the demon of hate, who lurked behind the fact that Jeanie hated herself. I helped Jeanie to see a crown on her head and a lovely gown, signifying who she really is, a child of the King (see 1 John 3:1) and, therefore, a princess. This thought excited her, and she was able to agree with Jesus that she was acceptable and forgivable and, on that basis, to choose to accept, forgive and love herself. Once this was done, the spirit

225

of hate admitted that he and his cohorts had no more right to stay within her. And soon we got them locked in another box.

We found several other demons as well. They had names like Rejection, Fear, Worry, Abuse and Death (since Jeanie had contemplated suicide and had also had a miscarriage). Each had helpers, and I commanded them, along with their helpers, to be bound together and locked in boxes.

Sending Them to Jesus

When all the demons I had identified were in the boxes, I asked the angels to gather any demons that I may have missed into another box. Then I asked the angels to take the locked boxes to Jesus and to ask Him to dispose of them and their contents, separating the demons from the person forever.

I said something like:

> I separate these demons from Jeanie as far as the East is from the West and place the cross and the empty tomb between Jeanie and these spirits forever. I forbid any of them to ever return or to send any others.

Then I asked Jesus to show Jeanie what He did with the boxes. She was able to see the boxes and told me that Jesus had flung them out into the ocean. Sometimes He throws them into darkness or into the ocean or into fire.

When Jesus had disposed of the boxes, I said something like, "Let the empty space, vacated by the demons, be filled with peace." Then I blessed Jeanie with blessings like courage, patience, love and strength. Next, I spoke the filling of all the empty space from where the demons had been in Jeanie with peace, love, patience, courage and a number of other blessings.

I then like to ask the client how he or she feels. Jeanie responded that she felt lighter and very peaceful in her mind and heart. Over the following days, she reported that there were no more voices in her head and no more negative emotions pushing her to live in anger. The change was so great that Jeanie reported she was going through an identity crisis, as she was learning how to live in the newness that became possible through the ministry session. Her husband noticed the difference right away and made an appointment with me to deal with his own problems.

Administer Post-Deliverance Counseling

Jeanie's experience of feeling herself going through a bit of an identity crisis leads me to the next important point: It is important to counsel the newly freed person. The person needs to know what is likely to happen next and what to do about it. What should he or she do if the problems were not completely dealt with or if the demons try to come back?

For most people, these seem to be non-issues. That is, the problems we worked on together seem to be solved or so greatly changed that the person can "finish up" on his or her own. But for a significant minority, there continue to be issues and a need for help in changing the habits that have been empowering the problems.

At the end of a ministry session, then, I like to seal all that the Holy Spirit has done by saying something like:

> I seal in Jesus' name all that He has done here. We close all doors through which the demons gained entrance and remove all vulnerabilities in Jesus' name but speak the continuance of any processes that are still incomplete.

It is important to remind the person of who he or she is in Christ. The enemy has been lying to the person about this, for he does not want any of us to know who we are. Now the freed person needs to assert his or her will in a new way to make the truth of his or her position in Christ real. This person is Jesus' child (see Romans 8:14–17; 1 John 3:1–3; Galatians 4:5–7), set apart to become like Jesus (see Romans 8:29) and called by Jesus to be His friend (see John 15:15). Jesus Himself chose (see John 15:16) and empowered him or her (see Luke 9:1). And any fear that we feel is to be banished, since fear is not from God (see 2 Timothy 1:7).

The enemy knows who we are, and it frightens him to think that we might find out. But remember: We are like spiritual elephants. The enemy is like a spiritual mouse. The mouse only wins by bluffing, but the elephant holds the real power.

We are, therefore, to take authority over any demons that try to return and to send them away again. Eventually, they will get tired of trying and go somewhere else. If the demons do not give up right away, neither should we. Demons may try to get back in because they feel they own the territory we have just taken away from them. But if they have been forbidden to come back, they cannot—unless the person invites them in again. The person needs to know this and that the demons cannot come back if they have been forbidden to come back. But demons can try to fake it by working from outside the person if allowed to try.

On one occasion after a ministry session, demons came back the same night, announcing their presence to the person by saying, "We're back!" The man came to, trying to wipe the sleep from his eyes, and eventually was able to ask, "Are you inside or outside?" The demon replied, "Outside." The man, then, claimed his authority by saying something like, "Okay, then get out of here! Your rights are gone." The demons left and never came back.

To prevent demons from coming back, I like to use words such as the following:

> In Jesus' name, we forbid any of these spirits to return or to send any others. We declare that this person belongs totally to Jesus Christ and allow no further trespassing by enemy agents. We place Jesus' cross and His empty tomb between this person and the spirits.

It is often important to remind clients concerning their authority in Christ and the right they have to use Jesus' power to ward off any further attacks. I like to point out that they have the same Holy Spirit as I do and, therefore, the same authority. James 4:7 says, "*Resist* the devil, and he will flee from you" (NIV, emphasis mine). The implication is that we are to continually resist. It may not be just a one-time thing.

The person will need to get into a support group and also perhaps begin working with a professional Christian counselor. Healing often requires more support and perhaps also therapy while the person is learning new habits. Either inner healing or professional counseling is considered therapy, while a small group or accountability to a friend is considered support. Often the best arrangement is for some or all of the ministry team members to continue with the person as a support group. Close relationships with other Christians can help ward off most of what the enemy brings to us. Enfolding into a church and Sunday school class can be ideal. In addition to the support they give, the members of such a group can advise if the person needs professional counseling or more inner healing.

It is very important for the person to keep clean of the stuff to which the demons had attached. The person needs to be willing to change habits, attitudes, friends and whatever else may be necessary to keep the healing and freedom God has given and to build on it. Getting back into old patterns or associating with former friends can open the door for further infestation.

One woman I was working with opened herself up to further infestation by reverting to a pattern she had engaged in prior to our ministry session. We had cast several demons out of her, including a strong spirit of death. But she got very discouraged, took a razor blade and cut her thumb just enough to draw blood. Then, reverting to the pattern she had practiced before our ministry session, to gain more power, she put the wound to her mouth as if she were kissing it. This invited another spirit of death to enter her.

Realizing what she had done, she called me. I asked the demon if he was the same one we had cast out. He said, "No, I'm a different one. That one could not get back in because you forbade him to." I asked when he had gotten in and he said, "When she kissed me!" I then asked where he had come from and he said, "I was just flying around, waiting for her to invite me in." So we kicked him out.

The person needs to work at getting healed in any related areas not yet dealt with, lest any such areas afford opportunity for demons to re-enter. He or she also needs personal spiritual growth. Prayer, praise, worship, Bible study and one's devotional life need to be worked at. These practices bring growth and protection against practices that provide openings for demons to enter.

Address the Issue of Habits

As I have mentioned, though we had gotten the roots healed, Jeanie still had to deal with the habits that were fed by those roots, and I warned her that could be a challenge. Inner healing deals with the roots of people's problems. Once the roots are gone, there still are habits, many of them long-standing, that if not addressed could lead the person back into emotional, spiritual or demonic problems.

I want people to retain the freedom God has given them during our deep-level healing sessions. Many clients will automatically do what they need to do next; many others, however, may find old habits to be tenacious as they try to conquer them. In addition, demons that have been cast out will often try to harass their former hosts from outside and to convince them that nothing has changed. Though now on the outside, they would like the person to believe they are still inside and still have power over him or her. New "freedom habits" need to be developed, and clients need to assert the authority they have in Christ to chase away any harassing demons.

> **Once the roots are gone, there still are habits.**

Habits are notoriously hard to break. But they are much easier to break once the roots are gone. However, just as we have had to work with Jesus to heal the roots, so we need to work with Him to change the habits. Many women struggling to deal with body hatred, for instance, have found it helpful to work with a full-length mirror, standing in front of it and talking to themselves. They usually say something like, "I love you," "Jesus says you're beautiful" or something similar and are in this way able to break the habit of hating their bodies. They then can replace the hatred habit with the habit of loving their bodies. It may not be easy, and it may take some time, but it works. It worked for me.

I have worked with people whose habit was to take on other people's problems. Such people need to learn to place the blame where it belongs rather than on themselves. I have also worked with people whose habit was to blame others for their own choices. They need help developing the habit of taking responsibility for their own attitudes.

I was once asked to minister to a man who had been beating himself up for about thirty years because of an accident in which a gun he was holding went off and killed his brother. He was marvelously healed from the root issue of the guilt he felt as he experienced Jesus' freeing love and power. But his lifelong attitude, or habit, had been to blame himself for the accident, as if he had deliberately killed his brother, and to condemn himself in situation after situation that had no relationship with the accident. This

230

latter habit needed to be addressed after the root issue had been healed. We did this, and he went free.

In my own case, I spent time with my bathroom mirror, telling myself that I loved myself. The change from self-hatred to self-love has been dramatic over the years. But it did not come automatically, such as when I first dealt with the rejection I felt at my conception because my mother did not want to be pregnant. I had to work with Jesus to change the self-hatred habit that I had been living with for fifty years.

For my part, I simply looked at myself in the mirror from time to time and said, either out loud or to myself, "I love you!" This was extremely difficult for me—at first I had to wink as I said the words. But I forced myself to do it, and it worked.

After months of doing this, I found that I began to feel differently about myself. This, in itself, since it was favorable, was a huge thing for me. But the exciting thing that happened after a couple of years was a bigger surprise. I looked at myself one day, enjoying my new attitude toward myself, and all of a sudden the thought came: *I not only love you, I like you!* Like is above love in our attitude toward ourselves. We can choose to love ourselves with little or no emotion. But it takes real, positive feeling to like ourselves. I seemed to have crossed an invisible line from love to like. This feeling, then, had become a habit or attitude—an attitude that has never left me.

The same kind of exercise can be used if the issue is self-forgiveness, guilt, shame, fear or most any other habitual attitude we might have toward ourselves. The idea is to do something regularly that confronts the negative habit and replaces it with a positive one.

Talking to oneself in a mirror is the most effective way I have found to work on changing the habit of self-hatred or self-rejection. We can look into a mirror regularly and say such things as "I love you" or "You are beautiful" or "God has forgiven you; you are free to forgive yourself" or "You are deeply loved by Jesus" or any of a number of positive things that confront the lies we have been hearing. I suggest a person do this daily for weeks or months or longer until the habit is changed. Changing self-image is a very important thing for most people to focus on, and changing negative habits is a good way to get it done.

Other habits may need other strategies. If a person's previous habit was using drugs or alcohol, he or she obviously needs to keep away from those substances. It is important to find something to take their place, and organizations are widely available to help with that.

With this chapter, we conclude our treatment of ground-level demons. We have dealt with what demons are and what they do. We have looked at how to challenge and get rid of them. Now we turn to dealing with cosmic-level, or higher-level, demons.

Part 5

Cosmic-Level

SPIRITUAL WARFARE

14

Cosmic-Level Spirits

The upper level of spiritual warfare is ordinarily known as *cosmic-level warfare* (called *strategic-level warfare* by C. Peter Wagner). At the cosmic level, we have to deal with at least five kinds of higher-level satanic spirits. These are territorial spirits, institutional spirits, vice spirits, household spirits and ancestor spirits. The order in which I list these spirits does not necessarily represent a hierarchical ordering of the spirits. For example, I am not sure that vice spirits are less powerful than institutional spirits. It is probable, however, that territorial spirits have greater power and authority than the others.

Everything we have learned leads us to believe that Satan is just as active at the cosmic level as he is at the ground level. Thus, cosmic-level spiritual warfare is just as crucial as ground-level warfare. We get a glimpse in Scripture of what is going on at this level in Job 1, then again in Daniel 10 and again in Jude 8–9, as well as in other places. Cosmic-level spirits are the spirits mentioned in Ephesians 2:2, where Satan is called the "ruler of the spiritual powers in space." The listing of spirit types in Ephesians 6:12, then, suggests a hierarchy in the evil spiritual world.[1] As the author

1. My theory is that each of the levels (territorial, institutional, vice, etc.) is organized in hierarchical fashion with labels such as those given in Ephesians 6:12.

of the book of Daniel correctly saw, God's host of His own spirits (angels) counters those of the enemy (see Daniel 10:12–13, 20–21). But the activity of both God's and Satan's emissaries is at least partially dependent on human partnership.

Cosmic-level satanic spirits seem to be in charge of ground-level spirits, assigning them to people and supervising them as they carry out their assignments. For example, when people commit themselves to occult organizations such as Freemasonry, Scientology, Mormonism or Jehovah's Witnesses, ground-level demons representing the higher-level spirits inhabit the membership. Likewise, cosmic-level vices, such as abortion and homosexuality, bring automatic ground-level demonization.

Though most of what goes on at the cosmic level is not clear to us, what is clear is that there is a war going on at that level. We can assume that there is war in the heavenlies as well as at ground level. But what is our involvement to be?

Second Corinthians 4:4 tells us that our enemy blinds the minds of unbelievers to keep them from coming to an experience of the truth. Satan wants to keep us blind to cosmic-level reality so that we cannot oppose him at that level. And some people seem to be going along with Satan by believing we should not try to fight the enemy at this level. They do not see Jesus engaging in cosmic-level warfare. They question whether it is scriptural to confront the enemy at a higher level.

So we ask, Can anything be done to confront Satan's blinding activity so that efforts at evangelism may be more successful? I believe we can and should confront the enemy at this level. And there are some impressive experiments going on that, I think, prove my point, some of which I share in the next chapter. But we need to be wise, cautious and working in dedicated groups rather than individually. And Scripture endorses plenty of ground-level activity that can influence what goes on at higher levels.

Evidence That Cosmic-Level Spirits Exist

The first thing I turn to is the existence of cosmic-level spirits. Though some may deny it, the following Scriptures support the existence of these spirits.

Two very convincing passages are located in Daniel 10 and Daniel 12. In Daniel 10:13, an angel appears with the answer to a prayer Daniel had prayed three weeks earlier. The angel explains that he was sent to deliver the answer to Daniel's prayer but that "the angel prince of the kingdom of Persia opposed [him] for twenty-one days. Then Michael, one of the chief angels, came to help [him], because [he] had been left there alone in Persia." After the angel delivers his message, he then states, "Now I have to go back and fight the guardian angel of Persia. After that the guardian angel of Greece will appear. There is no one to help me except Michael, Israel's guardian angel" (verse 21).

Then in Daniel 12:1, we find further reference to Michael as the guardian spirit of Israel, where it says, "The angel wearing linen clothes said, 'At that time the great angel Michael, who guards your people, will appear.'" I believe this kind of guardian spirit is a reference to God's cosmic-level spirits assigned to protect nations. These spirits seem to be more powerful than those like the unnamed angel chosen by God to carry to Daniel the answer to his prayer in Daniel 10. And since they seem to live in the air, they probably are "the spiritual powers in space" spoken of in Ephesians 2:2.

In 2 Kings 17:24–28, we find a fascinating story of spirit activity in relation to the land, even though the people of Israel were not being faithful to God. The emperor of Assyria had conquered Israel and, as was the custom when a land was conquered, took the leaders of Israel into captivity and replaced them with people from cities that already belonged to Assyria. These Assyrian people, however, "did not worship the LORD" (verse 25). So God sent lions that killed some of the newcomers. The emperor was told that this was because "the people he had settled . . . did not know the law of the god of that land, and so the god had sent lions, which were killing them."

> Cosmic-level spirits seem to be more powerful than ground-level spirits.

The emperor agreed with this interpretation. So he ordered that one of the Hebrew priests be chosen and sent back to teach the newcomers how to worship the God of the land of Israel. This they did, and it stopped the problem with the lions. I consider it likely here that God had assigned high-level angels to oversee the land that had been dedicated to Him. The pagan newcomers, serving other gods, were, therefore, trespassing and deserved to be punished.

In 1 Kings 20:23–30, it is recorded that in a war between Israel and Syria, the Syrian king made a serious mistake by insulting Yahweh. The Syrian army had been defeated by Israel, but its leaders planned to challenge Israel again. The Syrian king's advisers interpreted Syria's defeat as stemming from the fact that the fight took place in the mountains rather than on the plains. They advised the Syrian king, "The gods of Israel are mountain gods, and that is why the Israelites defeated us. But we will certainly defeat them if we fight them in the plains" (verse 23). So they prepared to lure the Israelites down onto the plains.

But the Syrians had insulted God by saying this, so He sent a prophet to King Ahab of Israel, saying, "Because the Syrians say that I am a god of the hills and not of the plains, I will give you victory over their huge army, and you and your people will know that I am the LORD" (verse 28). Even though the Israelite king was the evil King Ahab, God gave Israel the victory to prove both to Syria and to Israel that He is the God of all the earth, not just of the mountains. God's high-level territorial spirits would have been the ones who carried out God's revenge, bringing defeat to a much larger army than Israel could muster.

Throughout the Old Testament, we see God objecting to being treated by the Israelites as merely a local god. God is fighting against this animistic perception, contending that He is the God of all the earth, not simply one of many cosmic-level gods over a certain territory, Israel.

We see this further supported in Deuteronomy 32. Verses 8–9 speak of God assigning lands and angels to each of the peoples of the earth, saying, "The Most High assigned nations their lands; he determined where peoples should live. He assigned to each nation a heavenly being, but Jacob's descendants he chose for himself." Here we see that God assigned angels to the various nations but took Israel for Himself. Each nation was given a guardian angel, but Israel had God Himself looking after them.

God's spiritual connection to the land is highlighted again in the story of Naaman in 2 Kings 5. Naaman, the commander of the Syrian army, had contracted leprosy. On the advice of an Israeli servant girl, he came in desperation to the prophet Elisha in Israel to seek healing. He was, then, miraculously healed and attempted to pay Elisha. But the prophet refused to receive payment. Naaman then said, "If you won't accept my gift, then let me have two mule-loads of earth to take home with me, because from now on I will not offer sacrifices . . . to any god except the LORD" (verse 17). Naaman planned to follow Yahweh but felt he needed some sanctified Israeli earth on which to worship. He, as all the people of that day, believed that different gods were in charge of different real estate.

In Mark 5, we have the story of the man with a legion of demons in him. It is interesting that these demons "kept begging Jesus not to send [them] out of that region" (verse 10). We can infer that the demons had a special relationship to the region. They were territorial spirits, asserting satanic authority over that region. The demons were, however, foiled. They got Jesus to send them into the pigs, but the pigs took them over the border, into the water and out of that region.

In the temptations Jesus faced in the wilderness, Satan showed Jesus all the kingdoms of the world and claimed that he could give Jesus "all this power and all this wealth." He said, "It has all been handed over to me, and I can give it to anyone I choose" (Luke 4:6; cf. Matthew 4:8–9). Satan's claim was a claim that the world belongs to him. He is a cosmic-level spirit who heads up the whole satanic authority over the cosmic-level realm. It is his spirits that exercise a certain amount of control over the regions of the world.

Then in Ephesians 6:12, we are explicitly taught that we wrestle not only with humans but also with wicked cosmic-level spirits. The apostle Paul assumes the existence of several kinds of these spirits, possibly ranks of them, with names such as "rulers, authorities, and cosmic powers of this dark age." These spirits operate at the cosmic level we have been describing.

In Acts 19, we find a crowd of people in Ephesus rallying in support of their god Artemis. Artemis would be considered a cosmic-level spirit, portrayed as "the great goddess Artemis . . . worshiped by everyone in Asia and in all the world" (verse 27). In this way, Artemis, being a cosmic-level spirit, was given authority by the people to rule over Asia. And the people perceived her to be upset by a challenge made by the apostle Paul, who they said was teaching that "hand-made gods are not gods at all, and he

[had] succeeded in convincing many people, both . . . in Ephesus and in nearly the whole province of Asia" (verse 26). The Ephesians were naming the cosmic-level spirit/god that they were worshiping, and Paul was challenging her. This disturbed the people greatly, and they rioted to challenge the threat.

Another reference to a cosmic-level spirit belonging to a whole people or land is found in Jeremiah 50, where Jeremiah prophesies, "Babylon has fallen! Her god Marduk has been shattered!" (verse 2). Israel's God had bested the god Marduk. The wars of Old Testament peoples were assumed to be fought between their gods as well as between the human armies. When, then, an army won or lost, the result was attributed to their god or gods.

Then there are the angels of the churches addressed in Revelation 2 and 3. These would be considered cosmic-level spirits assigned by God to look after the seven churches mentioned in these chapters. From what is said here, it looks as though these angels were not as successful as God wanted them to be in their work because their human partners were not as faithful as they should be in their faith.

These Scripture passages give us some insight into the existence and activities of cosmic-level spirits. I assume that there are both good and evil spirits at this level. Each probably has lower-level spirits assigned by either God or Satan to serve the cosmic-level spirits. The battles that happen here on earth, then, are paralleled by battles taking place between cosmic-level spirits in the air. Both demons and angels are partnering with their human hosts as humans do battle.

Five Types of Cosmic-Level Spirits

Most of what we deal with when we look at cosmic-level spirits and their activities is invisible. We are, therefore, left to draw conclusions from inferences in Scripture and in life. Our analyses, then, are to be taken as educated guesses, not as fixed portrayals of what is actually there. In what follows, I will address each of the five types of cosmic-level spirits mentioned above. Remember that the order of the listing does not necessarily represent a hierarchical ordering of the spirits.

1. Territorial Spirits

The first of the cosmic-level spirits are called *territorial spirits*. These are principalities and powers assigned to create a "force field" influence over nations, cities and regions. We read about two of those assigned to nations in Daniel 10:13 and 21, called the "angel prince of the kingdom of Persia" and the "guardian angel of Greece." These spirits were powerful enough to hinder the delivery of an answer to Daniel's prayer.

Daniel was living in Persia at this time, so the picture that emerges is one of a high-level satanic spirit protecting that nation from intrusion by God. This spirit was powerful enough to keep the angel sent by God to answer Daniel's prayer from getting to Daniel. To counter this blockage, the angel sent to Daniel went to the archangel Michael to get the help he needed to get through to Daniel. What we are seeing here is a battle in the heavenlies between the emissaries of Satan and those of God. We do not know very much about how this conflict is waged, but we gather that it both affects and is influenced by humans.

To state this further, territorial spirits have legal rights given by humans to influence the people of a given territory and, as we see in Daniel, even to hinder God's workings in those territories. These rights are given to them by humans who have dedicated a territory to Satan either verbally or by use. God, of course, assigns His angels to operate in these territories as well. But rules govern the power each type of spirit wields.

These rules relate primarily to partnership between humans and spirit beings. Thus, when we refer to territories, we are referring to the people more than to the geography. It is people, especially people with authority, who give rights to territory. When they partner with God, they give rights to Him. When they partner with Satan, they give rights to him.

As we see throughout the Old Testament—starting with Adam's sin, continuing through the murder of Abel and then on throughout Israel's history—the sinful acts of humans bring curses on the geography in which those sins are committed. Genesis 3:17 and 4:10, as well as many passages thereafter, give references to spiritual damage done to the land.

In the New Testament, it is likely that it was cosmic-level (territorial)

241

spirits that Jesus cast out of the Gerasene demoniac (see Mark 5:1–20). Probably through regular use by servants of Satan, the region that those spirits inhabited was Satan's territory, held tightly by the "legion" of demons that were carried by the demoniac. By freeing the afflicted man, then, Jesus was able to disrupt Satan's hold on both the man and the territory.

So it is scriptural to assume that the geography is affected by the behavior of people, especially those in authority, both past and present. In keeping with the spiritual warfare theme of Scripture, the effect of such sinful behavior is to give a personal being (Satan) rights over the land. Just as the Fall gave the enemy certain territorial rights, so contemporary or past human sin—especially the sin of allegiance to Satan—gives him rights today.

Through the Fall, Adam gave the enemy rights over the kingdoms of the world. This fact is what gave Satan the right to claim in Luke 4:6 that the kingdoms of the world and all their power and wealth have "all been handed over to [him], and [he] can give [them] to anyone [he chooses]." This is a territorial outcome at the cosmic level. And these general rights of Satan continue, affecting generation after generation until Jesus comes to take those rights back.

So we recognize Satan's authority over the world and the organization of his kingdom into something like the hierarchy described in Ephesians 6:12—a hierarchy that I see as the organizing structure of each of my five categories. This leads many to postulate the existence of territorial satanic rulers that have been given rights by the people who inhabit the territories or, more likely, by their ancestors. Most of the animistic peoples of the world, including those in the Old Testament, assume that territorial spirits are in charge, and they can usually name the spirits that rule over various places.

We observe that people who live in certain areas often specialize in particular types of evil. This suggests that there are spirits over those people that encourage and empower that sin. Likewise, concentrations of sinful and occult institutions and/or organizations exist in particular localities. Businesses promoting such things as drugs, pornography, prostitution and gambling as well as occult bookshops often congregate in the same locales. I will deal with this issue further when addressing vice spirits below.

As John Dawson[2] and others[3] point out, when we look at the history of many of these places, our attention is drawn to the fact that these locales usually were committed, even formally dedicated, in earlier generations to satanic influence. Such observations, then, suggest that concentrating in geographical locations in this way is one of the ways in which the spirit world interacts with the human world.

We wonder, then, how God's angels go about countering such concentrations of satanic activity. We can assume that angels implement the protection we receive from God to keep satanic spirits from doing their worst. I am certain that we all have been protected from accidents over and over again through the activity of angels. Jesus refers to the fact that angels are assigned to children (see Matthew 18:10).

Those of us involved in spiritual warfare have experienced satanic darkness and sometimes attacks in certain areas of the world. In response to our prayers and the assertion of our authority in Christ, then, we assume that God's angels are able to counter such satanic activities. On a visit to Israel once, I felt this type of oppression. But we prayed over the places where we did seminars, and God did some important things in these places. On another occasion, the wife of a colleague of mine reported an unusual surge of sexual feelings while staying alone in a New York hotel. The feeling left, however, when she took authority over the room in the name of Jesus Christ to cancel any rights the enemy had been given over that room by previous occupants.

On several occasions, I have spoken in places where I experienced a freedom in teaching that felt truly supernatural. These were occasions when the places had been "cleaned out" spiritually through round-the-clock prayers that preceded the meetings. On other occasions, I have listened to primary school teachers report big differences in the behavior of schoolchildren when the teachers pray authoritatively over the rooms in which they teach. In such cases, I believe God's angels are active in taking charge over the space on God's behalf.

2. Dawson, *Taking Our Cities for God.*
3. Wagner, *Engaging the Enemy.*

2. Institutional and Religion Spirits

Institutional and religion spirits are those assigned by God or by Satan (depending on which side they are on) to churches, governments, educational institutions, cults, occult organizations (e.g., Scientology, Freemasonry, Mormonism) and non-Christian religions (e.g., Hinduism, Buddhism, animism). They have two types of assignments: 1) enhancing their interests and 2) opposing the interests of the opposite side.

Those on Satan's side are assigned to empower religions and occult institutions, to enhance occult activity and to oppose God's activity. Those on God's side are assigned to partner with God's people to empower godly activity and to oppose ungodly activity. Satanic spirits are assigned to disturb and hinder churches, Christian institutions and other organizations committed to God. God's angels are available to counter occult and religious activity and to empower the activities of organizations committed to Him when humans partner with Him (such as was the case with the angels of the churches in Revelation 2–3).

The religions of the world are counterfeits of what God seeks to do in the human context. They are clever counterfeits, masterminded by Satan to deceive humankind into partnering with him rather than with God. There is a lot of truth in these religions, and adherents frequently manifest high commitment. But the people practicing these religions are partnering with Satan, giving him a legal right to influence them and to take over the territory in which they live. Whether it is Buddhism, Hinduism, Islam, animism, Mormonism, Freemasonry, Jehovah's Witnesses, the Church of Religious Science, Western naturalism or any of the other varieties of satanic deceit, high-level satanic spirits are active in the process.

Though the guiding spirits operating in these religions are cosmic, the adherents are always carrying ground-level demons. That is, the adherents of these religions and institutions are demonized and need to be freed from their demons. Jesus seemed to deal with cosmic-level demons by freeing individuals from ground-level spirits rather than by confronting the cosmic-level spirits directly.

Cosmic-level spirits sometimes take up residence in a person, whether temporarily or permanently. I do not know what the rules are, but I think

I have met cosmic-level spirits on at least two occasions. I am guessing that when we meet cosmic-level spirits, we find that they are extremely difficult to cast out. I remember clearly the frustration of attempting to deal with what I suspect was an institutional spirit in a Lutheran pastor in Switzerland and with a similar one in a woman in Israel. To my dismay, I was not able to cast out either of these spirits, though I later heard from the woman that she finally had gotten free. Could this be the kind of spirit Jesus identified as requiring more prayer and perhaps fasting (see Matthew 17:21; Mark 9:29)?

In occult organizations, people either consciously or unconsciously commit themselves to Satan, partnering with him and participating in his deceit. Those who join Freemasonry organizations, for example, in the very first of their degrees (levels or ranks) renounce all light they have found in any other activity and pledge themselves to seek "the light" in Freemasonry. In doing so, usually without knowing it, they commit themselves to Lucifer as the god of light, regarding the true God as the god of darkness. Since the Bible

> **Jesus dealt with cosmic-level demons by freeing individuals from ground-level spirits.**

is used in their practices and many of the statements and rituals imitate Christianity, most of those involved in Freemasonry have no idea they have committed themselves to Satan.

As with false religions, the adherents of such religions and organizations become demonized. This happens subconsciously to those who join such organizations as Freemasonry, Scientology, many secret societies on university campuses (e.g., the Skull and Bones Society), New Age, satanism and others. With occult organizations, higher-level spirits are assigned to the organization while individual spirits live within the individual adherents. The individual demons, then, are passed down to later generations through spiritual inheritance—even to those who do not themselves become members of the organization.

Institutional and religion spirits can also infiltrate Christian churches. We have already deduced from the fact that letters were written to the angels of the churches in Revelation 2–3 that God assigns angels to His churches. These angels combat satanic beings assigned to harass churches and other Christian organizations. Both theological liberalism and legalistic fundamentalism portray some of the results of demonic activity in their theologies and practices. Nominalism and the ignorance of spiritual warfare in so many evangelical churches also reflect such demonic activity. Paul's warning to Timothy against teachings encouraged by demons (see 1 Timothy 4:1) and his mention of a "table" of demons (1 Corinthians 10:21) certainly point to such cosmic-level demonic activity.

When, for example, a theologically liberal church allows and even campaigns for same-sex marriage, abortion rights or any number of anti-God practices or doctrines (e.g., denying the virgin birth, the deity of Jesus or the inspiration of the Scriptures), they are opening their doors wide for enemy infestation. Or when, for example, hyperfundamentalist churches practice a legalistic enslavement to rules and a critical, loveless spirit, they, too, invite demons into their churches and into their people.

Further, many ground-level spirits gain entrance into individuals through churches and theologies that may speak of love but show little of it in practice. Examples of this are demons in persons who are controlled and manipulated by Christian leaders in such a way that their right to think for themselves is taken away. Further evidence of institutional spirits influencing Christians is the exclusivity based on lifestyle or overemphasis on small doctrinal points of many very conservative groups. These demons are assigned by higher-level demons. And such domination creates satanic soul ties.

Does God assign angels to counter such satanic beings? Of course. And many Christian organizations demonstrate clearly that they are working in partnership with God and His angelic servants to honor Jesus Christ in a world where enemy activity is often very obvious.

3. Vice Spirits

Vice spirits are cosmic-level satanic spirits assigned by Satan to oversee and encourage vices, such as prostitution, abortion, homosexuality, gambling, pornography, war and the like. People with spiritual sensitivity often feel the presence of satanic spirits in and around establishments that are involved in these activities. When we claim God's power to challenge these spirits, interesting things often happen. A former student of mine, though a committed Christian, once worked in an abortion clinic where, as Christians prayed outside the clinic, what was going on inside was crippled. In fact, she said she felt the power of God so obviously that she left the clinic and never returned.

The high-level satanic vice spirits are assigned to enhance satanic activity in establishments and activities whose main purpose is to entice their adherents into sinful behavior. Again, cosmic-level institutional spirits seem to supervise vice spirits whose task is to encourage prostitution or alcoholism or abortion or drugs.

To be more specific, vice spirits of gambling are probably supervised by cosmic-level territorial spirits in Las Vegas, Atlantic City and the many American Indian gambling establishments. Abortion establishments crawl with spirits of murder and death. High-level spirits of homosexuality and/or pornography reign over certain areas of our country (e.g., San Francisco). High-level spirits of death are present wherever unjust killing takes place, as in theaters of war or abortion clinics. And again, one of the major concerns of such cosmic-level spirits is to move their demonic underlings into the people who participate in these activities.

God, of course, assigns cosmic-level angels to confront vice spirits in response to the authoritative prayers of His people. When people gather to pray for the disbanding or banishment of a sinful organization, God's angels are engaged to fight vice spirits. I have heard several reports of churches successfully using authoritative prayer to banish vices from their neighborhoods. I wish more churches took such initiative. When cosmic-level spirits are not confronted by churches, they run roughshod over the people of the area for which the churches are responsible.

4. Household, Item and Nature Spirits

This category makes up a miscellaneous grouping of spirits that inhabit dedicated houses, rooms, work implements, rocks, trees, bodies of water, material items, rituals, music and everything else that their dedication covers. Under this heading, we focus especially on such things as household spirits, music that has been dedicated to Satan, certain computer games, dedicated items brought home from overseas by travelers and missionaries, certain medicines (often bought at certain health food stores), martial arts (e.g., tae kwon do) and yoga, as well as the nature spirits that inhabit certain lakes, forests, rocks, trees and water.

In many societies, spirits are invited in routinely by their human partners when the implements and places the people use are dedicated to such spirits. And many people—including missionaries—who have brought souvenirs from overseas that, to them, are art items testify that obvious enemy activity entered their homes when such items were brought inside. In addition, much contemporary popular music is dedicated to Satan either formally or informally. Christians should be aware of such things and use the authority of God to counteract their effects.

I am not sure whether this group of spirits really is a single category or should be divided up into two or more categories. Or perhaps it should be considered a separate ground-level type. But we will treat it as a single type at cosmic level.

In animistic societies, people regard anything out of the ordinary as the work of spirits. Thus, if someone drowns in a pond, the likely interpretation is that the spirit of that pond took the person's life. Or if there is an automobile accident, the interpretation is that the spirits of the place where the accident occurred were the cause. Animists, then, offer sacrifices or do rituals intended to change the spirit's attitude from harmful to kindly. Even though, due to our Western worldview, we might scoff at such supernaturalistic interpretations, we should be open to the possibility that enemy spirits are indeed very active in such events.

Examples of household spirits are the gods in Taiwan that are attached to stoves, furniture, clothing and other household goods. These are the spirits in focus in Paul Hiebert's important article on the "excluded middle."[4] Hiebert points out that we Westerners believe in ground-level things like nature and humans, and as Christians we believe in God high above us. But we miss the fact that an enormous number of invisible spirit beings are between us and God—in a kind of middle zone.

These spirits are active in the human sphere and are assumed to exist by the peoples of most societies outside of the West. They are assumed in

4. Paul Hiebert, "The Flaw of the Excluded Middle," *Missiology* 10 (January 1982): 35–47.

the Bible, as well, but are ignored and disbelieved by most Westerners, even Christians. Though these spirits are active in, around and among humans, they seem to be quite separate from what I call ground-level demons that live inside of humans.

Music dedicated to Satan, such as that of Marilyn Manson, Eminem, the Grateful Dead and other musical groups, is very dangerous, especially since Western young people have no idea what is attached to such music. Nor do they recognize how dangerous a pastime are occult computer games such as *Dungeons & Dragons* and many even worse ones. Certain books can also be very dangerous. Among them would be the Harry Potter series, which, according to William Schnoebelen, portrays at least seventy high-level witchcraft techniques.[5] Through such dedicated music, films, computer games and books, and through dedicated items brought home from overseas, the enemy sneaks into many homes and into the people themselves.

> **An enormous number of invisible spirit beings are between us and God—in a kind of middle zone.**

Through the activity of cosmic-level spirits such as these, people and places become demonized. If dedicated items are present, households can be disrupted greatly. Disturbing dreams, accidents and family arguments can become common. Many health food stores are New Age outlets, and it is standard for martial arts masters to dedicate their activities to their gods. Christians need to claim Jesus' protection when going into places possibly dedicated to New Age or pagan gods. Furthermore, we should be discerning in our choices of which of such places to enter at all.

Christians can combat household, item and nature spirits through building dedications, Christian rituals (including worship and preaching) and anointed music and by placing blessings on items like anointing oil and the Communion elements. I do not know if these dedications mean that angels actually live inside these items and places once they are blessed, as we assume demons do in things dedicated to Satan. But we can be sure

5. Taken from his private remarks. See William J. Schnoebelen, "Straight Talk on Harry Potter" (January 30, 2004), http://educate-yourself.org/mc/straighttalkonharrypotter30jan04. shtml.

that there are angels whom God sends to empower our blessings and dedications.

5. *Ancestor Spirits*

Lastly, we turn to ancestor spirits. This is pure deceit. These spirits are satanic, assigned to deceive people into believing that their dead ancestors still participate in human life. Many of the peoples of the world believe that their dead bring blessing when they are honored and punishment if they are neglected or otherwise not treated right by the living. Such belief is not scriptural. God does not assign angels to deceive. He does send angels to minister to and serve His people. But these angels are not the spirits of dead ancestors.

Those who believe that dead ancestors are active in relation to the living are being deluded. They believe the living are required to honor or even worship these "living dead" by doing such things as setting up altars, performing certain rituals to honor or worship the spirits, providing them with food and even offering sacrifices to "keep them happy." The individuals believe that when the ancestral spirits are happy, the family will be blessed. When, however, any family member displeases the ancestors, the family can expect revenge.

The Bible speaks of judgment—not ancestorhood—following death (see Hebrews 9:27). So it cannot be the spirits of dead ancestors who should receive a person's honor or worship. Those who believe in ancestral spirits have real experiences with spirits, but these experiences are the working of demonic spirits, not their departed loved ones. This belief in ancestral spirits and the experiences that go with such a belief constitute a form of satanic deceit carried out by demons. Satan, then, assigns certain demons to keep this lie alive.

Ancestral beliefs are difficult for people to give up. Often the beliefs continue even after people come to Christ. For instance, a prominent Korean pastor with an important deliverance ministry believes that when he does deliverance, he is releasing people from being troubled by the spirits of dead ancestors. I believe he is completely wrong in his analysis. I do not believe the spirits he casts out are ancestral spirits. They are demons, but he misnames them. Even so, he is very effective in freeing people from them.

As should be clear by now, discussions of spiritual warfare ought to take into account all of these levels and types of spirits. This chapter has presented us with what might be called the "inventory" of the cosmic-level spirit world. The question now is how the cosmic level relates to the ground level in the spirit world and what to do about it.

Jesus, of course, frequently encountered and cast out ground-level demons. He seemed, however, not to take notice of higher-level spirits except in His encounter with Satan himself (see Luke 4:1–13) and in dealing with the Gerasene demoniac's spirits. It is likely that in confronting and defeating Satan in the wilderness (considered to be Satan's territory), Jesus broke much of Satan's power over at least that part of Palestine.

I believe that the demons afflicting the Gerasene demoniac (see Mark 5:1–20) were territorial spirits. This interpretation is supported by the fact that the demons begged Jesus not to send them out of their region (see verse 10). Furthermore, in spite of the freed man's begging to be allowed to join Jesus' followers, Jesus sent him back to testify to the people of the region concerning his deliverance (see verses 18–20). And I have heard that history records that a revival broke out in the region as a result. If these were territorial spirits, they were concentrated in one man like ground-level demons. And though they were undoubtedly more difficult to cast out than other demons, Jesus dealt with them in the same way that He dealt with purely ground-level demons.

Now we turn to the dynamics of cosmic-level spiritual warfare.

251

15

Authority in Cosmic-Level Warfare

Jesus gave His twelve disciples power and authority "to drive out all demons and to cure diseases" (Luke 9:1). He then sent them out "to preach the Kingdom of God and to heal the sick" (verse 2). Later, He chose 72 of His followers and sent them out to do the same thing (see Luke 10:1).

Some say this authority to heal and cast out demons was given just to the disciples. But in John 14:12, Jesus says, "Those who believe in me will do what I do." This would seem to extend the power and authority to all of us. The early church leaders certainly believed these ministries were for everyone. Healing and deliverance have been part of Christian practice from that day to this.

The disciples were amazed when they tested this authority. On their return from an excursion into Jewish villages, they exclaimed, "Even the demons obeyed us when we gave them a command in your name" (Luke 10:17). I think we can assume that the disciples were conducting ground-level ministry. But there appears to have been cosmic-level fallout as well, indicated by Jesus when He said in response, "I saw Satan fall like lightning from heaven" (verse 18).

In other words, when the disciples cast out demons on the ground level, something significant seems to have happened at the cosmic level. The enemy was knocked down when the disciples used their authority to free people. Their authority, then, went even further than freeing people, even to the extent of "overcom[ing] all the power of the Enemy" (verse 19). "Nothing will hurt you," Jesus said (verse 19).

The disciples' discovery of their use of God-given authority and power plus what Jesus saw happening in the heavenlies as a result challenge us to obey as the disciples did. It is a heady thing to experience the same thrill that they expressed when they found the demons did obey them and to know that something is happening cosmically while we are challenging ground-level spirits. I can attest to this thrill. I experience it every time I work with Jesus to get people free from demons.

But then Jesus warned His men not to get proud over their God-given ability to conquer demons. He said, "Don't be glad because the evil spirits obey you; rather be glad because your names are written in heaven" (verse 20). The big thing to be glad about here is our relationship with God. It is on the basis of that relationship that we get to do lesser things like casting out demons. This is not a matter of gifting. Everyone who has a relationship with Jesus gets to do it. We are expected to obey our Master. And obedience precedes gifting.

Contrast this with the experience of the sons of Sceva (see Acts 19:11–20), who attempted to cast out demons but had no relationship with Jesus to give them the authority and power to do so. They may have done and said the right things. They certainly claimed the right Source of power—Jesus. But since they had no relationship with Him, their formula did not work with the demon, though it may have worked with others.

> **We have a power relationship with Jesus as well as a saving relationship.**

All of us who have this saving relationship with Jesus automatically have access to all the authority and power we need to cast out demons. If our names are written in heaven, we have a power relationship with Jesus as well as a saving relationship with Him. Demons respect that relationship and have to obey us. We, for our part, are responsible for exercising the power Jesus gives us, remembering always that it is *His* power, not ours. It is His gift to us, but it is our privilege to use that gift to carry out His purposes. We get to rejoice in our relationship with Him above all, but we can also enjoy the thrill of forcing demons to obey us, thus freeing people from them.

A lesson we learn with the disciples is that doing ground-level spiritual warfare has cosmic effects. Satan has apparently not fallen forever—yet. But I think Jesus is saying that what we do here on earth affects him. When we use the authority God has given us to free people, Satan falls.

How It Happens

The question of what to do about cosmic-level spirits is a controversial one. Many notice that Jesus seems never to have dealt directly with demons above the ground level, suggesting that we should not be concerned with cosmic-level beings but should simply do what Jesus did by freeing people from ground-level spirits. Contrary to these critics, I believe that Jesus, in dealing with ground-level spirits, did deal with cosmic-level spirits, though indirectly, and that we can legitimately follow His example. As mentioned above, when Jesus' disciples cast out ground-level demons, Satan fell. Dealing with ground-level garbage affects the cosmic-level rats.

For example, I have spoken of the fact that ground-level demons are governed by cosmic-level spirits. When, then, a ground-level demon is banished and loses his grip on his host, that diminishes the power of the cosmic-level spirit that is over the demon that was cast out. Part of his army has lost presence and power. The cosmic-level spirit in charge has one less member of his army to depend upon. If, as is usual, we are able to cast out many demons living in a client, the cosmic-level spirits above that person then take a big hit. Furthermore, the victim gets free, resulting in less of a satanic presence in the area in which those demons had lived.

The rats/garbage analogy gives us a way of approaching cosmic-level warfare, just as it did with ground-level warfare. If the higher-level spirits are like rats, we can look for the garbage in the human being that gives them legal rights and deal primarily with that. Such garbage is anything that enables cosmic-level rats to gain control over groups of people, their land and other meaningful things that keep the people captive to cosmic-level spirit influence.[1]

My experience in ground-level warfare teaches me that the two levels are parallel, allowing for insights gained from ground-level warfare to apply to cosmic-level warfare. We see, therefore, cosmic-level rats and seek to get at them through tackling cosmic-level garbage.

What, then, is cosmic-level garbage? First, as with garbage at the ground level, it is something to which cosmic-level demons are given legal rights. And these rights are given them by humans. When a building or a city or a vehicle or a child is dedicated to evil spirits, whether consciously or unconsciously, that item or place or person is put under satanic power. And the dedicated items, places or persons constitute one part of the garbage we have to deal with to get persons and places free.

So, formal dedication is one way cosmic demons can get attached to items, places or persons. Another way is through usage. This is a kind of informal dedication. If an item, place or person is used to serve either Satan or God, even if there was not a formal dedication to that power, that item, place or person then serves whichever spirit being it is dedicated to. A Masonic temple, for example, even without a formal dedication, gets taken over by satanic spirits as it is used to serve Satan. A church building, on the other hand, becomes a place where God dwells as long as the members are faithful to God. If the members devolve into apostasy, however, the enemy gets to take over buildings and other items used to serve God.

Next, just as there are activities that people do and commitments that people make that give legal rights to ground-level demons, there are activities and commitments that give cosmic-level demons legal rights. Unrighteousness is one thing that gives Satan rights. When a nation or a city or a church gives itself to unrighteousness, whether consciously or unconsciously, the enemy moves right in. I know of a church that supports and even campaigns for so-called gay marriage. That and other liberal causes

1. By speaking of human-level garbage that gives cosmic-level spirits rights, I am referring to things like the misuse of power, oppression, blatant sin, murder (including abortion) and the like. These are corporate sins that stand at a higher level than emotional issues, though they are related to emotional issues at the individual level.

deliver that church to the enemy. Likewise a nation that has banned the Bible, murdered millions of preborn babies and supported so-called gay rights. Our unrighteousness on the ground gives Satan a lot of control in the air (see Ephesians 2:2).

A number of things go along with unrighteousness, such as dishonesty, treachery, blasphemy, the shedding of innocent blood, abortion, same-sex "marriage," gambling and the like, that give legal rights to the enemy. All such rights are given to the enemy through choices made by people to participate in sinful activities. When people agree to participate in such activities, and especially when officials use their authority to allow and encourage those activities, the people enter into sinful behavior that gives the enemy rights. When sizeable numbers of people in a given area sin in one or more of these ways, cosmic-level demons gain substantial power over the people and the places they inhabit. The demonic strength of homosexual principalities over parts of San Francisco and other places would be a case in point.

> **Our unrighteousness on the ground gives Satan a lot of control in the air.**

Demons are given rights over groups through the activities of group leaders as well. People appointed or elected to leadership carry heavier responsibility in the spirit world than do ordinary citizens. If leaders stand for unrighteousness, that gives permission to Satan to move in. We see this in the Old Testament where certain kings led Israel into unrighteousness and other kings led them into righteousness. If the leaders stand for righteousness, God moves in. And this provides a formidable barrier against the enemy and his plans.

Cursing and blessing are additional means of committing things, places and people to Satan or God at both the ground and cosmic levels. These curses and blessings can be offered consciously or unconsciously. Unconscious curses can come on people through negative thoughts, music dedicated to Satan, movies and other vehicles of communication. Almost any cultural form can be cursed, giving Satan control of it, or blessed, giving God control.

All these are examples of what I am calling cosmic-level garbage.

Challenging cosmic-level spirits, then, is done through dealing with both cosmic-level and ground-level garbage. Below are two tables that list the kinds of things in ground-level and cosmic-level garbage.

Ground-Level Garbage

Unforgiveness	Ungodly commitments
Death	Drugs
Anger	Bitterness
Fear	Worry
Shame	Guilt
Curses on people	Occult involvement
Rejection	Abandonment
Lust	Pornography
Pride	Arrogance
Control	Domination
Abuse	Violence

Cosmic-Level Garbage

All on ground-level list	Lack of repentance
Sin	Refusal to confess sin
Disunity of leaders	Curses on land
Witchcraft	Dedications
Prostitution	Abortion
Gambling	

How to Respond

To counter cosmic-level rats, then, we must do several ground-level things, most of which are clearly taught in Scripture. A key verse is 2 Chronicles 7:14: "If my people, who are called by my name, will humble themselves and pray and seek my face and turn from their wicked ways, then will I hear from heaven, and I will forgive their sin and will heal their land" (NIV).

Several of God's requirements for spiritual breakthrough are listed here. If God's people are to win or regain God's favor and defeat cosmic-level spirits, God here outlines the way. I believe this is a divine message to churches and all other groups that claim to follow Jesus. Originally spoken to Israel, it is applicable to anyone, anywhere.

Humble Ourselves

The first of these requirements is that we humble ourselves. This is a group activity at ground level with cosmic effects. We are to give up our pride, humbling ourselves before our God and repenting. This humbling and repentance involves each individual in the group, especially the leadership, since human authority is honored in the spirit world. Thus, if those in authority give up their pride and repent, the enemy army at the cosmic level takes a major hit.

Pray and Seek God's Face

Having humbled ourselves and repented, we are then to pray and seek God's face. Prayer is partnership with God. It connects us with Him in cosmic-level spiritual warfare. There are many great things that God wants to have happen, but He often finds no partner to work with Him to bring them about.

Intercessory prayer is especially important. God wants us all to be continually in prayer (see 1 Thessalonians 5:17), but He especially works when those with the gift of intercession pray. Intercessors are people who love to pray and who hear from God what they should be praying for as they pray. Though everyone should seek God's face, gifted intercessors seem to make better contact with Him more often.

Turn from Our Wicked Ways

Then we are to turn from our wicked ways. Once we have turned to God in prayer, we must deal with our problems. The requirement is group righteousness. Such righteousness is abhorrent to our enemy and wounds him deeply. On the other hand, this and all other obedience to God enhances God's cause, empowering His angels to accomplish what He wants in the human sphere.

It is especially important for those in authority to lead in doing the things that bring victories over cosmic spiritual forces. When the spiritual leaders of a community get together in unity, giving up their competitiveness and criticisms of each other, God is greatly empowered to defeat satanic principalities and powers. And when these leaders take the lead in fostering reconciliation between people who have been oppressed or otherwise mistreated and members of the community or their forebears who have oppressed them, the enemy is put to flight.

Christian leaders have participated in what seem to be great victories through accepting responsibility for the actions of their forebears who perpetrated past wrongs and through apologizing to God and to representatives of those who were hurt. We call this "identificational repentance." It is what Daniel (chapter 9) and Nehemiah (also chapter 9) did when they took on themselves the blame for the sins of their ancestors and asked God to forgive them as if they had been the perpetrators. The rule seems to be that the guilt for communal sin remains until persons from that community who have authority in the present take responsibility for the past sin and repent. We see this spiritual rule in effect in 2 Samuel 21:1–14, as well, where King David was held accountable for King Saul's sin in breaking the covenant made by Joshua years before with the Gibeonites.

How to Locate Them

We have talked about the five types of cosmic-level spirits and have learned how they get in and what we need to do to counter them. But how do we find them in the first place?

Those specializing in cosmic-level spiritual warfare have developed a research technique called "spiritual mapping." Spiritual mapping involves research into both the secular and spiritual history of a community. The aim of such research is to discover what Satan and God have been doing in the community over the course of time. Researchers seek to find out the kinds of things Satan has done, what allowed him to do those things and what the results have been and are now. On God's side, the quest is to discover what God has been doing and what resources are available if a spiritual attack is to be attempted.

Spiritual mapping is a contemporary form of spying out the land (see Numbers 13). When God wanted to take the Promised Land, He instructed Moses to send spies to discover what would help them later when they

259

attempted to take it. So spiritual mappers advocate "spying out" whatever can be discovered about the ways in which the enemy has been working in any given area. When preparing for war, common sense demands that we investigate and experiment with whatever we can to aid us in promoting the cause of our side.

In seeking to discover what God has been doing, John Dawson suggests we also seek to find what he calls the "redemptive gift" of each community.[2] The redemptive gift is God's reason for wanting the community to be formed. From such research, strategy can be developed for attacking cosmic-level satanic forces and encouraging the exercise of a community's redemptive gift.

> **Identificational repentance and spiritual mapping are relatively new terms for old biblical ideas.**

Though some of our critics do not like terms like *identificational repentance* and *spiritual mapping*, these are simply relatively new terms for old biblical ideas. As mentioned, both Daniel and Nehemiah identified with the sins of their ancestors, taking responsibility for them even though they personally had no part in committing those sins. And spiritual mapping is simply about research and reconnaissance, similar to what Moses instructed the spies to do when the Israelites were seeking to enter the Promised Land.[3]

How Others Fight Back

There are a number of experiments going on today that challenge cosmic-level spirits in the way I have been outlining here. Many of these fall under the label *prayer initiatives*. Such initiatives involve those with intercessory gifts going to places that have been under satanic control and then praying to break the enemy's power. Such intercession is designed to reclaim from the enemy these particular places. During and after such prayer initiatives,

2. Dawson, *Taking Our Cities for God.*
3. For more information on spiritual mapping, the best teaching I have found is George Otis Jr., *Informed Intercession: Transforming Your Community through Spiritual Mapping and Strategic Prayer* (Ventura, Calif.: Renew, 1999).

numerous things happen that show that God is doing something special in response to the faithfulness of His people.

For example, in an exciting book entitled *The Peacemaking Power of Prayer*, the authors describe prayer initiatives and their results in Bosnia, Kosovo, Cambodia and Rwanda.[4] In each of these places, things changed politically after a group went there and specifically challenged the spirits. Skeptics attribute the changes to chance and expertise in negotiation. We note, however, that in each case, the major changes occurred immediately after the prayer initiatives.

Additionally, the *Transformations* videos put out by George Otis Jr. record several situations that were radically changed as a result of people engaging in cosmic-level spiritual warfare. One spectacular example of spiritual transformation took place in a Guatemalan town called Almolonga with a population of just over twenty thousand. Over the past 25 years, that town has changed from a carousing, drunken place into a peaceful place with only one tavern and no jails. In the carousing days, the town's four jails could not hold all those who violated the law. Officials regularly had to take prisoners to other cities to lock them up. It has now been more than 25 years since they needed a jail!

By confronting the cosmic-level territorial spirit of the area, a demon named Maximon, and by breaking that spirit's power, a radical transformation has occurred even in Almolonga's agriculture. Whereas the people used to send out one truckload of produce per week to sell in other towns, at the time of the publication of the first *Transformations* video in 1999, the people were sending out *forty per day*! And the size of the produce was almost beyond belief. The video shows carrots the length of a man's arm and cabbage the size of a basketball. Some crops now have three growing seasons, in fact.[5]

Cosmic-level spiritual warfare has resulted in another powerful demonstration of transformation in Argentina. For years, evangelists such as Carlos Annacondia and Omar Cabrera have used an approach to evangelism

4. John D. Robb and Jim Hill, *The Peacemaking Power of Prayer: Equipping Christians to Transform the World* (Nashville: Broadman and Holman, 2000).

5. Otis's *Transformations* videos also document significant transformations that have taken place in Cali, Colombia; Hemet, California; and Kiambu, Kenya. These DVDs can be purchased at www.revivalworks.com.

that involves several weeks of warfare praying prior to an evangelism crusade. Annacondia even conducts open, visible challenges to the cosmic spirits at the beginning of each meeting.[6] When he senses that the covering of Satan's power is broken, then and only then does he begin to preach. The response rate is incredible.[7]

Additionally in Argentina, Ed Silvoso led a three-year spiritual attack in the city of Resistencia aimed at opening the people up for evangelism by breaking the power of the cosmic-level spirits over the city. This approach involved persuading the pastors (the spiritual "gatekeepers") to repent of their sins and their disunity and to unite. They then trained pastors and lay church leaders in spiritual warfare prayer, repentance, reconciliation, prayer marching and eventually all-out evangelism. The results have been spectacular.[8]

The success of such experiments in Argentina and elsewhere in the world suggests that a direct approach to warring against cosmic-level spirits is legitimate. But just as in ground-level warfare, we must deal with the spiritual garbage first. This we do through such things as confession of sin, repentance, reconciliation and the uniting of the spiritual gatekeepers. Taking care of these issues is the first order of business if prayer against territorial bondage is to be successful. This first action weakens the demons, which allows us to then easily kick them out. Also, as mentioned, dealing with ground-level demons can cause the enemy to fall, as it did in Jesus' day (see Luke 10:18). And dealing with cosmic-level garbage, such as breaking curses and dedications on land and buildings, should also be done.

As we have already seen is usually the case, though the critics of this approach to cosmic-level warfare can be harsh, they usually work from theory rather than from experience. They criticize without having taken into account the results of this approach. If they look at results, they will find that there is a lot to praise God for.

6. See Carlos Annacondia, *Listen to Me, Satan!* (Lake Mary, Fla.: Charisma House, 2008).
7. Other exciting examples of the success of warfare evangelism in Argentina are recorded in C. Peter Wagner and Pablo Deiros, eds., *The Rising Revival* (Ventura, Calif.: Gospel Light, 1998).
8. Silvoso, "Argentina: Evangelizing in a Context of Spiritual Warfare." Numerous DVDs produced by Ed Silvoso can also be purchased at www.transformourworld.org.

With all that looks like success in cosmic-level warfare, I believe we should encourage teaching and practicing it. But we must be cautious. There are stories of people challenging cosmic-level spirits without enough prayer support and losing—in some cases, losing their lives. Yet the success stories encourage us to consider paying the price to take territory from our enemy. It is warfare and not to be entered into lightly.

Fortunately, there are helps. I have mentioned some already, but I will say here that George Otis Jr. has written an excellent guide to spiritual mapping called *Informed Intercession*. Tom White's chapter in my *Behind Enemy Lines* lays out a strategy for mounting a challenge to higher-level spirits. The *Transformations* videos prepared by George Otis Jr. and Ed Silvoso are extremely helpful. And several other books listed in the bibliography help us go to war at this level. The "generals" in this war are George Otis Jr., Ed Silvoso, John Robb, C. Peter Wagner and John Dawson.

16

What Now?

We have come to the end of our study, and hopefully you have become convinced of the fact that we are at war with a cruel enemy. Now, what can you do about all this? I have several suggestions.

Be Aware

The first issue is awareness. Like almost everything else we do, awareness is a matter of habit. As I contended in the early chapters of this book, we have learned, as part of our Western worldview, to assume that things we cannot see cannot hurt us. So we are habitually unaware of the invisible world. This habit must be changed if the material in this book is to be of any use.

We have noted the assumption of the apostle Paul, articulated in 2 Corinthians 2:11, that his readers were aware of the enemy's schemes. But it is not the same for our people. We, in our day and culture, are not naturally aware of the enemy's schemes. We have to learn as adults what the people of Paul's day learned as children. Most of our people, then, remain ignorant of Satan's activities unless we force ourselves to become aware of that dimension of our human condition.

In considering the matter of awareness, some refer to those who have gone too far, saying, "I don't want to be one of those who believe there is a demon under every rock and behind every bush." Nor do I. But I think it is important to find out which rocks and bushes demons *are* hiding behind. It is not wise to turn aside from the whole matter just because some carry it too far. Satan loves to see us go to one extreme or the other.

So let me suggest that we risk overdoing things for a while in order to school ourselves to the fact that there are malevolent beings out there working full-time to try to mess up our lives. I have found it helpful to go through a little ritual each morning that on the one hand brings protection and on the other hand keeps me alert to the presence of the demonic world and its devices. I suggest saying something like this:

We have to learn as adults what the people of Paul's day learned as children.

> In the name of Jesus, I claim protection from any enemy spirits that seek to hurt or harass me or my family today. I forbid them to affect me or any of my family spiritually, emotionally, physically or in any other way.

Claim What Is Yours

As our awareness grows, we need to learn to claim what is rightfully ours. We should not get frantic, but we should recognize that we live in enemy territory and therefore need to claim such things as protection from harm and freedom from harassment. I live in consciousness of the fact that this is a hostile world and that I need to calmly claim God's protection as I go about my daily business.

Whenever I get into my car or enter a dangerous situation, I will say something like, "In Jesus' name, I claim safety and protection," and then go on my way, knowing that both God and the enemy spirit world are listening and that angels are carrying out God's orders.

When it seems that I am being harassed or interfered with in some way, I use the expression, "If this is the enemy, stop it!" This helps not only to diffuse impending arguments but also to minimize disruptions of public meetings and even headaches or occasional physical problems if they are caused by demons. (Some are; many are not.) People tell me that sometimes when they experience emotional downs, they are able to get over them by breaking the enemy's power in this way. Even lustful thoughts or thoughts of anger and bitterness can be banished by commanding the enemy to stop feeding them into one's mind.

Assert Your Authority

I have mentioned the canceling of enemy rights to places, property, artifacts, music and other things that have been dedicated to him. And we have discussed the authority we have to cancel rights obtained through curses, vows, sin and in other ways. All these are matters of authority.

As I have taught on spiritual warfare, I have found that the most difficult change for many people to make is the taking of authority. When we debrief after they have attempted to minister, they say things like, "I just didn't feel comfortable asserting Jesus' authority." My reply is to invite them to try it—to experiment with it because that authority is already theirs. It is not some sort of intrusion into an area where we are trespassing. Jesus said, "I have given you authority" (Luke 10:19), and we are being irresponsible if we have that authority and refuse to use it. It is like having a credit card that someone has given us to enable us to purchase something but then we refuse to take the authority given us to use it.

I have spoken of ministry as warfare. And one of our most important weapons is the authority Jesus has given us. We must learn to use it. I have not gone into the detail I might have in this area because I have written eight other books on the subject (all available via online retailers). The one most relevant to the authority issue is *I Give You Authority*. Here are brief descriptions of each of the books:

Christianity with Power offers a general treatment of worldview and the use of authority in ministry.

Deep Wounds, Deep Healing explores ways to use our authority in a ministry of deep-level healing that gets at problems of an emotional or spiritual nature.

Defeating Dark Angels speaks of our use of Jesus' authority in dealing with demonization.

I Give You Authority is one of very few books on the authority of believers. It is the book of mine that occasions the most positive response.

Confronting Powerless Christianity continues the theme of attempting to awaken evangelical Christian leaders to the present use of spiritual power.

Behind Enemy Lines is a compilation that covers a broader use of authority in dealing with various matters, including territorial spirits.

The Rules of Engagement presents a quest for a science behind the relationship between the spirit world and the human world.

Two Hours to Freedom offers a quick approach to inner healing and is highly praised by many.

Change Your Worldview

We spent quite a bit of time reviewing worldview in this book and the need among evangelicals to broaden their worldview to include the spirit realm. It is important to acknowledge that several principles are involved when we want to change our perspective or worldview. First, it must be said that no one changes an entire worldview. There is just too much there. Rather, we change *parts* of a worldview.

How many parts get changed depends on the degree of the change. For example, when we choose to follow Jesus, there may be many things that get changed if our pre-Christian life was very pagan. However, if we choose to follow Jesus as young people who are pretty innocent, we will not experience as much change, either in our worldview or our behavior. A change from a "no God" life to a godly life can be a very big thing. But coming to Christ in a family where the worldview change is minimal due to the perspectives taught by parents requires only small changes.

Second, if we desire to change our worldview, we need to open ourselves to new experiences. We can diagram this principle as follows:

Old Perspective → New Experience → New Perspective

Though a worldview is nestled deep below the surface, it is strongly influenced by behavior. It also strongly influences behavior. When, then, behavior is changed and interpreted, pressure is put on people to change their worldview perspective.

My change from "ordinary" evangelical to "warfare-conscious" evangelical was mediated by seeing people get healed and delivered, along with teaching on healing. I sort of believed in healing, but it always occurred hundreds of miles away. When I saw healing and deliverance in people I knew (my students), I became a full-fledged believer.

As I look back, I always felt that there must be more to Christian faith than I was experiencing. Under John Wimber's guidance, I discovered what it was that was missing and went for it wholeheartedly—and I have not looked back. I am finished with powerless Christianity!

Not infrequently, we want to at least consider changing our perspective. I trust that this book has opened you to change in this area and at least started you in the process toward powerful Christianity. The path to change involves change in at least four areas.

1. Change in Attitude

We need to change from an attitude of closedness to an attitude of openness. If we are closed to change in any given area, it is unlikely that we will change in that area. The pastor I mentioned in chapter 1 did change his attitude, like the apostle Thomas, who believed when he saw. But he might have taken the attitude that he was quite comfortable with his present position and closed to change. Instead, he changed his attitude from closed to open and became a believer in deliverance from demons in our day.

2. Change in Exposure

Those never exposed to contemporary faith healing are unlikely to change. Personally, I went to Nigeria after training up to seminary level never having been exposed to contemporary faith healing and deliverance. When the Nigerian leaders told me that their major problem was demons, I knew I could not help them. I sort of believed in healing but had never been exposed to it and did not know where to start. When, then, the opportunity came for me to seek exposure in 1982, I sought it.

3. Change in Belief

At the time, I sort of believed that there were some spiritual giants in our day who were effective in healing and deliverance, so I was not rejecting an understanding of Christianity that included healing. But along with most of the evangelicals that I spent time with, I was not embracing it either. And I considered those in healing ministry to be unbalanced. Again, when the opportunity came to change my belief from rejecting such a ministry to accepting it, I changed my worldview belief. This came in response to my felt need for such a change and my exposure to a credible witness, John Wimber.

> I changed my worldview belief in response to a felt need and a credible witness.

4. Change in Practice

Built on top of whatever changes we make at the deep worldview level, we need to change our practice. Even if we make all of the above changes, we can still avoid the practice toward which those changes point. For example, in the days in which I was making the changes that brought me into healing ministry, I experienced quite a bit of fear. I wanted to avoid getting too involved in healing. However, I eventually decided to listen to my mentor and to experiment. And this was decisive. When I saw people getting transformed as a result of my prayers, I was hooked.

In summary we come up with a chart that outlines the following:

Attitude	From closed → to open
Exposure	From avoiding → to seeking
Belief	From rejecting → to accepting
Practice	From avoiding → to experimenting

We can speak, then, of two shifts that need to take place when moving into spiritual power. The first is what we call a *paradigm shift*, where our attitudes and beliefs get changed at the worldview level. The second is a *practice shift*, which is a change in our behavior so that we are actually doing something other than thinking about it. This shift is built upon the changes that have taken place at the deep worldview level.[9]

Continue to Experiment

I have pointed out that there is a lot about the spirit world we do not understand. It used to be that although many had ideas and practices in this arena that worked, they kept those ideas and practices secret or found them acceptable only within a limited circle of acquaintances. But today, more and more people are venturing into this realm and learning and writing about it.

And whenever people begin sharing ideas, theories and experiments more openly, the process of learning escalates. Someone advances an idea and someone else critiques it, offering what he or she considers a better approach. Then someone else comes along with a radically different suggestion and different traditions develop, each tradition practicing its own approach and conducting experiments based on its own theories. In this way, new ideas and techniques get developed, less effective ones get dropped and the science that the experimentation produced moves forward.

If the same regularity exists in the interactions between the spirit and human worlds that exists in the physical world (and I believe it does), we can speak of developing a *science of the spirit realm* by means of the same process. Thus, I make no excuses for experimentation in spiritual warfare as long as there is enough prayer support to overcome enemy pushback. As with the physical and human worlds, where God has left much for us to discover on our own (that is, without the benefit of special revelation), so it is in the spirit world. We must start with whatever the Bible shows us, but there is much more to discover through practice, theorizing and experimentation.

We know from the gospels, for example, that Jesus gives His followers authority and power. We read in the scriptural casebook some of what Jesus

9. See my book *Christianity with Power* for more on this subject.

and the apostles did with that authority and power, but the descriptions of those events are simply outlines of what happened. We are told few details of what they did as they healed or delivered people from demons. Nor are we given such information as to how long the deliverance sessions took or whether they or others did any follow-up to bring the freed people to complete wholeness.

Scripture does not answer all our questions as we assert the authority Jesus has entrusted to us. So we experiment, praying all the while that we are not going beyond what pleases God. In this way, we develop practices that are not explicit in Scripture but that work consistently to set captives free. Not infrequently, as I have mentioned before, we are criticized by those who feel we go too far. Usually these critics have little or no experience themselves. Nor would they ever launch out themselves to experiment with the authority and power Jesus gives us.

It is all right for people to critique ministries like ours, for that is how we learn and how a science of the spirit realm will be developed. But our critics often have had zero experience in most of the areas in which they find our approaches off base. And, as nearly as I can tell, they do not plan to tackle these areas in practice, only in theory.

> Scripture does not answer all our questions, so we experiment.

In a meeting with one of these critics, I suggested that it was difficult to take his criticisms seriously, given that he has never faced in ministry most of the problems we deal with regularly. The critics are nearly always criticizing from theory alone, without practice to back it up. When we face challenges in our practice, though, we soon run out of biblical information concerning what Jesus or the apostles did in such situations. With the theory being challenged in practice, we are forced to use our own creativity under the guidance of the Holy Spirit. "When you have worked with 25 demonized people," I said to him, "and discover that you, too, must go beyond approaches specifically indicated in the Bible, let's talk again."

I continue to take critiques seriously, but I will not stop working in Jesus' authority merely because people do not like what I am doing. If I must choose between ministering to a person by using approaches not found in Scripture (though they are not anti-scriptural) and allowing that person to remain in bondage, as evangelicals typically do, I choose ministry, even if my method is not specifically taught in Scripture.

The fact that God blesses our efforts so regularly, using them to bring freedom to people in amazing ways, encourages us to continue both ministering and experimenting to find better ways to help people, in spite of the criticism. I take the approach of D. L. Moody, cited earlier, who defended himself in response to a person who did not like the way he did things: "I don't always like the way I do things either, but I like the way I do things better than the way you don't do them."

Put It in Practice

When I teach on the subject of spiritual warfare, those who would like to get involved often ask, "How do I get started?" They have usually been unaware that they are living in enemy territory and are being harassed by Satan. When these facts are pointed out, however, they can often identify circumstances in their lives that they suspect are the result of enemy activity. So what do they do now?

I am concerned, first of all, that we know what our enemy is up to. As I mentioned at the beginning of this chapter, awareness is crucial. No army goes into battle without studying their enemy thoroughly. And from what Paul said in 2 Corinthians 2:11, it looks as though God expects us to be on to our enemy and his devices. Since he works 24/7 to thwart what God is doing in, with and through us, no weak-kneed, mild-mannered approach to defeating him will work. Though we are to be gentle toward people, our stance in relation to the enemy of our souls is to be all-out warfare.

In answer to the question above, I say, "Get involved in ministry." Specifically, get involved in inner healing, since it is through inner healing that the basic issues Satan uses to cripple us are dealt with.

So, how does a person go about getting involved in the ministry of inner healing? What I did was to get my hands on as many books as I could find and to talk to as many practitioners as I could find and to find a couple of people to link up with. These may be people already practicing or people who are learning. A team of three is ideal for ministry.

In my case, I knew two fellows who had a bit of experience, mainly with physical healing. We began applying what we were learning and began to see results, mostly in inner healing. The three of us read and discussed and began hesitantly practicing on people who admitted they were struggling with inner problems. We then arranged to sponsor a seminar to which we invited some experts to join us in teaching on inner healing and deliverance and doing ministry demonstrations.

In this way, we began an organization that we named Intercultural Renewal Ministry, with our eyes on working primarily with missionaries and international students. We focused on this group in seminars for which we produced teaching notes, some of which were influenced strongly by John Wimber's seminar notes. Later, in recognition of the fact that our audience was broader than we originally anticipated, we changed our name to Deep Healing Ministries.

What has developed is a teaching ministry, a ministry to individuals and a writing ministry. I have resisted becoming a large organization since I observe that large ministries tend to get tangled in administration at the expense of ministry. So, my one associate and I minister to people one-on-one (several hundred a year) and train people with the aim for the ones we train to start their own ministries. We encourage them to use and adapt our materials and to develop their own materials and their own approaches to ministry.

The books that have been most helpful to us appear in the bibliography of my first book on inner healing, *Deep Wounds, Deep Healing*. Several of the seminars we have offered (to date, five of them) are recorded on DVDs and CDs and are available for purchase. Our materials can be obtained by contacting judy@heartssetfree.org.

So, let's learn the enemy's schemes and how to go about using the authority and power God gives us to minister, to teach and perhaps to write against those schemes. Let us go forth to demonstrate God's love by using His power to free people from the enemy. Beyond this, let's speak God's power when and wherever we can to squelch what the enemy is doing or wants to do. It is as if God has placed in our hands a credit card entitled

In Jesus' Name, backed by the authority of Jesus' resurrection defeat of Satan and all his followers. Let's use the power represented by that credit card to bring freedom to God's precious children.

I pray that this book has been effective in challenging you to be and do all that God wants you to be and do, in and with His authority. I bless you to that end.

Select Bibliography

Anderson, Neil. *Victory Over the Darkness*. Minneapolis: Bethany House, 2000. (Previously published Ventura, Calif.: Regal, 1990, 2000.)

Annacondia, Carlos. *Listen to Me, Satan!* Lake Mary, Fla.: Charisma House, 2008.

Arnold, Clinton E. *Powers of Darkness: Principalities and Powers in Paul's Letters.* Downers Grove, Ill.: InterVarsity, 1992.

————. *Three Crucial Questions about Spiritual Warfare*. Grand Rapids, Mich.: Baker Academic, 1997.

Bubeck, Mark I. *The Satanic Revival*. San Bernardino, Calif.: Here's Life, 1991.

Cabezas, Rita. *Struggling Against Demonic Principalities*. Published privately. San Jose, Costa Rica: 1992.

Chandler, Russell. *Understanding the New Age*. Rev. and updated ed. Grand Rapids, Mich.: Zondervan, 1993.

Crow, D. Michael. "Spiritual Authority." Unpublished Fuller Seminary doctoral tutorial. 1996.

Dawson, John. *Taking Our Cities for God: How to Break Spiritual Strongholds*. Rev. ed. Lake Mary, Fla.: Charisma House, 2002.

Decker, Ed. *What You Need to Know about Masons*. Eugene, Ore.: Harvest House, 1992.

Dickason, C. Fred. *Demon Possession and the Christian*. Chicago: Moody, 1987.

Friesen, James G. *Uncovering the Mystery of MPD*. Eugene, Ore.: Wipf & Stock, 1997.

Groothuis, Douglas R. *Confronting the New Age: How to Resist a Growing Religious Movement*. Eugene, Ore.: Wipf & Stock, 2010.

————. *Unmasking the New Age*. Downers Grove, Ill.: InterVarsity, 1986.

Guelich, Robert. "Spiritual Warfare: Jesus, Paul and Peretti." *Pneuma* 13 (1991): 33–64.

Hiebert, Paul. "The Flaw of the Excluded Middle." *Missiology* 10 (January 1982): 35–47.

Hunt, David A. and T. A. McMahon. *The Seduction of Christianity*. Eugene, Ore.: Harvest House, 1985.

Kallas, James G. *The Satanward View: A Study in Pauline Theology*. Philadelphia: Westminster, 1966.

Kelly, Bernard. *The Seven Gifts*. London: Sheed & Ward, 1941.

Kittel, Gerhard and Gerhard Friedrich, eds. *Theological Dictionary of the New Testament*. Translated by G. W. Bromiley. Grand Rapids, Mich.: Eerdmans, 1985.

Koch, Kurt E. *Demonology Past and Present: Identifying and Overcoming Demonic Strongholds*. 1973. Reprint, Grand Rapids, Mich.: Kregel, 2000.

Kraft, Charles H. *Anthropology for Christian Witness*. Maryknoll, N.Y.: Orbis, 1996.

—————. *Christianity in Culture: A Study in Biblical Theologizing in Cross-Cultural Perspective*. Rev. ed. Maryknoll, N.Y.: Orbis, 1979, 2005.

—————. *Christianity with Power: Your Worldview and Your Experience of the Supernatural*. Rev. ed. Eugene, Ore.: Wipf & Stock, 2005. (Originally published Ann Arbor, Mich.: Vine, 1989.)

—————. *Confronting Powerless Christianity: Evangelicals and the Missing Dimension*. Grand Rapids, Mich.: Chosen, 2002.

—————. *Deep Wounds, Deep Healing: An Introduction to Deep-Level Healing*. Rev. ed. Minneapolis: Chosen, 2010. (Originally published Ventura, Calif.: Regal, 1993, 2010.)

—————. *Defeating Dark Angels*. Minneapolis: Chosen, 2011. (Originally published Ventura, Calif.: Regal, 1992, 2011.)

—————. *I Give You Authority: Practicing the Authority Jesus Gave Us*. Rev. ed. Minneapolis: Chosen, 2012.

—————. *Two Hours to Freedom: A Simple and Effective Model for Healing and Deliverance*. Minneapolis: Chosen, 2010.

—————. "What Kind of Encounters Do We Need in Our Christian Witness?" *Evangelical Missions Quarterly* 27 (1991): 258–265.

—————. *Worldview for Christian Witness*. Pasadena, Calif.: William Carey Library, 2008.

Kraft, Charles H. and David DeBord, *The Rules of Engagement: Understanding the Principles That Govern Our Lives*. Eugene, Ore.: Wipf & Stock, 2005.

Kraft, Charles H. and Marguerite G. Kraft. "The Power of God for Christians Who Ride Two Horses." In *The Kingdom and the Power*, edited by Gary S. Grieg and Kevin N. Springer, 345–356. Ventura, Calif.: Regal, 1993.

Kraft, Charles H., ed., with Mark White. *Behind Enemy Lines: An Advanced Guide to Spiritual Warfare*. Eugene, Ore.: Wipf & Stock, 2000. (Originally published Ann Arbor, Mich.: Vine, 1994.)

Larson, Bob. *Satanism: The Seduction of America's Youth*. Nashville: Thomas Nelson, 1989.

McAll, Kenneth. *Healing the Family Tree*. London: Sheldon Press, 1991.

Murphy, Ed. *Handbook for Spiritual Warfare*. Rev. and updated ed. Nashville: Thomas Nelson, 2003.

Otis, George Jr. *Informed Intercession: Transforming Your Community through Spiritual Mapping and Strategic Prayer*. Ventura, Calif.: Renew, 1999.

———. *Transformations*. Lynnwood, Wash.: Sentinel, 1999. Videocassette (VHS), 60 min.

———. *Transformations II*. Lynnwood, Wash.: Sentinel, 2001. Videocassette (VHS), 60 min.

———. *The Twilight Labyrinth: Why Does Spiritual Darkness Linger Where It Does?* Grand Rapids, Mich.: Chosen, 1997.

Peretti, Frank E. *Piercing the Darkness*. 1988. Reprint, Carol Stream, Ill.: Tyndale Momentum, 2002.

———. *This Present Darkness*. 1986. Reprint, Carol Stream, Ill.: Tyndale Momentum, 2002.

Priest, Robert J., Thomas Campbell, and Bradford A. Mullen. "Missiological Syncretism: The New Animistic Paradigm." In *Spiritual Power and Missions*, edited by Edward Rommen, 9–87. Pasadena, Calif.: William Carey Library, 1995.

Reddin, Opal, ed. *Power Encounter*. Springfield, Mo.: Central Bible College, 1989.

Robb, John D. and Jim Hill. *The Peacemaking Power of Prayer: Equipping Christians to Transform the World*. Nashville: Broadman & Holman, 2000.

Rommen, Edward, ed. *Spiritual Power and Missions*. Pasadena, Calif.: William Carey Library, 1995.

Seamands, David. *Putting Away Childish Things*. Wheaton, Ill.: Victor Books, 1993.

Shaw, James D. and Tom C. McKenney. *The Deadly Deception: Freemasonry Exposed by One of Its Top Leaders*. Lafayette, La.: Huntington House, 1988.

Sherman, Dean. *Spiritual Warfare for Every Christian: How to Live in Victory and Retake the Land*. Seattle: YWAM Publishing, 1990.

Silvoso, Ed. "Argentina: Evangelizing in a Context of Spiritual Warfare." In *Behind Enemy Lines*, edited by Charles H. Kraft, 263–283. Eugene, Ore.: Wipf & Stock, 2000. (Originally published Ann Arbor, Mich.: Vine, 1994.)

Smalley, Gary and John Trent, Ph.D. *The Language of Love*. New York: Pocket Books, 1991.

Unger, Merrill F. *Demons in the World Today*. Wheaton, Ill.: Tyndale, 1971.

————. *What Demons Can Do to Saints*. Chicago: Moody, 1991.

Wagner, C. Peter. *Confronting the Powers*. Ventura, Calif.: Regal, 1996.

————, ed. *Engaging the Enemy: How to Fight and Defeat Territorial Spirits*. Grand Rapids, Mich.: Baker, 1995.

————. *The Third Wave of the Holy Spirit*. Ann Arbor, Mich.: Servant, 1988.

Wagner, C. Peter and Pablo Deiros, eds. *The Rising Revival*. Ventura, Calif.: Gospel Light, 1998.

White, Tom. *The Believer's Guide to Spiritual Warfare*. Rev. ed. Minneapolis: Chosen, 2011. (Originally published Ventura, Calif.: Regal, 2011.)

Wimber, John and Kevin Springer. *Power Healing*. 1987. Reprint, San Francisco: HarperOne, 2009.

Index

Charles H. (Chuck) Kraft is retired from the faculty of the School of Intercultural Studies at Fuller Seminary (formerly the School of World Mission) after forty years as professor of anthropology and intercultural communication. He taught anthropology, communication, contextualization and spiritual dynamics (inner healing, deliverance and spiritual warfare) to missionaries and prospective missionaries.

He holds degrees from Wheaton College (B.A., anthropology), Ashland Theological Seminary (B.D., theology) and Hartford Seminary Foundation (Ph.D., anthropological linguistics). He served as a pioneer missionary among a tribal group (Kamwe/Higi) in northeastern Nigeria for three years, followed by five years each on the faculties of Michigan State University and UCLA teaching linguistics and African languages.

Chuck is the author of thirty-three books and numerous articles in the fields of his expertise. He spends most of his time now ministering to those with emotional and spiritual problems and conducting deep healing (inner healing) seminars in churches worldwide. God has used him to lead hundreds to spiritual and emotional freedom in Jesus Christ.

Those who would like to book Dr. Kraft for a seminar, or who seek assistance with spiritual warfare issues, may contact Dr. Kraft at ckraft@ heartssetfree.org or his associate, Rev. Judy Taber, at judy@heartssetfree .org. Visit www.heartssetfree.org for more information.

More from Charles H. Kraft

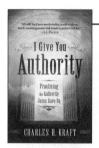

After His resurrection, Jesus passed His authority on to you—but do you know how to wield this amazing power? In this insightful book, you'll find out how to exercise and release this authority properly and wisely into your own life and the lives of others.

I Give You Authority

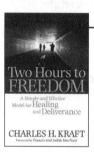

Past wounds and hurts don't disappear the moment we are saved, and they can keep us from experiencing the intimacy we long for with Christ. Using a simple, proven process, Charles Kraft leads you, step by step, on the path to deep-level inner healing and true freedom.

Two Hours to Freedom

In this solidly biblical book, you'll discover why spiritual power is the "missing dimension" in evangelicals today. You'll also learn how to develop a more robust faith that is powerful enough to heal, free others and bring about real life change.

Confronting Powerless Christianity

✔Chosen

Stay up-to-date on your favorite books and authors with our free e-newsletters. Sign up today at chosenbooks.com.

Find us on Facebook. facebook.com/chosenbooks

Follow us on Twitter. @chosenbooks